Cognitive and Emotional Study Strategies for Students
with Dyslexia in Higher Education

Amanda T. Abbott-Jones provides practical and motivational guidance
for students with dyslexia in higher education. The book presents effective strategies appropriate for dealing with an array of study tasks including note taking, essay writing, reading and exams, while also delivering
targeted emotional support. Pragmatic methods are delivered from the
voices of students with dyslexia who have first-hand experience of
fine-tuning study techniques, making learning suitable for how the dyslexic brain processes and memorises information to become successful
in the academic world. As such, this book does not simply present strategies from an educational perspective, but instead draws on the wealth
of empirical knowledge from the source of dyslexia – the dyslexic people
themselves. This gives readers a collective shared identity, which has been
previously lacking, teamed with valuable advice on ways to overcome cognitive and emotional difficulties by using appropriate strategies to enable
people with dyslexia to flourish in the university environment.

Amanda T. Abbott-Jones is an accomplished dyslexia practitioner. Her
own late diagnosis of dyslexia has driven her passion to work with and
support students with dyslexia. She received her doctorate in education,
focusing on anxiety and dyslexia, from University College London, UK.
She is the author of *Dyslexia in Higher Education: Anxiety and Coping Skills*
(2022).

Cognitive and Emotional Study Strategies for Students with Dyslexia in Higher Education

Amanda T. Abbott-Jones

Independent Dyslexia Consultants

CAMBRIDGE
UNIVERSITY PRESS

Shaftesbury Road, Cambridge CB2 8EA, United Kingdom

One Liberty Plaza, 20th Floor, New York, NY 10006, USA

477 Williamstown Road, Port Melbourne, VIC 3207, Australia

314–321, 3rd Floor, Plot 3, Splendor Forum, Jasola District Centre,
New Delhi – 110025, India

103 Penang Road, #05–06/07, Visioncrest Commercial, Singapore 238467

Cambridge University Press is part of Cambridge University Press &
Assessment, a department of the University of Cambridge.

We share the University's mission to contribute to society through the pursuit of
education, learning and research at the highest international levels of excellence.

www.cambridge.org
Information on this title: www.cambridge.org/9781009219068

DOI: 10.1017/9781009219044

First published 2023

A catalogue record for this publication is available from the British Library

Library of Congress Cataloging-in-Publication Data
Names: Abbott-Jones, Amanda T., 1969– author.
Title: Cognitive and emotional study strategies for students with
dyslexia in higher education / Amanda T. Abbott-Jones.
Description: Cambridge, United Kingdom : New York, NY : Cambridge
University Press, 2023. | Includes bibliographical references and index.
Identifiers: LCCN 2023005184 | ISBN 9781009219068 (hardback) |
ISBN 9781009219044 (ebook)
Subjects: LCSH: Dyslexics – Education (Higher) | Emotions and cognition. |
College students with disabilities – Psychology. | Study skills.
Classification: LCC LC4818.38 .A339 2023 |
DDC 371.91/44–dc23/eng/20230517
LC record available at https://lccn.loc.gov/2023005184

ISBN 978-1-009-21906-8 Hardback
ISBN 978-1-009-21905-1 Paperback

I would like to dedicate the work in this book to all dyslexic students within academia who continue to struggle through the difficulties and self-doubts, but whose strengths have provided the inspiration for bringing this work to fruition.

Contents

Contents

Contents

Contents

Contents

Contents

Contents

Contents

Contents

Contents

Contents

Contents

xviii

Contents

Contents

Contents

Contents

Contents

Contents

Figures

Preface

Students with dyslexia in higher education are in need of an effective study skills book that uses a clear step-by-step approach to learning targeted at their level, and that also addresses strategies for reducing negative emotion, such as anxiety and stress. This book closes that gap by providing practical and motivational guidance delivered from the voices of the potential readers' more experienced dyslexic peers and the dyslexic author, who have first-hand experience of fine-tuning study techniques by making learning suitable for how the dyslexic brain processes and memorises information to become successful in the academic world.

As such, the book does not merely present strategies from an educational perspective, but instead draws on the wealth of empirical knowledge from the source of dyslexia, the dyslexic people themselves. This helps to give readers pragmatic and valuable advice on how to overcome cognitive difficulties through using appropriate study strategies for how people with dyslexia productively learn.

Additionally, current study skills books have not integrated aspects of social–emotional development with cognitive development. This book, however, is enveloped in a deep understanding that students with dyslexia do not just require fitting study techniques to succeed academically, but also, if not more so, need support on overcoming emotional difficulties. Thus, the book, unlike other study skills books, provides cognitive technique chapters by focusing on and exemplifying how methods presented can productively be used to alleviate negative emotion. For example, in Chapter 2, *Organisation Techniques and Meeting Deadlines*, organisation methods are delivered to help the student to manage time around their studies, yet chiefly are designed to help with reducing anxiety around deadlines. The strategy of rehearsal in the *Presentation Techniques* chapter (Chapter 9) is discussed as a way of ensuring presentations are successful on the day whilst simultaneously focusing on this as a technique for overcoming nerves and panic about the presentation.

These cognitive concepts are ultimately bolstered by Chapter 11, *Emotional Coping Techniques and Looking After Your Wellbeing*, which delivers a range of themes on constructive ways of supporting positive emotion and wellbeing. This includes techniques for developing mental resilience, persistence and determination.

Acknowledgements

Very special thanks go to the students with dyslexia who so gener-
ously gave their time and shared their experiences with me for the
purpose of providing valuable research for this book.

Warmest thanks are also extended to my husband for his support
and encouragement and for giving me the strength throughout all
stages of this project to just keep going.

Preview of the Contents of the Book

After Chapter 1, the *Introductory Chapter*, which helps to explain the reasons why certain study tasks are difficult for students with dyslexia, the arrangement of chapters draws on the order of tasks that students encounter during a typical academic year. For example, a student's first challenge on arrival at university is to manage their timetable in terms of knowing when and where their lectures and taught sessions are, which is why Chapter 2 provides the skills for the student to develop this ability. Early in the academic term, the student must attend lectures and acquire the skill of efficient note taking. Hence, Chapter 3 supplies strategies for developing proficient note-taking ability. The *Reading Strategies* chapter also appears early in the book (Chapter 4), as, after organisation and note taking, reading and developing appropriate reading strategies is a requisite for progression. The *Making Learning Memorable* chapter appears as Chapter 5, as once students have knowledge of reading strategies and can use this skill to be selective, they then need to know how to memorise what they are learning, crucial for retrieving information for essay writing and exams. Hence, Chapter 6 delivers productive writing techniques, and Chapter 7 covers practical and productive spelling methods. As exams and essay assessment typically occur at the end of semesters to test students' development of knowledge during the term, constructive ways to revise and exam techniques are presented as Chapter 8. Chapter 9 looks at useful presentation techniques, and Chapter 10 covers beneficial methods for tackling seminar discussion and debate in addition to delivering effective strategies for developing public speaking skills. This chapter will also be useful for final-year students, graduate and postgraduate students, or any students in higher education currently looking for employment, as it includes productive methods for dealing with different types of job interviews. The final chapter, *Emotional Coping Techniques and Looking After Your Wellbeing*, is positioned at the end of the book, as a resource for learners to dip into whenever they are feeling unmotivated, anxious or stressed, and as a way of signifying the importance of this aspect of learning as underpinning all the previous chapters. More detail of what is included in each of the chapters is presented below:

Chapter 1 – Introductory Chapter: Dyslexia and Difficulties with Study Skills

From work experience as support tutor of students with dyslexia, whilst students tend to be aware of areas where they are academically weak, they are not always fully conscious of why they find certain tasks difficult, so this chapter helps the reader to know more about what underlies their barriers to study.

Chapter 2 – Organisation Techniques and Meeting Deadlines

Effective organisation techniques and the ability to break down larger projects into a series of more manageable time-framed steps are key to student progression and success. As such, this chapter, told from the dyslexic learners' perspectives, provides advice on developing proficient organisation strategies.

Chapter 3 – Note-Taking Strategies

Note taking in lectures is one of the most problematic tasks for students with dyslexia, because of processing, retention, and retrieval difficulties. Consequently, strategies delivered in this chapter to help with vanquishing these barriers include using active learning methods, using multisensory methods that utilise all the learning senses, and using technology.

Chapter 4 – Reading Strategies

This chapter features what dyslexic students say is helpful to tackle academic reading. Hence, advice is provided on using appropriate methods, such as the 'preview, ask and answer questions, summarise, and synthesis' (PASS) strategy, employing skimming and scanning approaches, and reading using selectivity to minimise the amount of unnecessary reading.

Chapter 5 – Making Learning Memorable

This chapter focuses on cognitive strategies to assist with overcoming difficulties due to working memory deficits. These techniques range from highlighting keywords and using image association, selecting and extracting information using the Q Notes (Burke, 2000) method to condense down learning, mind mapping, and using multisensory methods and technology.

Chapter 6 – Essay-Writing Strategies

This chapter covers effective techniques that students with dyslexia say they use to support essay-writing tasks. These involve using sub-headings to help with essay structure, applying the 'point, example/evidence, comment/criticism' (PEC) method of writing, designating proofreaders to check through written work, and using assignment cover sheets on coursework.

Chapter 7 – Spelling Techniques

This chapter provides strategies to assist with spelling difficulties. These range from using mnemonics to help with remembering spelling of difficult words, using sounding out words, using repetition by using the Look, Say, Cover, Write, Check method, copying words down from academic papers and dictionaries to become familiar with the visualisation of the word.

Chapter 8 – Revision and Examination Techniques

This chapter has three main purposes:

- To advise on ways of setting a purpose for revision to keep motivated and to cover equally the topics to be examined.
- To deliver useful revision methods to overcome memory difficulties.
- To provide guidance on applying effective exam techniques.

Chapter 9 – Presentation Techniques

The basis of this chapter is methods that students with dyslexia find productive for dealing with presentations. These include making a plan, using visual images, preparation by continuous rehearsal and timing, using activities for audience participation to take the spotlight off oneself, and ensuring the topic selected for presentation is interesting and enjoyable.

Chapter 10 – Public Speaking, Interviews, Seminar Discussion and Debate Techniques

Key techniques include ways of dealing with anxiety connected to providing ideas verbally in front of an audience. Strategies and tools are also presented to develop confidence when undertaking any form of public speaking. Finally, advice is provided on how to plan for and to feel reassured when tackling job interviews.

Chapter 11 – Emotional Coping Techniques and Looking After Your Wellbeing

This chapter presents a range of productive emotional coping methods, as used by students with dyslexia, that readers may want to consider as mechanisms for helping to deal with negative emotion. These include talking to someone, planning and using strategies, implementing breaks, participating in exercise, seeking comfort, and using mental resilience.

1
· · · · ·

Introductory Chapter: Dyslexia and Difficulties with Study Skills

1.1   Introduction

The Introductory Chapter will set the scene on the nature of dyslexia within the context of higher education by, firstly, presenting useful definitions of dyslexia. 'Useful' definitions are those that characterise 'dyslexia' as an umbrella term to describe a range of heterogeneous conditions. This explanation of dyslexia helps to highlight the array of difficulties that the student diagnosed with dyslexia may face whilst at university, rather than narrowly focusing on literacy difficulties.

   As we have drawn attention to the diverse spectrum nature of dyslexia as a condition which leads to complex problems, the second part of the chapter is a discussion outlining types of cognitive difficulties that students with dyslexia may meet when undertaking academic tasks. For instance, difficulties range from the phonological (which, in the case of students with dyslexia at university level, may be more likely to be moderate to mild, but can still present as problems with reading speed, the recognition and pronunciation of unfamiliar words, and trouble with spelling) to deficits with short-term/working memory which manifests as obstacles when it comes to remembering learning for exams. Or there may be sensory processing difficulties, which become noticeable when the student is trying to listen and keep pace with the lecturer during taught sessions, or when the student is attempting to follow spontaneous group discussion in seminars. The production and reception of verbal language may be an area affected, so there could be anxieties around contributing ideas during seminars, or an avoidance of presentations. If dyslexia is comorbid with dyspraxia, there will be difficulties with motor coordination, so tasks involving manual dexterity, such as handwriting and learning to drive a car, will be problematic. Dyspraxia may also affect the student's ability to be organised, so they could benefit from support with time-management strategies. If a magnocellular deficit (problem with the visual system) is present, the student will have visual difficulties and may get headaches when reading black text on white backgrounds. They may also miss lines of text when reading and require support with selecting appropriate coloured overlays to make reading easier.

Consequently, tasks involving reading, writing, spelling, exams, presentations, organisation, seminar discussion and note taking all present barriers for students with dyslexia. These difficulties are explained in relation to each study skill, and reasons for these problems are specified. In essence, the reader will gain an understanding of how dyslexia deficits such as problems with phonology, information processing, working memory, retention and retrieval impact negatively upon the ability to competently undertake study tasks. The ways in which this affects students with dyslexia emotionally are presented, and it is explained how negative emotion such as anxiety can also impede academic performance, perhaps to a greater extent than the cognitive difficulties associated with dyslexia.

1.1.1   Definitions of Dyslexia

Historically, definitions of dyslexia have been riddled with uncertainties, and there has been little consensus regarding the characteristics that constitute dyslexia. For instance, some definitions focus solely on difficulties with literacy learning and development at the 'word level'. An example is the explanation provided by the British Psychological Society (BPS), who suggest that 'dyslexia is evident when accurate and fluent word reading and/or spelling develops very incompletely or with great difficulty' (Reason et al., 1999). Other definitions, however, provide a more comprehensive description of dyslexia by taking co-occurring difficulties associated with dyslexia into consideration, which helps us to understand the types of difficulties encountered when studying at university. For example, Rose's (2009) six-part definition, embraced by Dyslexia Action (2009), not only describes the characteristic features of dyslexia at the cognitive level as 'difficulties in phonological awareness, verbal memory and verbal processing speed' (Rose, 2009, p. 10), it also acknowledges that there are other connected difficulties experienced by some (but not all) individuals with dyslexia: 'Co-occurring difficulties may be seen in aspects of language, motor co-ordination, mental calculation, concentration and personal organisation, but these are not, by themselves, markers of dyslexia' (Rose, 2009, p. 10). These co-occurring difficulties are often prevalent in individual students diagnosed with dyslexia, and they require a varied range of interventions. Another useful definition for understanding adult dyslexia and types of problems encountered with study skills is provided by the British Dyslexia Association (BDA). This describes dyslexia as a condition that is 'likely to be present at birth and to be lifelong in its effects. It is characterised by difficulties with phonological processing, rapid naming, working memory, processing speed, and the automatic development of skills that may not match up to an individual's cognitive abilities' (BDA, 2007).

Another valuable definition is provided by psychologist David Grant in the book *That's the Way I Think: Dyslexia, Dyspraxia and ADHD Explained* (2010). Grant's work as a psychologist involves screening for dyslexia and diagnosing it if evident. He argues that clients he diagnoses with dyslexia have what he refers to as 'spiky profiles' which reveal not only cognitive weaknesses, but also strengths in certain areas. For example, in Grant's testing for dyslexia, he uses the Wechsler Scales of Intellectual Abilities, which consist of a series of subtests used to measure 'performance on a range of different skills including knowledge of vocabulary, mental arithmetic, three-dimensional thinking and speed of copying symbols' (Grant, 2010, p. 31). Grant suggests that a typical Wechsler dyslexic profile will reveal high scores for verbal reasoning (the ability to understand and logically work through concepts and problems expressed in words) and visual reasoning (analysing visual information and being able to solve problems based upon it), yet scores will typically be lower for short-term memory and speed of visual processing. Grant argues that when no specific learning difficulty such as dyslexia is present, 'the Wechsler profile will be fairly flat, not spiky' (Grant, 2010, p. 32). In his text, he goes on to present a classic profile of a dyslexic student which shows that 'she scored above average on verbal and visual reasoning skills and below average on working memory and processing speed. Whereas her Verbal Comprehension (verbal reasoning) and Perceptual Organisation (visual reasoning) scores put her in the top 20 per cent and top 23 per cent of the population respectively, her scores for Working Memory and Processing Speed put her in the bottom 9 per cent and 32 per cent respectively' (Grant, 2010, p. 32).

Consequently, this discrepancy-based definition of dyslexia focusing on the amalgamation of both cognitive strengths and weaknesses is more useful for our understanding of adult students with dyslexia within higher education than the definitions that merely centre upon cognitive difficulties. Whilst the cognitive deficits exist and work to undermine the intellectual abilities which can be in the above average range, Grant's explanation of a typical dyslexic profile enables us to comprehend the types of frustrations faced by so many students with dyslexia in relation to their academic work. This is because, often aware of their intellectual ability, they become annoyed when they are unable to demonstrate this in exams owing to deficits in memory processes and speed of information processing.

Although the definitions provided by Rose (2009), Dyslexia Action (2009), the British Dyslexia Association (2007) and Grant (2010) are more appropriate in drawing attention to the varied range of strengths and difficulties associated with dyslexia, what is missing is mention of associated problems that may not be in the cognitive realm, but are connected with the behavioural realm, and are directly influenced by dyslexia, such as anxiety, stress and other negative emotional consequences. Whilst definitions of dyslexia have focused on the cognitive effects of dyslexia, behavioural effects have to a great extent been neglected.

1.2   Types of Cognitive Difficulties Faced by Students with Dyslexia

This section will present a brief explanation of some of the causes of dyslexia which have been theorised in the field of dyslexia: the phonological deficit regarded as a core characteristic of dyslexia; short-term/working memory difficulties; the cerebellar deficit; weaknesses in temporal processing; and finally deficits in the visual transient/ magnocellular system. However, rather than going into depth on each of the theoretical causes, discussing the theorists and research- ers who have focused on investigating them, and debating any crit- icisms or shortcomings of the individual causes as considered in the research literature, this section will instead supply a concise descrip- tion of each cause and outline how this might relate to difficulties in studying. This is in the hope that if a student diagnosed with dys- lexia sees a term such as 'phonology' or 'working memory', in their screening report, they will have more of an understanding of the implications of these difficulties for their studies. From practitioner experience, students can often be confused about the wording used in their psychological assessments and are not always sure what the problems identified from the assessment mean for them in connec- tion with their academic work. If the reader is interested in looking at a more detailed analysis of causal theories of dyslexia, please see Abbott-Jones (2022), *Dyslexia in Higher Education: Anxiety and Coping Skills*.

1.2.1   Phonological Deficit

Phonology relates to a child's perception of and production of the units of sounds used in language. In learning to read, a child is required to identify and manipulate sounds as distinctive units (seg- ments). For example, /p/ and /b/ are separate units of sound, referred to as phonemes. Basically, a child begins to map sounds (phoneme awareness) onto graphemes (the units and representations of letters in written language, for example the alphabetic letters). If a child has difficulty with or is unable to create these patterns of association, mappings, this impairs the development of the phonological path- way and delays the development of reading for meaning (semantics).

Consequently, if the mapping of sounds to letters is problematic, the child's progress in reading becomes significantly delayed.

When applied to an adult student with dyslexia in higher education, whilst the student may to an extent have compensated for difficulties in reading, if as a child they had a noticeable phonological deficit, they may still struggle with the sounds of unfamiliar words when reading for university. This is important to understand when students are taking specialist courses, such as medicine or pharmacy, where a lot of medical terminology is required. Some nursing students have commented on their embarrassment at being unable to accurately pronounce or read aloud names of certain medications.

Another symptom of the phonological deficit is that of word-finding difficulties which may interfere with the fluency of spoken language. Word-finding difficulties and problems with pronunciation of unfamiliar words help to explain the anxieties that students who present with these types of difficulties have when it comes to academic tasks, such as delivering presentations and verbally contributing to seminar discussion and debate. If there are problems with the acquisition and production of spoken language combined with word-finding difficulties (Hulme & Snowling, 2009) then, from practitioner experience, it is understandable that students with deficits that impact on speech rate and on speech production frequently attempt to avoid presentations and the delivery of verbal ideas during taught sessions.

1.2.2   Short-Term Memory and Working Memory Deficits

Other dyslexia theorists, notably Ramus and Szenkovits (2008) (please see Abbott-Jones, 2022), propose that the phonological deficit is caused by underlying processes of short-term/working memory, and it is a deficit in this area that is the cause of dyslexia. Short-term memory is defined as the capacity to hold a small amount of information in the mind for a short period of time and to be able to retrieve that information efficiently after the short period of time has elapsed. Working memory, as part of short-term memory, is a cognitive system responsible for the transient holding, processing and manipulation of information. Working memory is necessary for conducting mental multiplication tasks, such as when required to hold numbers in short-term memory to carry over, followed by retrieving the information whilst, at the same time, doing another component of the task.

Difficulties in short-term/working memory processes cause problems when the student is under time constraints in exam conditions where effective memory is an essential requirement for productive performance. Inefficient memory can also exacerbate the phonological difficulty. For instance, from practitioner experience, students have frequently commented on how they struggle to decode text and accurately read questions on the exam paper when placed under time pressure.

1.2.3 Cerebellar Deficit

The cerebellum refers to a part of the brain responsible for coordinating and regulating muscle and motor activity. If there is a mild disorder in the cerebellum, this will not just have an impact upon the development of reading skills, but will also affect balance, motor skills and sensory processes (see Abbott-Jones, 2022).

Students with dyslexia affected by the cerebellar deficit frequently present with a diagnosis of dyslexia which is comorbid with dyspraxia. As with dyslexia, which takes different forms and consists of a range of co-occurring difficulties, dyspraxia should also be used as an umbrella term covering a range of physical and cognitive difficulties.

Adult students who present with the combination of dyslexia and dyspraxia tend to need more support with developing organisational skills, implementing time management strategies, structuring written work, and developing skills for articulating ideas verbally and writing fluidly and fluently.

1.2.4   Weaknesses in Temporal Processing

Temporal processing refers to the perception of sound. If there are weaknesses in this area, this will present as a defect in perceiving rapidly changing auditory sounds, which can lead to difficulties in the linear sequencing of sounds and letters in a word.

Problems with temporal processing help to explain why students with dyslexia experience barriers when processing auditory, visual and sensory information in lectures and debates. There will also be obstacles in efficiently following rapid verbal information in the form of instructions. It has all too often been said by students with dyslexia that they find it difficult to keep pace with what the lecturer is saying.

1.2.5   Deficits in the Visual Transient and Magnocellular System

The visual transient and magnocellular system is the pathway required for visual input to be effectively signalled to the cerebellum. This pathway is also responsible for controlling eye movements and the allocation of visual attention.

A manifestation of the magnocellular deficit occurs when students have visual difficulties, often referred to as scotopic sensitivity. They may find reading black text on white backgrounds difficult and require use of either a background colour on a computer screen or a coloured overlay over printed hardcopy text to make reading easier. They may also get visual strain and headaches when reading without use of coloured backgrounds, overlays or glasses with tinted lenses. Text may look blurred or appear as though it is moving or swirling on the page. Additionally, the student may mistakenly skip words or lines of text during reading and may need to place a ruler under each line of text to focus more accurately.

The different causal theories discussed above are helpful for our understanding of adult dyslexia, as they reinforce our understanding that dyslexic university students' difficulties are not merely confined to problems with reading, but exist in all aspects of processing auditory, visual and sensory information. Whilst a phonological deficit is usually described as a core characteristic of dyslexia, other aspects may or may not be prevalent in a dyslexic student's profile, which is why support needs vary enormously with each individual. As such, it is useful to think of subgroups of dyslexics. For example, some students may just have a phonological deficit, whilst others could have a combination of phonological with short-term/working memory deficits, or phonological with sensory processing difficulties explained by both the temporal processing theory and the visual magnocellular theory. This demonstrates the spectrum nature of dyslexia and delves deeper into what underlies the specific individual difficulties manifested by the student's own unique profile.

Now that we understand the types of cognitive difficulties underlying dyslexia, next we look at barriers presented by various academic tasks required in all courses at university level, such as organisation, note taking, reading, spelling, essay writing, exams and revision, presentations and seminar debate. Consequently, the reader will gain an in-depth understanding of how the requirements of these various tasks produce obstacles for the dyslexic learner, together with the specific reasons for these obstructions.

1.3   Difficulties with Organisational Skills

Whilst organisation may be considered more of a strategy than an academic task like exams or writing, it is still categorised here as an academic task. This is because the skills of staying organised and using time efficiently are key components to achieving success at university and are a primary focus during dyslexia support sessions when working with higher education students. Organisation – such as using to-do lists, prioritising tasks and breaking bigger coursework assignments and projects into smaller time-framed steps – also helps to maintain student motivation and prevents procrastination of work. Having constructive organisation techniques can also have a significant effect on reducing negative emotion such as anxiety, stress and anger, as being more in control of study tasks and knowing what to do and when to do it lessens the distress caused by feeling too overwhelmed and confused by larger-scale study projects, or when several assignments must be completed at the same time. Once students with dyslexia have developed appropriate organisation strategies to help to deal with their studies and to assist with overcoming work pressures, they can become quite systematic in ensuring the management of their work is administered. For example, BSc Medicine student Naomi, terrified of making mistakes such as forgetting important deadline dates, referred to organisation strategies as making systems to be controlled by, to compensate for her short-term memory deficits:

> I try to make up systems which could control me. Calendars, writing things out, note making.

As we saw in the 'Definitions of Dyslexia' section, Rose's (2009) all-encompassing description of dyslexia acknowledges that personal organisation can indeed be a problem when outlining other associated difficulties experienced by some individuals with dyslexia.

As discussed above, organisation can be particularly problematic for students diagnosed with the amalgamation of dyslexia and dyspraxia, and these students will need more ongoing support with developing a daily routine and using effective time-management techniques to help to deal with their academic work. As seen in Naomi's case, the reason that students with dyslexia find organisation so difficult is largely due to inefficient memory processes. People with dyslexia also have a poor concept of time and find it difficult to accurately estimate the amount of time that has passed. Deficits in short-term memory cause challenges in remembering dates and times of appointments and meetings, whereas working memory deficits make planning and exercising conscious control of time and scheduling difficult. When a person with dyslexia must use working memory to juggle multi-tasking of meal preparation, this can cause complexities such as forgetting timings of certain ingredients and miscalculating or over/under-estimating how long something has been cooking. These are just examples of everyday tasks that a non-dyslexic person would be able to cope with more adequately.

These types of barriers with organisation can lead to feelings of helplessness and disorganisation which manifests anxiety. Lack of organisation ability causing high anxiety can impact negatively on study tasks. Mealey and Host, looking at causes of test anxiety, suggest that a source for this is when 'highly test-anxious students have deficits in the organisational stage of test preparation, primarily inadequate learning or study skills (Culler & Holahan 1980; Hodapp & Henneberger 1983)' (Mealey & Host, 1992, p. 147). This example is illustrative of how ineffective organisation in exam preparation leads to anxiety.

A couple of students more aware of their anxiety triggers and able to identify their cause are quoted here, to illuminate the destructive effect that lack of organisation can have on studying. Alan, a postgraduate MSc Sciences student, stated:

I think the disorganisation of myself impacts my anxiety. If I get better at organising, I could limit some of my anxiety or deal with it better.

In contrast, Fiona, a final-year BSc Sciences student, recognised:

When I'm not in control it all seems to start to go awry, so I will prepare to organise things. I end up taking control because the anxiety will get too much.

1.4   Difficulties with Note-Taking Skills

Developing good note-taking skills is essential for consolidating learning from lectures and for remembering key points in preparation for course tests and exams. Actively taking notes during lectures also helps with maintaining focus and with being better able to understand main concepts.

Reviewing well-organised notes after lectures is also necessary for developing understanding and memory of materials and for interacting further, through own thoughts and research with additional notes, to extend comprehension of key concepts.

The finding that note taking in lectures is problematic for students with dyslexia has, however, been documented by Mortimore and Crozier's study, 'Dyslexia and difficulties with study skills in higher education'. Mortimore and Crozier (2006) asked 62 male students with dyslexia to complete a questionnaire asking respondents to indicate whether they had difficulties with a list of aspects of learning. Although the questionnaire used in their study did not ask about exams and deadlines, it did ask participants to specify any problems with reading; spelling; note taking; organisation and time keeping; general study skills; expressing ideas orally; handwriting; memory and concentration. From the list, note taking, organising essays and expressing ideas in writing were rated as the most challenging areas

13

of study for the students. On note taking, Mortimore and Crozier (2006) say that 'lack of confidence in note taking and in retention of factual information has been described in previous research (Farmer et al., 2002; Klein, 1993; Riddick et al., 1997). Fuller et al. (2004) reported that virtually all the students with dyslexia in their sample of students with disabilities from one British university reported difficulties with learning in lectures: taking notes while listening and watching; lecturers talking too quickly or removing transparencies before the student could digest the information' (Mortimore & Crozier, 2006, p. 248). Whilst most lectures are now digitised for students to capture on computers during their own time, academic staff still need to be aware of their mode of delivery and should attempt to engage learners who have a diverse mix of learning styles.

The main reason that these difficulties exist for students with dyslexia is because note taking depends on the ability to listen, whilst simultaneously retaining, processing and writing down selected elements of the information. This is a particularly tall order for students with dyslexia who may have concentration difficulties teamed with weaknesses in retention and processing of information.

BSc Trainee Nurse Lisa highlighted the difficulties of note taking during lectures and would rely upon the online version of the lecture (most of her tutors uploaded their lecture content and slides onto Moodle after the lecture). This enabled Lisa to go through the content at her own pace. Additional worries, however, were caused if the content of the uploaded lecture had changed or had been added to from the original:

> I don't try to take notes. I can't filter the information very well. When you're following a lecture they put the slides online, but when the slides don't match and they've added slides, I'm like 'Oh right so I need to take this note' but then I get paranoid about the notes I'm taking. I won't be able to read them back to myself.

BSc Nursing student Tina summed up the difficulties of interpreting meaning from verbal dialogue when there are difficulties in auditory processing speed:

> You're thinking what do they mean? What does this link to? Taking notes is not good enough. You've got to be fast enough to catch what the lecturer says.

1.5   Difficulties with Reading Skills

Reading at university is one of the most common and important learning activities that the student is required to engage in. Reading is important for developing self-esteem as it increases a student's knowledge in relation to their studies. Additionally, participating in regular course reading helps the student to expand their vocabulary, not just on their topic and terminology and concepts used in connection with their topic, but also with greater understanding of words that the student can use in language on a more general basis. Thus, this leads to more confidence in terms of how the student speaks and writes about their topic. Reading also helps the student to have more enhanced critical and analytical thinking skills, which carries over into all aspects of their work.

However, students with dyslexia can have problems with reading and with developing good reading skills due to, as discussed above, a phonological deficit (the difficulty of matching sounds in spoken language to letters in written language). This interferes with reading development, and as such, reading comprehension and fluidity is delayed, as we have seen in the British Psychological Society's definition of dyslexia suggesting that 'dyslexia is evident when accurate and fluent word reading and/or spelling develops very incompletely or with great difficulty' (Reason et al., 1999).

Whilst a phonological difficulty is more noticeable in early years schooling when the child is learning to read, which helps educational practitioners to identify dyslexia, during adulthood a mild to moderate phonological deficit may still be present. This has consequences when reading for university, and the student with dyslexia may have slower reading speeds compared to their non-dyslexic peers, difficulties with spelling, difficulties with decoding text, and problems with producing the sounds of words accurately when reading aloud.

Academic reading can also be extensive and reading materials complex and difficult to comprehend. This was a problem specified by two postgraduate students, Charlie and Abu, who noted that reading was difficult because of the demanding materials they were required to go through for their level of study.

> It's all with reading, because I've never had to read so much, and I knew that would be the case. That's partly why I chose to do it (the course), because I thought I wanted to challenge myself with something that I knew I would find difficult. But this is like reading texts every week. It's constant and I find the lengths of the pieces I really struggle with. As soon as I know it's 30 pages, I'm thinking I don't know how I'm going to cope with this. (Charlie)
>
> I think it takes me longer to formulate thoughts and to read pieces of work, articles for academic reading, especially when the writing is complicated. It takes me longer to go through that. (Abu)

Ada, a PhD Sciences student, expressed that the key obstacles with her reading were associated with word recognition, decoding difficulties and the recognition of differences between homophones:

> I still can't identify certain words. For instance, if I see a word and I don't know how it's said, I will try and say it, but it won't be right. Sometimes I can look at a word and just won't know what it is. I have to ask someone to say the word to then know what it means. Also, identifying my own mistakes, you know, mixing up things like were and where.

16

Time is also a cause of frustration for students with dyslexia in connection with their reading. This is due to having to re-read academic texts to understand main points, thus spending much larger amounts of time on their reading than their non-dyslexic friends.

Difficulties with reading at university can also trigger anxiety. Anxiety leads to self-doubt, as in the case of Chloe, an MA Education student, on discussing difficulties with the volume of reading required by her course:

> I would tend to read thinner books because it's more manageable. I find the reading really difficult, and I feel like it sets up a lot of anxiety about whether I can do it.

An additional difficulty is that students with dyslexia may have stored in memory recollections of negative experiences from being asked to read aloud during school days. These memories can be reactivated at university, which creates fear around reading in front of others. This was described by Naomi, a postgraduate veterinary medicine student:

> I think when I was younger, I probably used to read out loud in school, but I always used to mess up my words and go wrong and things like that. So, I just kind of started to avoid it at all costs really.

1.6   Difficulties with Spelling Skills

Efficient spelling skills help to improve reading comprehension and can make the process of writing easier to master. If a student develops a good understanding of a word, they are more likely to recognise it during reading, spell it, define it, and use it accurately in speech and writing. Yet, poor spelling can create confusion and lack of clarity and meaning in written communication, from coursework essays through to important emails or job application forms.

The reason why students with dyslexia can find it hard to spell correctly is the phonological deficit. If the student has difficulties in segmenting a word into its phonemes and problems with memorisation of specific word patterns, this then becomes a barrier to developing accurate spelling.

Another difficulty with learning to spell words used in the English language is that English is an opaque language system. This means English has a complex phoneme–grapheme correspondence, with many irregular words. For just one example, many words in the English language start with *ph*, like *phone, photograph, physical*, yet we pronounce these words using the *f* sound. Words that are not pronounced how they are spelt are called *irregular words*, such as the word *yacht*. English is thus an overly complex language for students with dyslexia to grasp, owing to its lack of orthographic transparency. These complexities are specified by Spencer (2000) in the article 'Is English a dyslexic language?' Spencer states that 'readers in more transparent orthographies such as Italian, Spanish, Turkish, Greek, and German, where the words are spelt matching their sounds, have little difficulty in decoding written words, while English children have many more problems'. These problems become more profound when the learner is dyslexic, owing to the already existing problems of accurately mapping graphemes to phonemes.

In many professions, for instance teaching and nursing, an individual's spelling ability can be exposed. Teachers are required to write on boards in front of their pupils, and nurses are required to write down names of medications. This level of exposure can be a source of anxiety for students with dyslexia. Lisa, training to be a nurse, when asked about her spelling feared that weaknesses in this area could have a detrimental effect on her chosen career:

> It scares me a lot. I think especially in nursing, I had huge fears that I couldn't actually be a nurse because of my dyslexia.

Sam, training to be a teacher, pointed out that her main difficulties lay in the spelling and pronunciation of longer words:

> It affects me (dyslexia) with my spelling and my pronunciations. So, there's times when I really need to concentrate. It does affect me in a big way when it comes to spelling. I've got to take my time when I'm writing. Reading is fine, it's just maybe long words that I have trouble to pronounce.

Spelling can also be a source of embarrassment, not just in the university setting, but also in the work environment. MA Humanities student Charlie, who worked part-time in an office, was so embarrassed by her spelling that she would hide her computer screen from colleagues at her workplace and would avoid making handwritten notes during meetings.

> In work, I always put the computer at the right angle and the screen. You know, not giving hand-written notes and avoid things where my written language is visible.

1.7   Difficulties with Essay-Writing Skills

Academic writing is important at university as it provides a form of communication that demonstrates to teaching staff the level of knowledge that the student has acquired on a particular topic. Writing academically also helps students to develop analytical and critical thinking skills, as well as growing ability in conveying their understanding of their subject area. The practice of essay writing also advances student comprehension of the correct technique and style to use in different types and genres of academic writing.

To write proficiently, the student is required to show a capacity to effectively assimilate different ideas and perspectives on a topic. The research involved before essay writing begins, such as the reading of coursework materials and other academic textbooks and journal articles to develop student mastery of the subject they are writing about, also helps the student to learn how to scrutinise academic texts. This process enables the student to clarify in their own words their understanding and interpretation of what they have read. If the student is then also able to show a level of analysis and to exercise critical judgement, through their writing, of the source materials they have read, this displays successful essay-writing skills. Consequently, practising academic writing on a regular basis helps students to be more creative in their studies, which emanates into all aspects of their lives in terms of how they examine varying information, and extends into their judgement of situations. This helps to develop student confidence in applying unconventional ideas and approaches to issues arising from their topic area, and they also begin to look for solutions to problems in their subject that may not necessarily be obvious. In other words, the whole creative process involved in essay writing helps students to develop innovative approaches to their topic.

However, developing effectual writing skills takes time, practice and perseverance, particularly for students with dyslexia. According to the University of Reading's LibGuide (2021) on essay writing, developed for students with dyslexia and other specific learning difficulties, writing is difficult for students with dyslexia/SpLD because:

> It involves planning and working interchangeably between large- and small-scale levels of writing. (Large scale refers to the overall structure of the text, its form or genre, and the writing process as a whole. Small-scale, on the other hand, refers to the components of text, such as paragraph and sentence structure.)

This complexity is especially challenging for students with dyslexia/SpLD's. For example, a fragile working memory can make it difficult to hold in mind and manipulate large amounts of information at any one time. Processing differences may also make multi-tasking and sequencing difficult. (University of Reading, 2021)

Additionally, because of deficits in working memory, capturing ideas and getting them down on paper may seem inconceivable. That is because thoughts will come to mind but will disappear from memory almost instantaneously and before there has been time to capture them in writing. Another difficulty is due to problems with sequencing and organisation. This can lead to barriers in coherently structuring the essay, and ideas may jump around on the page, rather than being thoroughly developed before logically moving to the next point.

Students with dyslexia comorbid with dyspraxia tend to have difficulties with both writing and verbally articulating ideas fluidly and fluently. For example, Fiona, a BSc Sciences student, pinpointed her difficulty in structuring writing in essays and structuring verbal dialogue during talking:

I suppose where I notice it affecting me (dyslexia), is there are some things that my brain just doesn't seem to be able to work with. In an academic setting, structuring essays. I can have ideas about the subject, I can have a discussion with someone about the subject and I find I don't even really know where to begin when I'm thinking about structure. I find my brain does not work in that way. So, I find that's something that I definitely struggle with. Also, I don't think this is necessarily a negative thing, because sometimes people find it humorous, but the way I speak. My sentences, I kind of go a bit roundabout, or sometimes words kind of mix together. People know what I'm saying, but you know when you say a word and it's clearly not a word. I don't know, I think I notice, but how it affects me, definitely in structuring, sometimes I can't articulate myself in a way that other people know what I'm saying.

21

MA Arts student Cara recognised that her difficulty in writing was not only with putting ideas in the right order but was also due to getting her words in written sentences back to front, which she would have to repeatedly go through to change. This was having an impact on her confidence:

> Occasionally, I can get sentences back to front, so I would have all the right words in, which is just something to be aware of if I've got presentations, or I'm trying to learn quotes. I have to make sure that I've got it correct. When I'm writing, I know that it never comes out right the first way. Normally I'm writing all my ideas and they're all in there, but they are in the wrong order, so then I have to rearrange it all. I think it's something that knocks my self-confidence quite a lot.

1.8   Difficulties with Exams

Exams and tests are one of the most common forms of assessment at university. Educators tend to rely on this method to tap into whether learners have remembered key concepts from lectures and from course reading materials. Because of working/short-term memory deficits, though, exams tend to be an inequitable approach to checking the knowledge level and ability of students with dyslexia. Hence, for the student, the inability to excel in exams increases levels of anxiety in connection with this academic task. An interesting study examining dyslexic student anxiety levels in relation to exams is the work undertaken by Nelson, Lindstrom and Foels (2015). The study not only provides evidence that students with dyslexia present with a higher prevalence of anxiety than non-dyslexic peers when it comes to exams, but it also identifies that dyslexic students with higher deficits in non-verbal ability and working memory have higher rates of anxiety during exam-based situations.

Consequently, working memory deficits have an impact on the retention and retrieval of information required for exams. As the student becomes unable to remember learning they had previously absorbed from reading and lectures for the exam, their anxiety escalates, which further worsens their ability to recapture the information required. The frustration that this scenario causes is expressed by BSc Medicine student Naomi:

> I get really frustrated that I don't remember. It's not that I never read it. I know there's something I know, but I can't recall it.

Another difficulty during exams is that students with dyslexia may misread or misinterpret exam questions. Although dyslexic students at university have generally compensated for and coped with literacy difficulties and slower reading speeds to gain entry to university, having to deal with literacy during a high-stakes and time-pressured situation such as an exam produces further levels of worry and anxiety, which in turn cause mistakes to be easily made during the reading of exam questions. This was exemplified by BSc Nursing student Lisa, who spoke frankly about how the anxiety created by taking exams could lead to misinterpreting information and misreading questions on the exam paper:

> When you get into the exam, sometimes you're so anxious that you're not going to be reading the question properly.

As noted above, because of the nature of exams and the abilities they test – retrieval of information from memory and processing skills under time constraints – they place students with dyslexia at an unfair disadvantage; hence, dyslexic students' feelings of being distressed in connection with exams. An interesting study around the inequalities of exams for dyslexic students and the anxieties they raise has been undertaken by Camilleri, Chetcuti, and Falzon (2019), titled '"They Labelled Me Ignorant": Narratives of Maltese Youth with Dyslexia on National Examinations.' The research involved interviewing eight students with dyslexia on the challenges they face with exams and what in their opinion could make national examinations fairer. Challenges involved students being exposed to unwarranted examination stress and anxiety caused by the examination boards' lack of knowledge and examination invigilators' insensitivity to dyslexia. For example, being in a badly lit exam hall with other students was distracting for one participant, whilst another student had their scrap paper, which they had taken to the exam for the purpose of jotting down ideas, taken away by the exam invigilator. Suggestions the students made to make exams more equitable for students with dyslexia included changing the colour of the examination paper, using larger and more dyslexia-friendly fonts, including oral and practical examinations together with written examinations, allowing the use of technology such as computers, and having the examinations in a familiar setting such as the students' own school. These small steps, whilst not totally eradicating the anxiety felt by students with dyslexia around exams, could still go some way to making the experience fairer for the student.

Although additional time for examinations is provided and may to some extent compensate for slow reading speeds, there is still a problem with this. Because of the nature of exams as, basically, a test of how efficiently information from learning can be retrieved from memory processes, extra time still cannot place a student with memory difficulties on an equal footing with a student with no known learning difficulties.

1.9   Difficulties with Presentations

Developing effective presentation skills is crucial at university. Regular practice of presentations in the form of delivering speeches and messages to an audience helps to enhance competence in communication. This is a valuable skill that will help the student succeed not only in their academic lives, but also in their future career. Undertaking presentations also helps the student to unlock their creativity when it comes to communication as they can devise innovative ways to illustrate their talk, through slides, handouts for their audience members or visual aids. The preparation stage of the presentation also provides an important learning opportunity, as the student must learn about and become knowledgeable on the specific subject of their talk. The presentation delivery builds on the student's ability to speak articulately and meticulously to ensure the audience can follow the speech.

Presentations also provide teaching staff with a productive method of assessment, as they are a way for the student to demonstrate what they have learned about a topic and how constructively they have analysed and critically engaged with the subject of their speech. Presentations, however, are based on having acquired adequate language skills in its auditory form, both output (spoken language) and input (the processing of questions asked by audience members). As such, presentations require competence in use of vocabulary, phonology and grammar.

As we have seen above, though, if there is a barrier in the acquisition of accurate phoneme awareness, this will cause difficulties with the delivery of speech (output) for presentations; and to some extent, there will also be obstacles in the perception of the sounds of the words used in audience questioning (input). Ramus and Szenkovits's (2008) theory that the phonological deficit is caused by underlying processes of short-term/working memory goes some way with helping us to understand what is happening in this scenario. They claim that phonological representations are stored in what they refer to as 'buffers' in memory. They suggest there is an 'input phonological buffer' involved in speech perception and an 'output phonological buffer' for speech production and for retrieval of lexical phonological representations ('lexical' relating to the list of words stored in a person's vocabulary, and phonological representations being the mental representation of the sounds and combination of sounds that comprise a word). Thus, if there are difficulties in memory processes, then tasks requiring efficient use of spoken language, such as presentations, will be difficult. If there is a deficit with the 'input phonological buffer', then tasks requiring listening and responding to the auditory input of words will be difficult. If the deficit lies in the 'output phonological buffer', then the retrieval of words stored in the lexical pathway will cause problems, which is why people with dyslexia often have 'word-finding difficulties'.

If the student's dyslexia profile is based on weaknesses in short-term/working memory and if this affects the reception and production of verbal language, the student could display anxieties around contributing with ideas during debates, or in seminars, and they may want to avoid presentations. This anxiety can easily manifest into performance anxiety and fear of evaluative situations, such as presentations where weaknesses in language may be exposed.

From practitioner experience, students with dyslexia at university frequently have performance anxiety over speaking in class and particularly over delivering presentations. They fear being evaluated by the audience as stupid, largely owing to earlier phonological difficulties, and this is sometimes teamed with detrimental experiences from school. They are often afraid of being perceived as unintelligent by university peers and lecturers, which becomes exacerbated by the importance that is placed on assessed presentations as being highly relevant for academic progress and the student's own self-concept. The anxiety over public speaking arises from the student's perception that they are being judged against a perfect standard, and their belief that they are not able to achieve that standard.

Nevertheless, this fear of looking stupid in connection with the presentation can be a positive force. It can act as a driver for the student to practise and rehearse beforehand, and to reflect on the types of questions that may potentially be asked on the topic. For example, MA Arts student Cara talked about the amount of preparation work she would do for presentations to ensure she could effectively answer questions asked by her audience. This was probably driven by not wanting to feel humiliated, yet she believed the extra push to work harder than others had shaped her to become more resilient:

> I think the fact that it makes me work that much harder to find out things is a real bonus for when you're doing presentations. You have the five minutes of questions afterwards. I watch a lot of people get unstuck, but because I'm so prepared, that's probably my favourite aspect because I can really fire off all my knowledge that can't fit in the presentation. So, I think that overall, it's made me a really driven and resilient person.

1.10 Difficulties with Seminar Discussion and Debate

Seminar discussions and debates are timetabled regularly at university throughout the academic year and are generally scheduled to take place between the more formal lecture learning experiences. They involve smaller groups of students than the numbers attending the lecture setting, who are usually studying the same course, offering them a forum for interaction on a particular topic that has either been featured in the course reading materials or presented during a lecture. The benefit of this type of learning opportunity is that students can contribute and discuss ideas around the topic in a more informal setting than the lecture. As such, this type of more interactive learning enables students to learn from one another. Students can therefore utilise this safe space to try out evaluations of the material by articulating their own thoughts on an issue or subject.

Through this student-centred way of learning, participants can gain broad, multifaceted knowledge around their topic, as each contributor will be inputting their own unique notions on the area under discussion. The student's confidence and self-esteem can also be increased during this type of setting as they begin to feel more comfortable speaking and testing out ideas amongst their peers. Additionally, as discussion provides exposure to a range of perspectives, critical thinking skills are developed. The auditory articulation of ideas enhances the learner's ability to structure and organise their thoughts. Through the process of conveying their thinking verbally, the student can progress in their ability to form balanced, informed arguments using reasoning and evidence. This form of learning also helps to build the students networking and teamworking skills.

Nonetheless, as we have seen above in the section on presentations, difficulties with memory processes and phonology will also impact negatively on the student's ability to contribute confidently and in a coherent and logical way during the spontaneous type of discussion that seminars and debates lend themselves to. Adding to the work done by Ramus and Szenkovits's (2008) as mentioned above, which helps us to understand why there are barriers with speech, both output and input, for the student with dyslexia, another interesting study that looked at memory processes and speech production was conducted by McDougall, Hulme, Ellis and Monk (1994). The study investigated the relationships between reading, short-term memory and phonological skills. Participants selected for the study included 90 children, who, although they had not been diagnosed as dyslexic, were chosen because their reading problems were like those identified in children with dyslexia. The children were divided into three groups according to their reading ability. Hulme and Snowling, discussing the work of McDougall et al., noted that the study results showed that 'the poor readers have substantially lower memory spans (memory span is the longest list a subject can recall correctly) than the average and good readers' (Hulme & Snowling, 2009, p. 61). It was also discovered that differences between the groups in memory span was paralleled by the differences in speech rate. Hulme and Snowling suggest that 'the findings of McDougall et al., (1994) demonstrate clearly that short-term memory difficulties of poor readers are intimately related to problems in speech processing mechanisms (as indexed by slow rates of articulation). In short, there seems to be a basic inefficiency in the operation of this phonological code in children with dyslexia that might tentatively be related to an underlying problem with speech production mechanisms that also results in impaired speech rate' (Hulme & Snowling, 2009, p. 62). The McDougall et al. (1994) findings, when applied to considering types of difficulties faced by the student with dyslexia in higher education, could explain anxieties that such students have when it comes to academic tasks, such as verbally contributing to seminar discussions and debates. If there are problems with the acquisition and production of spoken language combined with word-finding difficulties then, from tutor experience, it is understandable that students with deficits that affect speed of speech rate and speech production frequently attempt to avoid participating with their own verbal ideas during taught sessions.

On the other hand, when a student does attempt to contribute to debate, rather than avoid it, this can also be problematic. Owing to deficits in short-term memory, word-finding difficulties and articulation disorders, some students need to verbalise their ideas instantly before the words they want to use fade from their memory.

29

The instant input of verbal dialogue may be at the expense of interrupting others and appearing rude, and this can lead to feelings of frustration and social isolation for the dyslexic individual. This scenario was experienced by MA Humanities student Charlie, as she explained:

> I find it quite frustrating if I can't find the appropriate time to talk. I'm not a great believer in putting my hand up if I have something to say. If I have an idea, I'm just going to come out with it and people have taken badly to that in the past. Last time I had to go and see the senior tutor for my year and say, I keep offending people, I keep getting these looks from people whenever I speak. I don't like it if people feel they're being interrupted or being cut off. People strop about it quite visibly.

Another reason that Charlie believed she had to blurt out a verbal expression of her ideas is that until she heard it, or could visually see it, the concept was not coherent in her mind. By hearing herself speaking it through, her ideas began to make more sense, as expressed:

> If I have an idea, I need to be able to either hear it, or see it, for it to be a complete idea. Otherwise, it's just these images, or concepts, it's nothing coherent. Until it's being spoken, I do have a panicky feeling, because there are ideas buzzing around in my head. Suddenly my head gets quite manic and the ideas need to come out of my head, so until I can say something, I will be on edge.

1.11   Emotional Difficulties

Wellbeing, as defined by the Oxford English Dictionary, is the 'state of being comfortable, healthy, or happy'. It is a necessary human condition for a student to attain to cope with university life. If a student has positive wellbeing, this can influence improved concentration, motivation and energy levels, all of which are beneficial for academic success. Students who make time to invest in their holistic wellbeing including their social, mental, physical and emotional health are more likely to achieve their personal and academic goals. Ultimately, wellbeing, and the way in which the student perceives themselves and the satisfaction they have with their life, is inextricably intertwined with academic progress.

Emotional wellbeing, which includes the ability to produce positive emotions, moods, thoughts and feelings, and to use resilience to be able to cope with adversity and difficult situations, is an essential state for the student to develop and maintain, not just in terms of dealing productively with the challenges of university, but also to have the capacity to overcome obstacles in everyday life. In fact, strengths in wellbeing and emotional wellbeing underpin and are the foundation stones for achievement in all the study skills listed above. For example, how can the student think positively of ways of working through the challenges presented by their reading, exams, presentations or essays, if they do not have the ability to withstand difficulties and/or to come up with different ways of tackling problems?

Despite the importance of developing emotional wellbeing to enable successful progression, emotional difficulties are often present for the student with dyslexia. This is generally caused by memories of negative, adverse experiences encountered during earlier education in the school years (Abbott-Jones, 2022). Research on emotional difficulties associated with dyslexia, although sparse in comparison to the work on dyslexia and cognitive difficulties of adult students, has begun to provide the necessary evidence to show that students with dyslexia at university can suffer from internalising disorders, such as depression, low self-esteem, anxiety, obsessive-compulsive behaviours, and dissociative disorders in relation to their dyslexia, which can have a more harmful impact upon cognitive ability and study progression than the cognitive deficits underlying dyslexia. The small number of studies that have looked at the relationship between dyslexia and emotional difficulties have found that university students with dyslexia report higher levels of somatic complaints (that is, physical symptoms) and social problems, lower self-esteem, and higher depression scores than their peers (Riddick, Sterling, Farmer & Morgan, 1999; Caroll & Iles, 2006; Ghisi, Bottesi, Re, Cerea & Mammarella, 2016). Other limited studies in the area that have looked at dyslexia and anxiety in specific subject areas, such as maths and statistics (Jordan, McGladdery & Dyer, 2014), and in specific study tasks, such as exams and timed tests (Nelson, Lindstrom & Foels, 2015), found a higher prevalence of anxiety in the dyslexic samples than in the non-dyslexic control groups.

Furthermore, in *Dyslexia in Higher Education: Anxiety and Coping Skills* (Abbott-Jones, 2022), new substantial evidence of the problem of anxiety for the dyslexic university student has been presented. This evidence is in the form of findings from an anxiety survey which was used to measure differences between 102 dyslexic students and 72 non-dyslexic students. The survey showed a statistically significant effect for the dyslexic sample for higher levels of academic anxiety, as compared to their non-dyslexic peers. Sako (2016) also declares that the most frequent emotional repercussions of dyslexia reported by dyslexic adults is anxiety. Anger and depression are also emotional symptoms of dyslexia, yet have not been as extensively researched as dyslexia and its association with anxiety in dyslexic adults (Caroll & Iles, 2006; Jordan et al., 2014; Nelson et al., 2015; Riddick et al., 1999).

Furthermore, anxiety acts as a block to cognitive functioning in relation to student progression in their studies. For example, during exams, if there are high levels of anxiety, the student will find it difficult to perform. It can also affect confidence and cause self-doubt, lead to social withdrawal and manifest in lack of structure or routine (see Abbott-Jones, 2022).

1.12   Social Difficulties

Social skills involve the ability to effectively interact and communicate with others. It is important to develop strong interpersonal skills at university, as these skills are required to progress and succeed in the academic environment and in the student's future workplace. Both environments involve the need to build relationships and to liaise and negotiate constructively with a range of people across a range of situations. The student will need to speak with tutors and lecturers to request extensions on coursework if needed, to ask questions one-on-one as well as during lectures, to raise concerns and to feel comfortable in being able to disclose any problems. Productive social skills are also needed to form friendships with university peers, to feel confident in making small talk with strangers, to effectively work in teams and to feel assured when public speaking during presentations.

Sako (2016), in 'The social and emotional effects of dyslexia', states that dyslexia can affect children's social life for five main reasons. Firstly, the child finds it difficult to understand jokes or sarcasm. Secondly, the child can have trouble with finding the right words to verbally articulate, particularly if they are required to respond quickly or must think on their feet. Thirdly, the child may miss or misinterpret social cues. Fourthly, the child could withdraw from sending messages either through text or email to their friends, owing to the embarrassment caused by having their written language on display. Finally, the child may remember things inaccurately because of difficulties with short-term memory, which others could perhaps interpret as the child being vague, misleading or distrustful (Sako, 2016). Whilst this literature is based on the social effects of dyslexia for children, some of these problems continue into adulthood. For example, in Abbott-Jones (2022), it was identified that university student social anxiety was mainly centred on discomfort during in class interaction with peers and tutors. This was caused by the fear of reading aloud due to being judged by peers/tutors, the fear of any type of evaluative situation where words and language are involved, the fear of being singled out as not understanding and the fear of looking stupid in front of others, the comparison with peers and feeling inferior, having imposter syndrome, feeling different and misunderstood, word-finding difficulties, and delayed thinking on feet, all of which affect social ability skills.

The fear of reading aloud due to being judged, and the consequences this has for the student socially, were exemplified by Dean, a nursing student:

> It probably affects me in social situations, such as I hate reading in front of people.

Dean also spoke about how other types of evaluative situations affected additional areas of his life, such as work and social activities with friends. He had a strong dislike of being observed by colleagues at work due to the embarrassment this caused, and he also hated being evaluated by peers when playing word games:

> I hate people looking at my work because I feel embarrassed. I hate playing word games. I don't know what you call it, Jingo, Scrabble. I don't like playing that because I don't really know words.

34

1.13   Summary

In summary, this chapter has:

- Provided useful definitions of dyslexia.
- Specified various causes of dyslexia.
- Outlined the types of cognitive difficulties faced by students with dyslexia.
- Listed the barriers and specified the reasons for the obstacles presented by the academic tasks of organisation, note taking, reading, spelling, essay writing, exams, presentations, and seminar discussion and debate for students with dyslexia.
- Presented a discussion of how dyslexia can affect the learner emotionally and socially.

2

· · · · ·

Organisation Techniques and Meeting Deadlines

2.1   Introduction

Effective organisation techniques, and the ability to plan and to break down larger projects into a series of more manageable time-framed steps, are key to student progression and success. That is because the 'one step at a time' approach turns what might seem an overwhelming and daunting task into a series of more manageable milestones. Competent organisation skills help to overcome academic weaknesses, and time management abilities can alleviate negative emotion such as stress around study tasks. Developing valuable organisational skills can help with effectively arranging your digital and physical spaces so you can easily locate pieces of work and objects without the unnecessary distress caused by not remembering where things are. Efficient organisation also assists with managing, prioritising and planning everything you need to do.

As such, this chapter told from the dyslexic learners' perspectives provides advice on developing proficient organisation strategies. The students whose viewpoints are featured in the chapter, and who so helpfully imparted this important information, are predominantly postgraduate and final-year undergraduate students who seem to have a passion and love for being organised which runs through all aspects of their lives. One explanation for this could be that by postgraduate stage, students – and particularly students with dyslexia – have clearly identified that being organised and having a more systematic approach to work is an essential strategy to ensure academic progress. This is exemplified by final-year BA Education student Sam, who noted, on the topic of organisation:

> That's one of the strategies I have to have, in order to move forth.

These strategies, therefore, include techniques such as developing systems to control events. This means investing in a set of materials – like calendars, diaries, to-do lists, either technology-based or paper-based – which work together as part of a mechanism or process to help to keep you organised and on track with your studies and other things in your life that you are committed to and/or enjoy, such as hobbies, social events and sporting activities.

The chapter covers, more specifically, techniques that can help to make organisation effective and give you control of your work and life. These techniques include using plans and breaking down work into steps; using technology; using multisensory methods; and creating and utilising materials such as visual plans, daily to-do lists, and timetables designed as creative posters to display on walls. All of these can help to make organisation enjoyable and something that works for you, to enable you to achieve your goals. Visual examples, derived from Hargreaves's (2012) valuable book, of different types of academic calendars, timetable templates and to-do lists are provided so that the reader can select methods suitable for how they work. Practical ways of being organised are covered, such as keeping filing in order and keeping desk space tidy. Metacognition (the awareness and understanding of how you need to work to be productive) is encouraged, and advice on using organisation to maintain motivation and prevent procrastination of work is supplied. Meeting deadlines and multitasking on several assignments due at the same time are anxiety-provoking experiences for students with dyslexia, so guidance is also presented on ways to cope with this, such as using support networks for motivation, starting work on assignments early in the term to meet deadlines, and identifying and breaking down tasks into smaller components by imposing self-made goals to make the work more manageable.

2.2   Techniques

2.2.1   Using Plans

Planning can be defined as deciding in advance what needs to be done in the future. It involves the process of thinking before doing. For example, you don't just launch immediately into writing an essay; instead, you plan what reading you need to do to obtain the necessary information, and you also plan what points you want to cover in your writing by breaking it up. To plan, you take your big goal – completion and submission of an assignment on the assigned deadline date – and transform this into a series of mini goals or milestones arranged in a logical order. You do this by listing the activities required to be undertaken to achieve each mini goal. For instance:

- Gather reading materials from library.
- Go through and make notes applicable for essay.
- Break essay question down into a series of bullet points or subheadings.
- Plan what days of the week to write, and your word target per day.

The process of writing your plan down, either by typing it into a computer document or handwriting into a notebook, is what is important. Writing a plan and reviewing it regularly helps to keep you on track with your work and provides you with a better view of what you need to do to achieve your goals and be successful.

Planning helps to maintain psychological wellbeing by providing you with a way to cope with your work, hence reducing anxiety. Planning also enables you to develop and progress with your work by keeping you focused and motivating you to get things done.

In relation to wellbeing, psychologist George Mandler (1984), known for his work on the theory of uncertainty, suggested that without plans in place to cope with work, or with other situations and life challenges, anxiety can be evoked. He argues: 'helplessness turns arousal into anxiety through the unavailability of plans or actions that are relevant to the task or to the situation. The one thing that leads to helplessness is the interruption of plans or behaviour. This may degenerate further into hopelessness if it builds up, goes on for too long, or if there are repeated failures. This in turn becomes related to the development of low self-esteem and may lead to depression' (Mandler, 1984).

Mandler's (1984) theorisation here of unattainable or interrupted plans leading to anxiety is illustrated by final-year BSc Sciences student Fiona:

> My organisation is poor. I actually think this is a big problem in my life as a whole and something that I kind of need to deal with, because I don't really write things down. I have a lot of things on in my head and I do have a planner. I bought a planner last year because my mate said, 'What's wrong with your life, because you're disorganised, get yourself a planner?' But then I've not used it for ages, so I have like loads of stuff, the things that are happening, but it's kind of just all like in my head and sometimes it surfaces and sometimes it doesn't, whereas if it all surfaces together then it's like aaah!

Other difficulties with planning that students with dyslexia may face (beside, as in the example above, purchasing planners and not using them) include not knowing how to plan, as in the example of MA Arts student Debra, below:

> Well, I know that I've got to plan, because I've been told that I've got to plan, but at the moment, I'm not even sure I know how to do that, because even in the essays that I'm writing, I don't think my planning is that effective for me. I write things, but they don't mean anything to me, and it's only when I'm writing that they make sense, so I feel like, well I can write bullet points about what I'm going to write, but it doesn't tell me anything.

Or students may not want to invest the time into planning as they feel that this aspect of their work takes up too much of their time, as stated by Nursing student Dean:

> I should really plan a lot better than I do but it's so hard to plan and it takes time. If I planned a lot better, I'd probably get better grades. But I think planning takes a long time and I'm a bit of a neat freak when it comes to that sort of thing.

Let us now start to unpick these difficulties and ambiguities around planning. By looking at how we can start using a planning approach to our work by breaking down bigger projects, we begin to learn how to identify the smaller tasks involved in the submission of our assignments.

2.2.2   Breaking Down Projects

Breaking projects, such as assignments, essays and revision, down into a series of steps enables us to see large tasks as more approachable and doable. This helps to reduce our inclination to procrastinate and to put off work on the project because we don't know where to begin. This whole overwhelming feeling of not knowing where to start and being uncertain and confused on what the smaller parts are that make up the project is illuminated here by MA Arts student Debra, who recalled being asked to write her first essay on entry to university:

> When I had to do my first essay, I remember changing my bedsheets and just breaking down crying. I had this panic and I just thought I have no idea what to do, I need to write an essay, I've no idea where to start.

BSc Nursing student Tina, aware of the need to make her projects less daunting and more manageable by breaking them down into smaller tasks, explained that she didn't always know how to identify what the smaller parts of the assignment were:

> I suppose I'm not an organised person. Sometimes I just don't know how to break it down. So sometimes it's good to ask someone, like what are you doing first?

The identification of the components that make up a project can at first be difficult to know. For example, when lecturers hand out essay questions, they very rarely say, 'Your first task will be to pick out the course reading that will help you answer the question. Your second task is to go through the reading highlighting relevant sections appropriate for developing a response to the question' and so

41

forth. It is usually more the case that questions are assigned, and the student is left to figure it out for themselves, as long as a piece of coursework is submitted by the due date.

The recognition of the smaller tasks involved does get easier with practice, though, and before too long the student will be able to work using a more systematic approach, as specified by Tina:

> I do think I've kind of improved with the timetables, making sure I break down the brief against my timetable. I find that helpful. But beforehand, I would just feel I need to do it and it would just be all over the place.

Let us have a go at turning this approach to assignments into the steps involved in breaking down projects to be more manageable.

Step 1

Identify the tasks by figuring out step-by-step what you need to do.

Step 2

Think about the logical order of completing the tasks. What do you need to do first, second, third?

Step 3

Create a timeline for completing each of the tasks you have listed.

Step 4

Make a visual plan. Put the time that you will spend on each step of your project into a schedule on your laptop, desktop, diary or calendar. That way, you can regularly check your progress and ensure you stay on track.

To help with starting to identify the stages of an assignment and allocating chunks of time to each of the steps, below is an example of ways you could break up an essay and assign a timeline. This is followed by an activity to help you to start to use this approach to your work.

2.2.3   Identifying and Breaking Up the Steps of the Project into Time-Framed Chunks

The timelines below are provided as an example. You will need to define your own when breaking down your own project.

Break Down the Question to Understand What Is Being Required from You

What information do I need to answer the question? – *A few hours*

Research to Gather the Information

Library catalogue searches for journals and books

Database searches for journal articles

Internet, e.g., Google Scholar – *A couple of weeks*

Reading and Note Taking

Using preferred reading and note-taking strategies (these are covered in Chapter 4):

Reading strategies

Q Notes

PASS

SQ3R – *3 to 4 weeks*

Mind Mapping/Concept Pyramids

Using preferred method to get down the ideas from reading and note taking into a concise structure. – *A couple of days*

Organising Ideas into a Structure

Numbering branches on mind map/transforming into linear structure. – *A few hours*

Writing Using Selective Quotes from Reading and Notes

Quotes need to strengthen, back up, provide evidence of the points you make. – *3 to 4 weeks, dependent on word target set for each study session*

Presenting, Formatting, Adding Bibliography

Typing up in Word and making sure the essay follows the guidelines on the style conventions. – *A couple of days*

Checking

Proofreading, reading out loud – *A couple of days*

2.2.4 Activity on the Steps of Undertaking an Essay, Assignment or Project and Placing within a Time-Managed Framework

- Think about the **various actions or steps** that you need to take to complete an essay, assignment or project.
- What are these actions/activities/steps?
- Make a list of them in chronological order, **starting with what you would do first**, and finishing with what you would **finally do** before submitting your essay.

_____

_____

_____

_____

_____

_____

_____

_____

_____

- If you have a timescale of 4 weeks to write an essay, how would you allocate time to each action, activity or step?

Next, let us define and clarify what is meant by developing proficient organisation strategies.

2.2.5   Developing Proficient Organisation Strategies

Accomplished organisational skills are competencies you can use to establish structure and order in your daily life. They can help you work more competently and constructively and, as a result, increase your academic performance and productivity. When a student can develop strong organisational skills in relation to their studies, it typically means they will have a strong aptitude for time management, goal setting and understanding how to meet their objectives.

Organisational skills can fall into one of two categories. These categories are physical or reasoning. The physical refers to having a tidy workplace and tidy documents. Reasoning relates to using planning and time-management strategies to approach work.

Having strong organisational ability means having more than just knowledge on what organisation is. It involves a combination of knowledge and skills, matched with the ability to identify and apply appropriate strategies correctly in the right situations. For example, if you must multi-task by working on several assignments with the same deadline, then your organisation proficiency is developing if you initially invest in time to *make a plan* showing a well-thought-out timeline of when you will work on each piece of coursework. If you are unable to concentrate because your desk is messy, then aptitude for organisation would cause you to identify that untidiness is distracting you and you would *take some time* from your studies to put things in order, so you are able to continue to work more effectively.

45

Therefore, developing good organisational skills is all about activities. You need to grow the expertise of knowing when and how to use a range of organisational strategies that work well with how you work, in a range of situations. To arrive at this level of expertise requires opportunities to apply your knowledge and techniques of organisation to real-world situations. What better way to foster these skills whilst at university? The complexities and demands required from you in trying to manage your work and maintain a healthy work life balance during your studies will provide ample occasions where you will need to test various time-management and organisation strategies. Don't be too concerned if some of your timetabling and organisation methods are unsuccessful at first. Failures through testing and trying it out are needed for you to learn how to fine-tune your techniques so they work well for you.

As a starting point, below are a few hints and tips of planners you could use. These will assist you by enabling you to know what work you are being required to do, when you need to do it by, and what smaller steps you will be doing on each piece of work, each day, to be able to keep on track.

Examples of different types of planners you can create and use, along with details of these planners, are provided in Section 2.4, 'Multisensory Techniques'.

2.2.6   Hints and Tips for Effective Personal Organisation and Time Management

- Use a **year planner** to plot subject sessions and deadline dates of all assignments, projects or essays. Use also to plot exam dates, presentation dates, etc. This will provide you with a visual guide of how many weeks you have to work on assignments.

- Use a **week planner** to plot the *steps of each assignment, project or essay*. Use also to plot revision sessions, and steps for completing a presentation. Aim to have these steps completed before the deadline dates, which will give you some space for checking, proofreading, updating, improving, etc.
- Use a **to-do list** every day which you write the night before, listing *around five or six items* to ensure that you complete the work aims, *little goals* that are specified for that day on the week planner.
- Remember to make time each day to **do the things that you enjoy** – sporting activities, hobbies, etc. These can also be listed on your *to-do list* to make sure that you remember to have time away from studies.

2.2.7   Developing Systems to Control Events

What we mean by developing systems to control events is to use resources that are created and designed to help with organisation, planning and time management, such as to-do lists, diaries, calendars, alarms on electronic devices, or apps on mobile phones: basically, any method that will help you to live a more structured life, and that will remind you of important events and appointments that you must attend.

Having these systems in place is important for all students, but particularly for students with dyslexia, for several reasons. These include, firstly, needing more time to work on assignments than non-dyslexic students. Secondly, owing to the nature of dyslexia whereby levels of intelligence in the average range or higher are undermined by cognitive weaknesses in working memory and information processing ability (Grant, 2010), the student can set too high expectations on what they can achieve in the time given, and when needing more time can become frustrated by their slower progress compared to their peers. Thirdly, difficulties with short-term and working memory make it easy to overlook key dates and/or to forget about things that must be done to help with progress on the work. This can lead to confusion, generate stress and cause anxiety.

As we saw in Chapter 1, two students with dyslexia, who were aware of their anxiety triggers and able to identify ways they needed to learn to reduce stress, pinpointed that the source of anxiety was either due to feeling out of control with their studies or was caused by their disorganisation. This was recognised by Fiona, a final-year BSc Sciences student, and by Alan, a postgraduate MSc Sciences student:

> I think the disorganisation of myself impacts my anxiety. If I get bet-ter at organising, I could limit some of my anxiety or deal with it better. (Alan)
> When I'm not in control it all seems to start to go awry, so I will prepare to organise things. I end up taking control because the anxiety will get too much. (Fiona)

To ensure that the anxiety caused by being disorganised does not get too intense, thus disrupting learning further, from practitioner experience, it is common for the more experienced student to become very accomplished at using their organisation resources to guarantee that they have an element of control over their lives. Recall BSc Medicine student Naomi from Chapter 1, who referred to organisation strategies as making systems to control her, to compen-sate for her short-term memory deficits and avoid missing deadlines:

> I try to make up systems which could control me. Calendars, writing things out, note making.

Students with dyslexia will frequently find it helpful and will feel the need to use 'systems' to be in control. These methods will vary from calendars, to writing things out, to making notes, depending on what you find useful. At first, it is best to experiment with a few options and then evaluate which methods helped you to stay on track, whether it was to-do lists, keeping notes in diaries or other methods. Furthermore, these organisational systems do not just apply to your work, but should also relate to your physical space, such as your desk and your computer. For instance, you could invest in stationery such as desk organisers to help with keeping your area decluttered, and you may want to come up with methods for keeping your electronic documents structured on your computer, so items are easy to retrieve – for instance, creating named folders and arranging them alphabetically.

2.3   Using Technology

In the United Kingdom, higher education students with dyslexia who are in receipt of the Disabled Students' Allowance (DSA) are entitled to receive a special equipment allowance for the purchase of items such as laptop computers (although from September 2015, changes to the DSA require students to make a £200 contribution towards a laptop), specialist assistive technology software, scanners, and recording devices for use in lectures and seminars. To meet the eligibility criteria, the student must provide the funding body with written proof of the disability by a medical professional. Students with a diagnosis of dyslexia would be able to use an assessment report from a recognised educational psychologist or specialist teacher as evidence of the disability.

The DSA comprises three supplementary allowances which can be claimed by the student after completion of the DSA application form. The first is the special equipment allowance mentioned above. This gives the student access to assistive software, which includes mind mapping, screen reading, and text to speech software. The second allowance, the non-medical helpers allowance, is used to fund training sessions for the student on using the disability software, and study skills support sessions with a specialist dyslexia tutor. In some cases, scribes to write down what the student dictates may also be funded from the non-medical helper allowance. The third general allowance covers the costs of books, printer paper and photocopying.

Students with dyslexia with access to specialist technology allocated from the DSA can therefore use this, combined with everyday technology such as Google and YouTube, to help with their organisation strategies. Here are some examples.

2.3.1 Using Technology as a Supplement to Hard Copies

If you use paper diaries, to-do lists, weekly planners and wall calendars, you may want to supplement these with online calendars and diaries. An advantage of using online schedules is that they can then be synched to your other electronic devices, such as watches, mobile phones and laptops. That way, wherever you are, you can always check the appointments and events you are to attend and what your to-do list looks like.

2.3.2 Using Speech-to-Text Software

Speech-to-text assistive software works by listening to the student's voice dictation and then translating this into a verbatim transcript of text displayed on the screen or in a computer document. Speech-to-text it is particularly effective for students with dyslexia who may prefer to verbalise their ideas aloud. Additionally, speech-to-text software enables students to capture their thoughts whilst freely moving around the room. If, as is common with students with dyslexia, the student suddenly remembers whilst making a cup of tea that they have forgotten to write down important dates, for instance, they can use the speech-to-text software on their phone or laptop to capture these recollections before they disappear from memory again. Once the verbalisation is captured on the screen or in the document, the student can input this into their more formalised academic calendar, to-do list or planner.

2.3.3   Use Event Reminders Which Display as Pop-Up Reminders You Can Set Any Time Before

Online calendars display pop-up reminders of appointments, events, things you have added to your calendar to do. These reminders can be synched with your other devices, such as your watch, phone or iPad, and you can set how long before the event you would like a reminder notification to pop up.

2.3.4   Setting Alarm Reminders Before Deadline Dates

The setting of alarms on mobile phones is also a useful device to ensure you are reminded of assignment deadline dates. BSc Nursing student Lisa combined the strategy of starting assignments early with having an alarm set exactly two weeks prior to the deadline date. That way, the alarm would help to ignite her motivation on the work if she had become distracted:

> I make sure I've got an alarm set two weeks before on my phone. Not to freak me out as it were, but to kind of just kick me up the bum and go, listen, remember there is a deadline.

51

2.3.5 If Going to Appointments or Lectures, Allow Time by Setting Alarm

It can be easy to get involved or distracted by something at home and realise you haven't left enough time to travel to an appointment or lecture. If you set an alarm on your phone that goes off before the time it usually takes you to travel to your lecture, allowing additional time for any anticipated delays, this should take away the stress caused from rushing and the fear brought on from arriving late.

2.3.6 Using Colour-Coded Excel Worksheet

Some students use technology in the form of computer spreadsheets to help with organisation, as in the case of MSc Humanities student Alison:

> I have an Excel to-do list for work and it's colour-coded, it's priority coded, it's like some amazing looking sheet.

This can work particularly well as a strong visual display for steps of work on different assignments, or attendance at various modules, all colour-coded, so the topic Politics, for example, may be indicated by pink, and Economics by blue.

2.3.7 Using Technology for Advice and Motivation

Some students would take inspiration from online videos and online web forums to help with organisation and keeping motivated in academic work, as mentioned by MSc Geology student Luke:

> The online web forum is really good. There is this sub-read on there called 'get disciplined' and one called 'get motivated'. Reading

through those and reading about other people's experiences, motivational quotes, and strategies for getting work done really helps.

2.4   Multisensory Techniques

Multisensory basically means to activate all your senses: visual (to see it), auditory (to hear it), kinaesthetic (to do it), and tactile (to touch it).

A multisensory techniques approach to keeping organised and managing time is particularly effective for students with dyslexia as it helps to make learning more memorable and can help the dyslexic learner to cope more effectively with processing, absorbing, retrieving and retaining information. Rather than just typing a to-do list into a computer document which can easily be forgotten, the act of making and creating a bright-coloured visual poster of a yearly and weekly academic calendar to display on the wall makes organising fun, practical and more conducive to keeping you on track.

2.4.1   Yearly Academic Calendar

Seeing events, deadlines and important dates throughout your academic year, visually and colourfully displayed and marked in a calendar on a wall near to where you work, helps to overcome any difficulties with short-term memory and the fear and worry induced by not remembering. A yearly academic calendar posted on the wall also provides a visual indication of how many days there are in between specific dates. Whilst it may sound simple to calculate days between dates, some students with dyslexia can easily overlook this, as was the case with BA English student Cate, who mistakenly booked a return flight from Germany for a month's rather than the intended week's time. After this mistake, she started to mark dates on a visual calendar:

> So, I put everything in a calendar, but yeah, I'm very bad for example at booking flights, because I don't book for a week from Monday to Monday, I book for a month. So, these things, I don't know how to deal with it because sometimes it just slips out of my sights.

For MA Education student Chloe, it was evident that her organisation methods needed to be visual, with colour-coding of calendars displayed as posters on the wall. That way, individual colours could be connected to different assignments and colour-blocked onto dates in the calendar to visually signify the deadlines for each subject:

> This task will get the pink coding and I will use colour coding when I write it down. Then I can just see that. It's on the wall at home, so I can see it. I can visually see.

MSc Sciences student Alan also benefited from the bright wall calendar by having a visual indicator of deadline dates, exam dates and various pieces of work to be done for different modules all colour-coded, as described:

> I know when my deadlines are going to be and I will plan it visually. I tend to have a wall calendar and I will be able to see and I will do that for exams, so that I can see when I need to be doing things. I tend to use colours for different modules and see when things are happening, just to see 'Oh, so I've got these happening' and that's… And I think oh that's happening here, this is happening there.

The link below provides access to an example of a yearly academic calendar created in Excel, as drawn from Hargreaves's (2012) text.
www.cambridge.org/abbottjones

You may want to use this as a template to customise your own version. Alternatively, you can search on the Internet for different types of academic calendars that will work effectively for you, or you may want to invest in colourful academic wall calendars from stationery shops, so you have choices of month to view, or year to view. Ideally, though, by investing a little time into creating your own yearly planner, you will find the process of organising your learning more enjoyable, which is conducive for memorisation. Additionally, the act of having your work/life organised in such a visual way will help to alleviate the stress and anxiety connected to not knowing when things are happening.

2.4.2 Weekly Calendar

To break down the events coloured in on your yearly planner, you can use a weekly planner (please see Section 2.2.6, 'Hints and Tips for Effective Personal Organisation and Time Management'). With a weekly planner, it is advisable to plan just one week at a time and then review at the end of each week, say on a Saturday or Sunday, before making your coming week's planner. That way, you are able to reflect at the end of each week on the tasks you have achieved, things you have not yet accomplished and reasons for this, whether you have been too ambitious with your weekly planning by expecting too much, or whether you have had too few tasks on the list and allowed procrastination to set in.

BSc Sciences student Fiona learned the hard way that she was overly planning by setting tasks for several weeks in a row, rather than just taking one week at a time, reviewing, and planning for the following week. This prevented her from being able to stick to her timetable, yet she still recognised that she needed to plan her week rather than leaving it unstructured, as this would help her to get into a routine and consequently would enable her to be more focused and productive with her work.

> For example, I've got loads of words to write for January. So, I have tried to plan-out like reading, writing days that I'm going to write these essays, but I've just written reading, reading, writing, reading, reading, writing, you know for the next few weeks.
>
> I've always been quite against timetables, and like 'Oh I don't want to stick to a timetable, I don't like it,' and I've realised that actually maybe it would really help me, because my anxiety is worse when I don't have a routine.

Testing out different ways of organising and getting into a structured routine with your work happens through trial and error until you find the system that works for you. The link below takes you to a few different versions of the weekly planner template (Hargreaves, 2012), which you may want to experiment with.

www.cambridge.org/abbottjones

The benefits of using each version are listed here:

Benefits of First Weekly Planner

- Each module for the course has been allocated a separate colour, and attendance at the lecture for that module together with time spent on working on the coursework for that module is signified by the coloured blocks.
- Ideally there should be, and is on this example, an equal amount of time spent working on each of the different modules represented by the different-coloured blocks. That way, an assignment or piece of coursework for a module is not neglected because of spending too long working on something else.
- Activities, hobbies, social events and time spent at part-time jobs are also coloured in. These events are just as important as study time and help to maintain a good work/life balance.

56

- Meal breaks and breaks from work are also indicated.
- Travel time, which can so often be overlooked, is also specified on the planner.

Benefits of Second Weekly Planner

- A weekly targets list is added, which will help you to focus on important tasks you want to achieve during the week and will give you a sense of satisfaction and achievement if you are able to tick them off.

Benefits of Third Weekly Planner

- Underneath the planner, you can list tasks such as reading, revision or writing. You then have a place to write your planned hours that you ideally want to spend working on these tasks, followed by a space to write down the actual hours that you were able to spend working. This helps to give you a more realistic view of what can be achieved in the time and will help to ensure that you don't over- or under-plan.

2.4.3   To-Do Lists

The to-do list breaks down the tasks that you have timetabled into your weekly planner into a series of more manageable smaller steps (see Section 2.2.6). There are many benefits of having a to-do list to look at each day. Firstly, they help to dissipate anxiety around the chaos of daily living by putting things into an organised, logical order. Secondly, they help to give our day a structure, a plan we can stick to; and thirdly, they help to boost confidence and self-esteem through the act of ticking off tasks on the list as we progress through the day.

It is advisable to get into the habit of writing out the to-do list late afternoon/early evening before the day the to-do list is intended for. That is because, at the end of each day, you have a better idea of what you want to achieve tomorrow. You then list these miniature goals for the day, and first thing in the morning, after reviewing your to-do list made the night before, you are ready for your day.

Whilst you can obtain examples of to-do list templates on the Internet to find ones that work for you (also see link below to access such a list), to make the process more multisensory, and hence more enjoyable and memorable, you can create your own. For example, you may want to purchase an attractive, colourful notebook for the purpose of making your daily lists. Allow one page for each day, and always handwrite the date at the top of the page. To handwrite your list of things to do, you can use colourful pens that are comfortable to write with, again making the process creative and customised for how you personally would like to see your list. The whole act of handwriting the list, using your motor skills and using attractive colours, makes the activity engaging, appealing, visual and kinaesthetic. This will enable you to make producing your to-do list a habit at the end of your day, as it is relaxing and pleasing.

www.cambridge.org/abbottjones

To make your to-do list achievable, do not overload it with too many things. If you do, it will just be too intimidating and cluttered, and you will not be motivated by it. Ideally, a list of six to eight miniature goals per day should be sufficient, and these should be a mix of personal, social, work and academic-related tasks. The key is, once you begin to develop the skill of identifying the small steps, compared to the bigger things you must do, ensure that the to-do list is only for the smaller tasks, whilst the bigger things should be marked on your calendar. This was a skill at which BSc Nursing student Lisa became very adept. She consequently began advising her non-dyslexic friends, whom she perceived as disorganised, on how they should keep to-do lists for small tasks and use sticky notes (such as Post-It notes) and paper to jot down larger things:

> I've talked to people who were really disorganised about dyslexia, and I said, 'I try to do to-do lists for everything, I do a list every day for the little things.' Now my friend, she's doing something important somewhere, it's politics or something. She's not dyslexic, but she does have an issue with her organisation, and I said, 'Listen, do your major points and write them on a piece of paper and have sticky notes and write down these are my major things and just tick them off when you've done it, and then have a list every day for little things, you know, just remind yourself.

Below is a typical example of what a to-do list could look like. As can be seen, it is not inundated with tasks, but has a nice balance of practical, personal, hobbies and study-related items listed, all in the order they would be done during the day:

- Have breakfast at 7 a.m.
- Get ready for spin cycling classes.
- Do pots, laundry and hoover.
- Catch the 08.39 a.m. bus to do spin cycle classes from 10 a.m.
- Have lunch.
- Write 420 words for essay.
- Do research gathering and reading for Politics assignment.
- Write out a to-do list for tomorrow.

Above, we reviewed using multisensory techniques for organisation in the form of creating yearly academic calendars, weekly planners and to-do lists. Let us now turn to more practical reflections by considering some useful stationery that can help with personal organisation in terms of making it easier to locate information, and that can also make your approach to learning multisensory and fun, hence aiding memory and engagement with your work.

2.5   Practical Things

2.5.1   Useful Stationery to Help You with Personal Organisation Over Your Studies

Once students with dyslexia begin to realise the importance of being organised to help with reliving anxiety and stress caused by unstructured routines and worry induced by forgetting important things, it is common to begin to invest in colourful stationery, sticky notes, to-do lists, diaries, calendars and folders to keep self and work organised. Bright and attractive stationery can be used as a way of keeping the work appealing, as explained by MA Education student Chloe:

> I buy nice folders. I like to look at it as well, I try to put it together.

BA English student Cate had a fun way of making reading more engaging by picking out important pages from an article. She would then mark pages with bright-coloured animal sticky notes if she wanted to return to them later. That way, she devised a pleasurable method which helped her to locate relevant information when needed:

> I have my animal markers, my little animal Post-It notes, because I just like playing with them.

Activities or stationery that make learning fun are important. As shown in studies of children's education (Parker & Lepper, 1992; Rea, 2000), if acquiring new knowledge is enjoyable, this makes learning easier to absorb and more significant. This remains as necessary in adulthood, particularly with students who may have cognitive deficits in memory and information processing, as it is when educating children.

Below is a list of some of the helpful stationery items you may want to consider to assist in organising the information that you accumulate over the course of your studies organised and making it easier to retrieve when required for revision or for writing essays:

- A4 file/plastic wallets with holes to keep in ring binder files.
- Sticky labels for labelling sources of information, and for labelling ring binder or lever arch files.

You can stick these onto the top right-hand corner of your A4 clear plastic wallets, writing down in a bright-coloured pen the source of the information contained in the wallet. For example, if the papers are reading material, you can write author name and title of paper onto the label. If the material is lecture notes, you can write the date and title of lecture. That way, when it comes to revision, you have all your documents labelled in an organised systematic way and can easily retrieve materials for each topic you are revising.

- A4 lever arch files using labelled numerical list at front to know where to file material and for easily finding materials/information.

Most lever arch files are sold with a contents template for you to fill in and keep at the front of the file, together with colourful A–Z index dividers so you can keep your papers separate within the file, dependent on subject, module and so on, or however you want to organise your papers.

- Colour-coded files using colours that match the colour you have chosen for each subject/module.

By colour-coding modules, you can block-colour your attendance at and your work on the module in your calendar and planner, as we discussed above. You are also able to keep the colour-coding consistent by using files in the chosen colour to arrange your paperwork for that module. That way, it is easy for you to know what material is in each of your files.

61

- A4 coloured plastic presentation/document folders for taking only paperwork required for a lecture/seminar/tutorial.

When you are attending lectures and tutorials, you don't want to be taking everything with you as this can easily lead to confusion and disorganisation during the lecture. Keep your materials to a minimum by only taking with you what is necessary for that lecture in an easy to carry colour-coded plastic wallet/document folder.

- A4 sketch pad for mind maps or mind-map templates.

Some learners with dyslexia prefer to mind-map lecture notes on blank paper with coloured pens, rather than write linear notes on lined paper. If that is the case, then it is advisable to purchase an A4 plain sketch pad for this purpose.

- A4 ring binder admin folder for important information related to studies: for example, enrolment info, fees info.

All the essential bits should be kept in one separate folder.

- Coloured pens for drawing mind maps.
- Coloured highlighter pens for identifying key points in photocopies of books/journal articles.

Now we have listed useful types of stationery that can be used to help to keep you organised, let us turn our attention to developing metacognition (an awareness of how you learn best).

2.6 Metacognition

2.6.1 Using Organisation to Prevent Procrastination

Using effective organisation strategies (like the examples discussed above) teamed with developing a metacognitive perception over how you learn can help you to prevent procrastination. Procrastination is the art of delaying or putting off tasks until the last minute. Instead of prioritising and/or dealing with tasks as they come along, a person who procrastinates will avoid doing what needs to be done. Usually, the procrastinator will immerse themselves into distraction techniques, such as using Facebook, watching films, or doing the cleaning, rather than tackling any demands from their work. Whilst these distraction methods can be useful to provide relaxation and sustenance when breaks from studies are required, if they are overly used as a form of avoidance, then the consequences could be that important deadlines are missed.

Developing metacognition – which is consciousness over how you learn, process, absorb, retain and retrieve information – is important for knowing how to utilise and implement organisation strategies to your work to keep you motivated and to help you avoid procrastinating. Examples of metacognition involve knowing whether you are a visual, auditory or kinaesthetic learner. The link below will allow you to access the visual, auditory, kinaesthetic (VAK) learning styles questionnaire, which will enable you to gain an understanding over your learning strengths when confronted with a series of tasks. Once you have established how you mainly approach activities in your life generally, whether through kinaesthetic, visual or auditory methods, or through a combination of these, you can begin to apply these approaches in all aspects of how you use organisation techniques and how you develop strategies for dealing with your studies. For example, if your strengths are in the kinaesthetic realm, you may benefit from physically creating your academic weekly planners by drawing them out by hand on coloured cards and through colouring in blocks of allocated time by hand. Auditory learners can profit from saying key dates aloud, repeating them so they become activated in memory processes. Visual leaners may find it easier to process information by making appealing posters to display on their walls so they can frequently absorb the data visually. This may sound quite simplistic, and usually a combination of the three methods for any activity is more effective, but if you recognise you do have more of a strength for one of the domains over another, then you need to utilise this in all aspects of your learning.

A free-to-use VAK questionnaire can be found on the Businessballs website which will help you to identify your learning style.

www.businessballs.com/self-awareness/vak-learning-styles/

BSc Sciences student Fiona, on recognising her visual strengths, began to mind-map notes during lectures with coloured pens on blank paper, rather than sticking to traditional methods of writing in a black/blue pen in linear format on lined notepads. She commented:

> I think I expected myself to be and to work like everybody else, but it doesn't, everyone's different and everyone learns in different ways.

Once students with dyslexia develop this metacognitive awareness, they can become more accomplished in using strategies suitable for how they need to learn information and solve problems. Other benefits of becoming more aware of how you think and work are that the knowledge can be used for psychological functioning and wellbeing during studying. Some examples are listed below:

- Being conscious of ensuring the environment is suitable for study.
- Being aware of the most effective times of the day or evening to work, whether this is due to external factors such as noise in shared households, or to internal factors such as knowing that your cognitive functioning is better in the morning or afternoon.
- Being conscious of whether breaks are required. BA English student Cate, rather than working ceaselessly on reading throughout the day, would break it into chunks and when feeling tired would do something else:

I portion it into specific bits, and the moment I find myself struggling, I get up and do something else for five minutes and come
back to it, because my brain needs a rest.

2.7   Deadlines

Many students with dyslexia can have negative emotion and frustration in relation to deadlines. This is usually due to the additional
amount of time that they feel they need to allocate to an assignment,
in comparison to their non-dyslexic peers, to submit a satisfactory
piece of work. Consequently, as the deadline approaches, feelings
of stress, worry, anxiety and panic can prevail, all of which interfere
with cognitive ability. This scenario was summarised by BSc Nursing
student Lisa, who revealed how the dread of deadlines impeded her
concentration:

> Each day it gets closer (the deadline), I'm just kind of dreading it
> even more, especially if I haven't started early enough. That dead-
> line just seems like I can't make it. I just kind of feel sick and just
> worried all the time. Even when I'm focusing on work, I just feel not
> able to put a hundred per cent in.

The example above signifies that constant worry of producing work
to meet deadlines has a profound effect over the student's ability to
perform effectively.

Another difficulty that students with dyslexia can have with
deadlines is missing or misinterpreting the detail, such as overlook-
ing or inaccurately reading dates, not having checked or not knowing where to submit work if taking in hard copies – just general
administration things. This point was illustrated by BSc Medicine
student Naomi:

65

If I miss them, I'd be very annoyed. Well, if they're the deadline I should know. If I don't know about it, I haven't done my research, and therefore it's made me miss something that I should have not otherwise missed. I've done that before with a few things. I've either skipped over something and haven't read something thoroughly and I've missed out a vital point, to do with things like accommodation, or when I have to get things in for certain forms and I just get angry thinking if I took the time to read that or look at it properly, I'd know about that deadline, and I wouldn't have missed it.

Let us now have a look at some ways of keeping on track when it comes to meeting deadlines, starting with some advice on multi-tasking when several assignments are due to be submitted at the same time.

2.7.1   Multitasking on Several Assignments

Multitasking – in this context, the switching between different module or topic projects – is frequently required at university when more than one assignment is due to be submitted on the same date. To cope with this demand, it is advisable to timetable one piece of work at a time. For example, if you have eight weeks to complete two projects, then one project should be allocated a four-week block of time, and the second project, the second four-week block of time. That way, the different pieces of work are given an equal amount of time and are timetabled so you can fully focus on each project without having to switch intermittently during the week from one to the other.

If, however, you can work on different assignments during the week and enjoy the stimulation and the variety that the switching may provide, then it is advisable to plot your weekly planner with work on one project for, say two days, followed by work on the other assignment for the following two days. Each piece of work should again be allocated an equal amount of time over the course of the week.

BSc Sciences student Fiona, preferring the method of working on one assignment at a time, explained how she approached this:

> So sometimes I would have two or three essays due at the same time. I would look at my diary and say I've got two months to write three essays, or two essays let's say, I say okay, so the first essay I will do on these days spreading out when I have to work or when I have other commitments, and I'd be like okay this is the time I'm going to concentrate on this essay, because I can only really write one essay at a time. I couldn't have two things, and I would set aside that time and I would complete that essay by the first month, so I know that the next month is only for the second essay, even though they're both due in at the same time.

2.7.2   Using Support Networks

Support networks, such as family members, support tutors and peers, can be a great source for helping to keep you on track and for providing encouragement and motivation with your work. If there is someone in your family, mother, father, sibling, partner, that you feel close to, you can provide them with a copy of your timetable and a list of the smaller steps involved in your project. They can then regularly check in with you to see if you are reaching each one of your mini goals. Having someone encouraging that you trust to hold you to account will provide confidence in your work and will help to push you forwards.

MA Arts student Debra used the support network of her family, particularly her sister, to help her to pace the work and to keep her motivated. On submitting her work, she felt reassured that because of the approach of applying small time-framed steps, she was able to hand in a good standard assignment. She also noted that many of her non-dyslexic peers, who left work on their assignments till later, would still be working up to the deadline:

> Through this whole time my sister was amazing. She kept saying to me 'You can do it, you're doing so well, you're ahead of other people.' I didn't really believe that until I actually handed it in, and people were in the library to the last minute writing it. I had already done it.

Dyslexia support tutors can also help by breaking up work on assignments and by setting a series of mini milestones negotiated with the student. During weekly or monthly support meetings, discussions can be based on whether the student has been able to stick to completion of their milestones.

MA Education student Chloe would regularly use her tutor for this purpose and was able to discuss with the tutor when things had progressed well. More importantly, she was able to retrieve support from her tutor when things had not worked out as planned:

> My tutor was amazing because she was so supportive and I could go to her crying, I could go to her whatever. The same with the disability centre and the libraries staff.

Groups of supportive peers, either from your course or from your university, whether dyslexic or not, can also provide the sustenance for motivation with work by setting each other tasks and small goals, as articulated by MA Arts student Debra:

> We supported each other and set each other tasks, like no, you have to do a presentation, we are all doing it and then we can have a laugh about it after. So, you don't feel so much alone. You can bring out ideas in the support network.

2.7.3 Starting Work on Assignments Early

Assignments set by university teaching staff are allocated at various times during a university term. Some universities will provide essay questions to students early on in a semester to enable the student to start the research work around their selected question. Other universities will leave the issuing of assignments until later in the term.

As students with dyslexia generally need longer than their non-dyslexic peers to complete work to a satisfactory standard, it is advisable to begin assignments as soon as they are designated. That way, during the first couple of days, after having read through the requirements, tasks involved in getting the project to completion can be broken down into identifiable smaller steps and can be time-tabled. This action will immediately provide you with a thoroughly thought-out written plan for reaching the deadline in a well-paced manner and will help to alleviate any stress and uncertainty in connection with the work.

MA Education student Chloe, who used the 'start early' strategy, would get irritated by her non-dyslexic friends' lack of understanding of how she needed to work:

> From day one, I would never leave it (the assignment). Actually, my peers at Uni, they always say, 'Oh don't be so stressed Chloe, you've got plenty of time,' and it irritated me, because I was like 'No, you might think so, but I don't work like this, I need to start,' and a lot of them laugh at me.

This strategy worked to her benefit, as she always managed to finish her work before the deadline date with enough time for checking and for any last-minute adjustments. In contrast, her friends, similarly to the observation made by Debra above, were getting anxious owing to having to rush their work to meet the deadline, because of having left it so late to start on the projects.

2.7.4 Identifying and Breaking Down Tasks

Let us now return to near where this chapter originally began, in Section 2.2.2, on 'Breaking Down Projects' into identifiable steps. This is the key to getting the work done and fundamentally the solution to being able to meet deadline dates. Every assignment with an end date for submission of work allocated to you during your time at university will lend itself to being broken down into a series of identifiable time-framed steps. One way of identifying the tasks that make up your project is to think about their dependency on each other. For example, in essay writing, you cannot write about a topic until you have done the reading and have understood the subject. You cannot do the reading until you have researched, found and gathered the relevant sources and reading materials, and so on.

Even with an academic activity like revision for exams, although a deadline is not usually prescribed by teaching staff, the 'end date' for that work is ultimately the date of the exam. Consequently, you can break up revision into a series of time-framed steps by making a list of topics you need to revise. Once you have the list, put these into a logical chronological order – for instance, are there any topics you should know about before moving onto other topics, because knowledge of one area may help you to understand another area better? Once you have considered this and have your list in logical order, just as with the steps of essay writing, you are able to allocate a completion time/date for revision of each individual topic.

In terms of allotting time to each of the steps you have identified and listed, this all depends on two factors: how long you have to work on the project before the deadline date, and the time available to you for your studies, bearing in mind your other commitments.

Section 2.2.3 provided a rough guide to how the steps of essay writing can be allocated chunks of time, but to be honest, at first, and earlier in your studies, these will be rough estimates of time, done through trial and error, before you begin to get a feel for how long tasks realistically take you to complete. The key, however, is to stick to your time allocations and to not spend too much time on any one task at the expense of others.

2.7.5   Sticking to Self-Made Goals

Finally, how do you stick to completing the smaller tasks, milestones, mini-goals and self-imposed deadline dates that you have identified and listed as necessary stages of a project? As well as making sure that the smaller tasks are doable within the timeframe you have allocated, another method to help with sticking to your milestones is to make an informal contract, verbally or in writing, with a person you have chosen to act as an accountability partner. The person should be someone you trust, such as a close friend, parent, dyslexia tutor or partner (as discussed for support networks above). You can then provide your accountability partner with a written copy of your time-framed milestone plan, and as each of your mini deadline dates approaches, you can have a chat with your partner about your progress.

Another way to help you to stick to your goals is to have a rewards and consequences scheme, either self-made or in collaboration with your accountability partner. For example, on completing and achieving a milestone, you treat yourself to something you enjoy, such as watching a favourite movie, or having a special evening out with friends. Likewise, if you find that you procrastinated and did not reach your goal, and this was due to your own doing, and not to

71

circumstances beyond your control, then you should impose con-sequences, such as working on a Saturday or Sunday when this is usually your free day, or forsaking watching your favourite TV show. You just need to create whatever treats and repercussions you personally feel would work best for you, to keep you on track and motivated.

2.8   Summary

This chapter has:

- Covered techniques that can help to make organisation and being in control of your work and life effective, such as:
  - Using plans
  - Breaking down projects
  - Identifying the steps/stages of the project
  - Allocating time-framed chunks.
- Provided examples of how technology can be used to help with organisation.
- Discussed ways of using multisensory methods to make organisation and important activities and dates more memorable, such as:
  - Creating and utilising materials such as visual plans
  - Making yearly academic calendars, weekly planners and daily to-do lists, designed as creative posters to display on walls.
- Presented practical ways of being organised by:
  - Listing useful types of stationery that can make learning fun and information easier to find.
- Supplied examples of metacognition and how this can be used to maintain motivation and prevent procrastination of work.

2.8   Summary

- Provided guidance on ways to cope with meeting deadlines, such as:
  - Ways of multitasking on several assignments
  - Using support networks for motivation
  - Starting work on assignments early in the term to meet deadlines
  - Identifying and breaking down tasks into smaller components
  - Imposing self-made goals
  - Sticking to self-imposed goals.

3

• • • • •

Note-Taking Strategies

3.1   Introduction

Note taking in lectures is one of the most problematic tasks for students with dyslexia due to processing, retention and retrieval difficulties under time-constrained conditions. These are summed up by the quote below from a student discussing the difficulties of interpreting meaning from verbal dialogue when difficulties in auditory processing speed are present:

> You're thinking what do they mean? What does this link to? Taking notes is not good enough. You've got to be fast enough to catch what the lecturer says.

Consequently, the information presented in this chapter taps into techniques that students with dyslexia have themselves devised to help with overcoming difficulties and barriers with note taking.

The quotes provided not only help the reader to identify with common dyslexic difficulties verbalised by their dyslexic peers, which helps the student to feel less isolated with academic obstacles connected to note taking; they also illustrate and provide examples of effective methods that students with dyslexia use to make the note-taking process work productively for the ways in which they think, learn, process and retain information.

Strategies delivered in the chapter that help with vanquishing barriers include active learning methods developed and adapted from proven and established note-taking techniques, such as the Q Notes method (Burke, 2000; www.englishcompanion.com), which uses two columns – a question column and answer column – and can help to make the lecture a more interactive learning experience. The Two-Column method – like the Q Notes technique, but a strategy that can help to develop the skill of condensing notes – is also considered. Examples of ways of using these methods to benefit appropriately from them are presented, such as using shorthand and symbols to replace sentences, and using drawings to replace words. The Four-Quarter method is also suggested: this is a system whereby the page is divided into quarters, with each quarter representing 15 minutes of the lecture, to encourage more concise notes to be taken in the limited space; as is note taking using the Mind Map method, helpful for students who find it difficult to work in a linear way and prefer to see the overall structure of a subject and its connections in colourful ways on one page.

The chapter also reviews types of practical materials that can help to make note taking fun and creative, like coloured pens and paper. Multisensory techniques, note-taking strategies that use all senses, thereby making the process more memorable, are also exemplified. Ways of using technology, such as recording devices to capture the lecture, supplemented by the assistive technology software Sonocent Audio Notetaker, are also discussed.

Finally, metacognition, and developing an awareness of how you can most effectively process auditory information for the purpose of note taking and to retain those notes in memory, is an important academic activity to master. Therefore, we look at an explanation of metacognition and how you can draw upon your visual, auditory or kinaesthetic strengths to select strategies that are suitable for how you think, work and process information.

Before we delve into presenting, trialling and implementing into practice these strategies, however, let us have a look at common difficulties with note taking. That way, we can begin to understand why note-taking difficulties are so prevalent for students with dyslexia.

3.2   Common Difficulties with Note Taking

As dyslexia centres around difficulties with language, both written and verbal, students with dyslexia struggle to listen to a lecture whilst simultaneously being required to identify and write down key points. Owing to processing problems associated with dyslexia, it is extremely challenging to translate the spoken word from the auditory input of the lecturer's voice into the written word, whilst at the same time trying to determine the most important parts of the speech to note down. These challenges are caused by several factors. First, some students may have a speed-processing deficit which makes the procedure of listening, interpreting and writing down points quickly difficult. Second, other students may have a short-term memory deficit as their dyslexia profile, which makes listening whilst writing and then trying to recapture or recall what was previously said to finish writing down a key point especially demanding. If the student has a comorbid diagnosis of dyslexia with dyspraxia, the ability to make quick handwritten notes or to type rapidly into a laptop will be affected.

Because of these multitasking requirements, for students with dyslexia, who may also have concentration difficulties teamed with weaknesses in retention and processing of information, efficiency in note taking becomes particularly difficult. As such, students with dyslexia can easily become frustrated or angry at their own inability to perform note taking proficiently (Abbott-Jones, 2022).

Other negative, and at times destructive, feelings that can be induced by the task of note taking for the dyslexic learner include annoyance, stress, panic, worry, and feeling drained and irritated if the pace of lectures is too fast. BSc trainee Nurse Lisa high-lighted the difficulties of note taking during lectures and would rely upon the online version of the lecture (most of her tutors uploaded their lecture content and slides onto Moodle after the lecture). This enabled Lisa to go through the content at her own pace. However, additional worries were caused if the content of the uploaded lecture had changed or been added to from the original:

> I don't try to take notes. I can't filter the information very well. When you're following a lecture they put the slides online, but when the slides don't match and they've added slides, I'm like 'Oh right so I need to take this note' but then I get paranoid about the notes I'm taking. I won't be able to read them back to myself.

Lisa also described problems when lectures were too long or contained too much information. For students with dyslexia, this is a concern, particularly if the learner gets easily overwhelmed when having to continuously process the delivery of large amounts of verbal dialogue (Brosnan et al., 2002). As Lisa described:

> I do have a problem when lecturers go on and you get an hour in. I know my brain just goes 'Yeah, we can't take this much right now, we're switching off.' Then I switch off and I will come back going 'Oh my God, I've missed most of the lecture. Did I miss something important?' I have no idea what he's been on about for the last five minutes and that is a worry.

BSc Sciences student Fiona had emotions of frustration and hate around note taking, when comparing herself to non-dyslexic peers who seemed capable of this task:

> It's quite an emotional reaction. I just get so frustrated with myself and I hate it when other people can make notes. I know what's being said, but to do it so quickly, especially if they're speaking quickly.

Now let us look at ways and solutions to overcome some of these cognitive and emotional barriers with note taking.

3.3   Techniques

3.3.1   Using Active Learning Methods

Active learning involves a learning activity in which the student participates or interacts with the learning process, rather than just sitting, listening and passively taking in the information. Studies on differences between active and passive learning, such as Bonwell and Eison (1991), have found that for students to be engaged and to learn effectively, they must do more than just listen. They must read, write, discuss and participate in solving problems. For example, early on in her studies, Medicine student Naomi made the mistake of passively sitting and listening to her lecturers as she relied on her Dictaphone (a device allocated to students with a formal diagnosis of dyslexia as part of the Disabled Students' Allowance package, for recording lectures) to do the work during the lecture for her. However, Naomi did not use the device after lectures to relisten to information. She thought this affected her performance in her earlier exams, as she did not do as well as expected. She subsequently learned note taking through trial and error, which enabled her to develop more effective active learning methods. She reflects:

> I got the Dictaphone for Uni and I started recording in the second term. I didn't take many notes and I think that's got a lot to do with the fact that I did worse in the exams because I think I should have taken notes. What I also should have done, and I never did, was to re-listen to it and then taken notes. I didn't do that, I never listened to it again.

Whilst the Dictaphone may be suitable for students with dyslexia, as it takes away the anxiety about missing important information, it is only effective in conjunction with relistening to what was recorded, or if it is supplemented by minimal note taking whilst in lectures to be more engaged.

The recognition that just recording and passively listening is not engaging or active also resonated with postgraduate Sciences student Ada:

> I did have a recorder, but I used it twice and I found that I wasn't as engaged as when I could see the person, see the slides and make the notes there on the spot.

So how can we be more engaged when note taking? Here are some ideas you might want to try.

3.3.2 Creating Questions from Handouts or from Learning Objectives

After realising that recording lectures and passively listening to them was not effective, BSc Medicine student Naomi (discussed above) began to make questions for her lectures, to engage with capturing the relevant information from the lecturer. Fortunately, Naomi's institution always ensured that lecture materials were uploaded onto the university's resources website a few days before the lecture. This enabled her to apply an active learning technique to her note taking during lectures. For example, her lecturers always specified learning objectives for each teaching session by presenting these as a series of bullet points on the initial lecture slide. Using the Q Notes method, described below, Naomi would create a series of questions around the learning objective statements. For example, a learning objective might specify: '*by the end of the lecture students will understand what T cells are*'. On an A4 sheet of paper, or on document on a laptop, Naomi could create questions in the left-hand column – the questions column – such as '*What are T cells?*' '*What do they do?*' etc. That way, her questions became hooks to interact with the material presented during the lecture. Questions also help to make the lecture more interactive as the student becomes focused on extracting the relevant answers to the questions from the verbal speech, as Naomi explained:

> It's more of an active learning thing rather than me passively just sitting there listening.

In the right-hand column (the Q Notes or Q-uiz column), Naomi would write down abbreviated answers to the questions using keywords and shorthand, as covered below.

3.3.3 Activity on Creating Questions from Learning Objectives

To become accustomed to the habit of making questions from lecture handouts and learning objectives presented at the start of a lecture, put yourself into the place of a medicine student and have a go at turning some of these lecture aims into questions to which you would want the answers for your notes during the lecture:

At the end of this session students will be able to:

- Identify and describe the interior and exterior parts of the human heart.
- Describe the path of blood through the cardiac circuits.
- Describe the size, shape and location of the heart.

Examples of some questions you could write down for the lecture in relation to the first statement could be:

- What is the name of the interior part of the human heart?
- What is its function?
- What is the exterior part of the human heart called?
- Does it have a different function from the interior part?

You will at first make your questions through trial and error and will gradually become more skilled in knowing what type of information you want to extract from your lectures. This whole process, however, of waiting for your questions to be answered and discussed by your teacher during the lecture can provide a key to helping you to be more involved and less distracted. That is because the questions provide a meaningful purpose that frames and guides your note taking throughout the lecture.

We now look at how the **Q Notes method** (Burke, 2000) can provide a useful template for helping you to create your questions,

81

interact during the lecture, and reflect on your learning by reviewing the notes made at the end/after the lecture.

3.4   Q Notes Method

The steps involved in the Q Notes process are as follows:

- Take an A4 sheet of paper and divide it into two columns.
- In the left-hand column – the Questions column – make up and write down questions that you want to know the answers to from the lecture/reading.
- Once the questions are written down, wait for the answers in the lecture (or find the answers in the reading) and write these down in summarised note form alongside the questions in the right-hand column of the paper – the Q Notes column.
- To place into memory, cover over the notes in the right-hand column, and see if it is possible to answer the questions without looking at the notes.
- Repeat the process, doubling the amount of time between attempts at answering the questions, until eventually it can be left for a couple of days, and answers to the questions can be given without looking at the summarised notes in the Q Notes column.

Thus, in addition to making it easier for you to make questions and take notes throughout a lecture, the completed Q Notes template can act as a useful resource for revising lecture content in preparation for your exams. The Q Notes method can also be used to make course reading more interactive and memorable. In the same way as you create questions to act as hooks for capturing the relevant information during lectures, you can use the Q Notes template to make questions before you read, so that you are approaching your reading with the purpose of extracting from the text the answers to your questions. Then in the same way that you can use your Q Notes from lectures as a revision source, you can also use Q Notes to make your reading more memorable by covering up the notes column and trying to answer the questions in your question column without looking. For example, MSc Geology student Luke used this two-step process to make his reading absorb into memory processes more effectively. He would first read through an important paper selecting and extracting key information by highlighting and making condensed notes. Then he would apply the Q Notes method to test himself on the information he had read and to put his learning into memory.

Below is an example of the Q Notes template. The link below enables you to print out the template to take along to your lectures. It has several key features:

www.cambridge.org/abbottjones

- By filling in the Date – Module – Subject/Topic, you can store the notes in your file, and in preparation for exams you can easily find your revision sources for each topic covered during the Module.
- The Q-uestions column encourages you to translate titles, subheadings and statements, or topic sentences from your lecture handouts into questions you want the answer to during the lecture. For example, if a slide on your lecture handout had the title **Cardiac Circuits**, in the questions column you might jot down – *What are cardiac circuits?*
- The Q-uiz Answers column gives you limited space to write down your answers, which forces you to be concise and to use abbreviations for your note taking.
- The Summary of the Lecture box enables you to reflect on the lecture and your notes and prompts you to write a few sentences in your own words on what the lecture was about.

83

3.4.1 Example of Q Note Method Template

Date _____

Module _____

Subject/Topic _____

Q-uestions	Q-uiz Answers
(Turn titles, subheadings and topic sentences into questions)	(Write the answers to the questions opposite. Use symbols, abbreviations and bullet points to help organise your ideas more efficiently)
Summary of the Lecture:	

3.5   The Two-Column Method

The Two-Column method shares similarities with the Q Notes method, as the template for this system again uses two columns with a Summary box at the bottom for recording the main points of the lecture. However, unlike the Q Notes method, the left-hand column, rather than being for writing questions, is called the Recall column and is there for the purpose of reducing the main notes made in the right-hand column – the Note-taking column – to **key points** and **cues**. That is why the left-hand column is much narrower than the right-hand column.

The main benefits of the Two-Column method are, first, it requires students to identify the main ideas and important information in connection with the topic, which are recorded in the Note-taking column. Second, it provides the student with practice in condensing notes down to keywords and abbreviations. Third, the learner can use the method as an effective revision device, by covering over their notes in the Note-taking column and by using key points in the Recall column to act as memory joggers for retrieving the covered information. This process, if repeated, helps to place the learning from the lecture into long-term memory. As such, this strategy is particularly suitable for students with dyslexia as it is a multisensory technique requiring you to listen to record notes, to act on visual information to reduce your notes into the Recall column, and then to be active by reciting, reflecting on, revising and reviewing your notes to commit them to memory. As with any strategy, though, students need to understand the point of the exercise, and to practise the method to feel more competent and comfortable in using the system. For that reason, the technique is broken

85

down into a series of easy-to-follow steps below, which you can use as a guide and as a starting point for becoming more familiar with this method.

Step 1

Before the lecture, either print out the template for the two-column note-taking system by using the link to the Resources below, or draw a vertical line on an A4 blank piece of paper about 6 cm from the right-hand edge. This is your **Recall column**. To the right of this is your **Note-taking column**, which should be 15 cm wide. If you would prefer to use a hard copy of this, the link below provides access to the template for the Two-Column method.

www.cambridge.org/abbottjones

Step 2

During the lecture, try to determine what the key important information is and then **record notes** in the Note-taking column as fully and clearly as you can. If possible, attempt to use abbreviations, symbols and diagrams, which we go through below, rather than trying to write full sentences. That way, it will save you time. If you are using lined paper, **skip lines**. If using blank paper, leave spaces as though you have skipped lines. You can do this for several reasons:

- To show the end of particular ideas or thoughts.
- If you lose your train of thought.
- You cannot keep up with the lecturer.
- If you don't fully understand what is being said.

In each case, **mark the gap with a symbol or word** to identify the reason for the blank space. Using words such as 'END' or 'MISSING', or

symbols such as **?** (Question mark), will help you afterwards to identify the reasons for the omission.

Step 3

After the lecture, reduce your notes by jotting down ideas and **keywords** (cues) in the Recall column (use **drawings and symbols** if you
prefer). These should immediately give you the idea and gist of the
main points of the lecture. This process should help clarify the meaning and **relationships of ideas**.

At this step, you should also complete the Summary box by writing
a couple of sentences on what the **main points** of the lecture were.

Step 4

Recite the main facts and ideas of the lecture by covering the Note-
taking column and using the cues in the Recall column. This process
helps commit facts and ideas to your **long-term memory**. At this
stage, you may also begin to reflect and come up with new ideas and
relationships.

Step 5

A quick **review** of the keywords in your Recall columns for a few
minutes each week will help you remember much of what you have
made notes on.

This method has many similarities to the **SQ3R Reading Strategy**
which is covered in the *Reading Strategies* chapter.

As you can see below, the template for the Two-Column Note-
Taking system, similarly to the Q Notes method, requires you to enter
date, module and topic in the right-hand corner of the page. Thus,
in the same way that the filed Q Notes become easy to retrieve for
revision purposes, this organisation is also achieved with the Two-
Column Note-Taking method.

3.5.1   Example of Two-Column Method

Date _____

Module _____

Topic _____

Recall Column	Note-Taking Column
Reduce main points to **key points** and **cues** for reciting, reflecting and reviewing	**Record** facts and ideas (as fully as possible) Use abbreviations, symbols, diagrams etc. Write as clearly as you can

←6 cm→	←15 cm→

Summary

Use this space for a brief overall summary.

88

3.6   Using Shorthand and Symbols to Replace Sentences

During the early stages at university, it is common for students to believe that they must make notes on everything the teacher is saying during lectures. This leads to panic and stress when the student struggles to keep up and finds that they have big sections of their lecturer's speech missing from their notes. Over time, the student gradually realises that it is more important to capture the main information and to make notes quickly. For this purpose and to save time when writing, they often begin to use abbreviations of words and their own variations of shorthand and symbols which they have devised as a recognisable replacement for words or sentences. This was an experience identified by BSc Sports Science student Sarah:

> When I first started in the first year, I'd be sat there writing out the whole thing.

On realisation that this was not only exhausting but counterproductive, she began to use abbreviations for longer words and terminology specific to her course:

> You're not writing shorthand, but you are in a way, like if you know that there's a shorter way or like a symbol that means what you need to write then you wrote that.

Below are listed some useful ways for helping you to create shorthand and abbreviations when you are note taking during lectures:

3.6.1   Forget the Unnecessary Verbs and Conjunctions

Some verbs, for example *be*, *have*, *do*, *say*, *tell*, are just not needed for you to understand your notes. Getting rid of them completely can help save you time when note taking. Likewise, articles and conjunctions, such as *the*, *a*, *and*, *but*, are unnecessary when note taking.

3.6.2 Shorten Words by Leaving Out Letters or by Using the Start and End of the Word

This is known as word truncation. Some examples below, to help you get into the process of doing this, are as follows:

- Me – medicine
- Pogy – phonology
- Ppl – people
- Ustand – understand
- Res – research
- Natl – national
- Gov – government
- Dep – department
- Ed – education
- Psy – psychology

3.6.3 Create Your Own Abbreviations and Symbols

Create your own abbreviations and symbols that you can use for commonly used words and phrases and/or for words specific to your course content.

So that you remember what the abbreviations and symbols stand for when you review your notes after the lecture, you should keep a list, like a glossary of terms, that you have created and that you can refer to. Additionally, to get you into the habit of consistently using shorthand, abbreviations and symbols for note taking, you could initially take this list with you and refer to it during lectures when the word is used and you want to note it down. This will help to place your symbols into memory, so eventually you will be attending your lectures without having to rely on looking at your list. To give you an idea of the sorts of symbols and abbreviations you could use, some common ones are listed below.

3.6.4   Common Symbols

- ∵ because
- ∴ therefore, OR consequently
- + & and OR plus
- ? question OR doubt OR possibility
- > greater than
- < less than
- # no. number
- £ or $ money OR cost
- Δ change
- / per OR each
- ↑ increase OR improvement
- → leads to OR causes
- ↓ decrease OR deterioration
- ↔ linked OR interrelated OR connected
- ↛ does not lead to
- = equal OR the same as
- ~ approximately OR around OR similar to
- ≠ not equal OR not the same as

- X strikethrough not
- ∝ varies with OR related to
- … etc. OR missing words

3.6.5 Common Abbreviations

- etc.   etcetera; and so on
- et al.   and the other authors
- e.g.   for example
- i.e.   that is
- NB*   note well OR remember this
- Approx.   approximately
- cf.   compared to
- am   morning
- pm   afternoon
- ASAP   as soon as possible
- DIY   do it yourself
- AWOL   absent without leave

3.7   Using Drawing to Replace Words

Drawing images to replace writing words whilst note taking is an effective method for keeping engaged during the lecture, as it requires active learning processes. This is because it enables inter-pretive techniques to take place, so the student is not just passively listening to the information. As the student processes the auditory information from the lecture, they can transform this into images that are meaningful for them. In that way, they are constantly identifying connections between topics and illustrations that represent those topics. Furthermore, images can be a productive form of unlocking information, particularly for students with dyslexia, and can act as powerful memory joggers for retrieving learning that has been covered during lectures. A study by Akhavan Tafti, Hameedy and Mohammadi Baghal, titled 'Dyslexia, a deficit or a difference: Comparing the creativity and memory skills of dyslexic and nondyslexic students in Iran', discovered that in students with dyslexia their visual-spatial memory (ability to remember the shape, colour and location of something in space) can be stronger than their visual-semantic memory (ability to remember how a word looks) (Akhavan Tafti et al., 2009). Consequently, visual memory is a strength for many students with dyslexia, and the strategy of converting spoken and written language to visual images can be a key to placing information into memory, as metaphorically expressed by MA Arts student Debra:

> Keyword or drawing something visual, then it's like, oh there it is. It's like the closet you open, when everything falls out, but it's sometimes finding that little thing that will open the door. It's finding the key basically.

One approach to note taking advocated by the learning platform Edutopia (www.edutopia.org) is called Sketchnoting, created by Mike Rohde. Sketchnoting is basically a form of visual note taking that helps to transform doodles into a tool for helping to deepen understanding of a concept. If you want to find out more about using Sketchnoting during lectures, there are YouTube videos on this which can help to get you started. Other ways to introduce yourself to visual note taking, as advised by Edutopia, include taking the basic steps below.

3.7.1   Rethink Your Paper

Rather than using A4 lined paper with margins, which because of its rigid structure can inhibit drawing, try using blank paper. The space on the paper allows you the freedom to experiment with the drawing of symbols and with how you would like your notes/drawings to be organised or arranged on the page. You may also want to use different-coloured paper or different-coloured pens, or to make mind maps or spidergrams. This will make the process creative and more engaging. Links between concepts can easily be made and visually seen by drawing arrows, links or circles to connect things together. This method was used by MA Arts student Debra, who, after struggling throughout her undergraduate degree in trying to make notes in the traditional way, had finally developed a version that was more suitable for the way she processed information:

> Then I realised colourful pens which were exciting and the images, the drawings. So, I'd actually turn my paper landscape, and my notes would be different kinds of circles or bubbles, so it's almost a bit like a mind map. It's actually sometimes upside down, or different, so I'd be constantly turning my paper around.

The constant turning of the paper into landscape, then back to horizontal, allowed Debra the freedom to be expressive and to easily make connections between the different concepts. If at first you would prefer a template for experimenting with this form of note taking, the link below will give you access to a concept map which you can print out, take along to your next lecture and test out. It can be turned around and drawn on; or if you don't want to be constrained by this, then have a go at taking a sheet of blank paper or a sketch pad to your lectures to trial your visual note taking.

www.cambridge.org/abbottjones

3.7.2   Develop a Symbolic Language

If you identify the main keywords or concepts most regularly used in your topic, you could develop a visual library of shorthand, with icons and characters representing these principal ideas. Over time, you could keep adding to your visual vocabulary, so that when it comes to revision of your subject, each visual image unlocks your memory of the semantic meaning it represents.

3.7.3   Keep Images Basic

You do not have to be an accomplished artist to use visual note-taking techniques. The idea behind visual note taking is not to try too hard in making the sketches and drawings look good, but to use images to make associations between concepts, and ultimately, to use them as visual memory joggers for unlocking the information behind them, as described by Debra above.

3.8   Four-Quarter Method

If you prefer to work in a more linear way and the unstructuredness offered by the visual note-taking method is not for you, then the Four-Quarter system may provide a more suitable format. The Four-Quarter method involves dividing your page into quarters (see the example below).

The link also allows you to print out a coloured template of the Four-Quarter method.

www.cambridge.org/abbottjones

3.8.1   Example of Four-Quarter Method

Date _____

Module _____

Topic _____

1st Quarter – 15 mins	2nd Quarter – 15 mins
3rd Quarter – 15 mins	4th Quarter – 15 mins

Each quarter of the page represents 15 minutes of the lecture. The benefit of this system is that it helps to keep you active and engaged, as you will need to set a timer on your watch to ensure that you move onto the next section after a 15-minute period. The limited space that the template provides encourages you to be concise with your note taking by using symbols, abbreviations and keywords as discussed above. Additionally, having to repeatedly switch after 15-minute intervals helps to keep you focused on the information during the lecture. Also, as with the Q Notes and Two-Column methods, you are required to complete the date, module and topic on the template, so once your notes are filed away, they are easy to retrieve and provide a good revision source.

A disadvantage of this method, though, is that students can be confused over identifying and capturing important parts of the lecture and knowing what information to note down. Combining this method with the Outline method below can go some way to resolving this.

3.9   The Outline Method

This method works more effectively when amalgamated with being able to view the handout of your lecturer's slides in advance. If your lecturer uploads their presentation before your taught session, you should ideally print out the handout and take it along with you to the lecture. This will help to guide your understanding of the content of the lecture and key areas to be discussed. Once you have the gist of what will be covered, the idea is to select four or five of the main points from the handout, perhaps by highlighting these on your printout. When your lecturer starts to talk about one of the key areas you have identified as significant from the handout, still using the 15-minute timed blocks, you write the name of this main idea or key point into your Four-Quarter template as a title. When your lecturer begins to elaborate on this topic, you can use bullet points to write more in-depth subpoints, based on what is being discussed on the topic, under the title. It may be useful to use two different-coloured pens, one colour to write the title of the main idea, and a separate colour to add the subpoints.

The advantages of this method are, because you have spent a small amount of preparation time before the lecture in identifying and highlighting what you predict the important aspects to be, you won't be overwhelmed by unexpected information during the lecture. You will also be able to focus more on the sections of the talk you have highlighted, in the aim of turning the extra information on these points into a series of mini bullet points. This system enables your notes to be fairly structured. They may look a little like the example below:

Date: Jan 15, 2022
Module: Cardiology
Topic: Heart Diseases

1st Quarter – 15 mins	2nd Quarter – 15 mins
Types of Diseases • Coronary Artery Disease (CAD) • Heart Arrhythmias • ♥ Failure • ♥ V Dis	Causes of Diseases • Obesity ≥ • In rest OR Diabet • ↑ Cholest • Fam Hist
3rd Quarter – 15 mins	4th Quarter – 15 mins
Symptomology • Chest	Treatment • Diet • Exercise • Med

Of course, with this system, you are also encouraged to get into the habit of using abbreviations, symbols, truncation of words, and diagrams, to take less time when note-taking and to use your visual memory strengths.

3.10   The Mind-Map Method

Mind maps, also known as concept maps or spider diagrams, can be an effective way of capturing and getting down ideas onto paper when you are struggling to know where to start. That is because the central idea (see the example below) forms the starting point of the mind map.

In this example, the main topic or central idea is Module Research, and the main branches, titled library, planning, lectures and computer, form the key sources of information for Module Research (see Figure 3.1).

If we placed the topic Heart Diseases from above into mind-map form, it would look something like this, with the main topic of the lecture – Heart Diseases – being the central idea, and the key areas of the lecture – types, causes, symptomology and treatment – forming the main branches and emanating from the central idea (see Figure 3.2).

As you can see from these two examples of mind maps, they enable you to see connections easily using branches and sub-branches. They provide a complete overview of a topic and, owing to the very visual way in which colourful images are associated with keywords, they lend themselves to being a memorable revision resource.

Mind maps were first popularised by author and educational consultant Tony Buzan. He argued that mind mapping based on radiant thinking, whereby connections and associations emit outwards like the branches on a tree, mirrors the way in which the

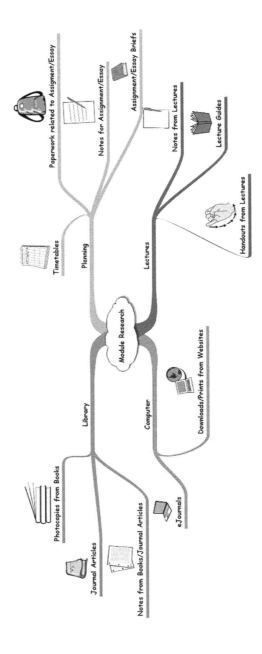

Figure 3.1 Module Research mind map

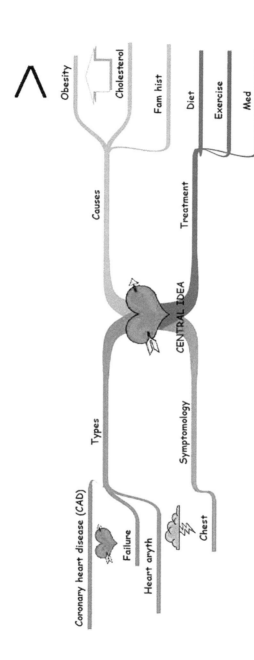

Figure 3.2 Heart Diseases mind map

brain naturally thinks. Thus, it allows the mind to think more easily and spontaneously, as it is not constrained by having to work in linear list format.

Despite the benefits of mind maps, there are some disadvantages with this method, and you will need to try it out a few times to see if it is suitable for you. Some of these drawbacks include: if you are note taking during a lecture using a blank piece of paper (which should be in landscape mode), you may be self-conscious about your drawing. As we discussed (in the section 'Using Drawing to Replace Words'), this does not matter, because you should only be attempting to use very simplistic images that are easy for you to remember anyway. Some students may think that mind maps are unprofessional; they end up looking scruffy; or they cannot hold enough information from the lecture, owing to using only one A4 sheet of paper, which must contain words, branches and images from an entire two- to three-hour lecture. Other students, owing to the way they prefer to think, or to being more comfortable with traditional modes of learning, may be more inclined to be linear thinkers.

If any of these disadvantages of mind mapping is true for you, there are solutions to these difficulties. One method is to transform your freehand mind map from your lecture into a computer-generated mind map.

3.10.1   Computer-Generated Mind Map

After your lecture, you could go over your freehand mind map to place it into mind-mapping computer software, such as Inspiration or X Mind. This transformation process enables you to review, reflect, recap and expand on the things you learned during the lecture, which is beneficial for memory and for consolidating your learning.

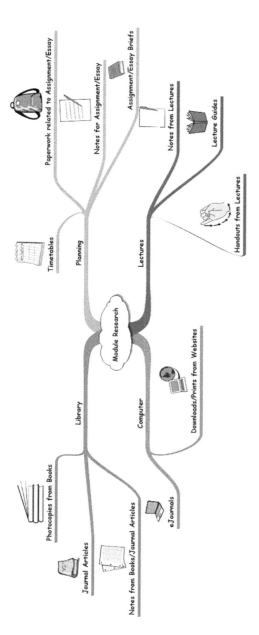

Figure 3.3 Module Research mind map (with linear list)

Module Research

I. Planning

   A. Timetables

   B. Paperwork related to Assignment/Essay

   C. Notes for Assignment/Essay

   D. Assignment/Essay Briefs

II. Lectures

   A. Notes from Lectures

   B. Lecture Guides

   C. Handouts from Lectures

III. Computer

   A. Downloads/Prints from Websites

   B. eJournals

IV. Library

   A. Photocopies from Books

   B. Journal Articles

   C. Notes from Books/Journal Articles

Furthermore, if you are dissatisfied with the drawings you made during the lecture, Inspiration software, which was used to create the two examples above, has a terrific, easy-to-use library of symbols and images. Visuals can be searched through the libraries by simply typing in keywords and selected by clicking and dragging into place on your mind map, so that an entire vocabulary of image word association can effortlessly be created.

If you are a linear thinker, or you like to combine the two approaches by first creating colourful, memorable visual mind maps, and then converting these into linear lists for the purposes of planning, timetabling revision of topics and so on, then the Outline view in Inspiration will make this transformation for you (see the example below of a mind map together with a linear list obtained by clicking on the Outline view) (see Figure 3.3).

This approach is effective if you want to combine a visual method with a more organised view of your notes.

3.11   Practical Methods

3.11.1   Materials

Using Coloured Pens and Coloured Paper

Let us now turn our attention to more practical matters and review some of the materials and stationery items that make the process of note taking more enjoyable, interactive and engaging.

Benefits of Using Colour

When reviewing your notes, if they are written in one colour, typically blue or black ink, they will appear the same throughout. There will be nothing standing out and not a single aspect to grab your attention. When you add colour, however, to draw emphasis to important points, suddenly the notes come alive. They become unique, unusual, more memorable, and interesting. That is because you have used your thought processes to interpret and transform the material into something that is meaningful to you, which enables you to be more absorbed in your learning. Another benefit of using colour for note taking is that you will be able to recall more effectively the various colours used throughout your notes, highlighting key aspects of your topic, than you would be able to do with notes of one colour, which ultimately hide the significant parts of the subject. Notes using colour will also be easier to review when it comes to revision.

Red Pens

Whilst it is advisable to select different-coloured pens that are meaningful to you for your note taking – favourite colours, or colours that you have coded, so that blue signifies important points, and green represents additional information, for example – an interesting study by the University of British Columbia revealed that the colour red 'boosted performance on detail-oriented tasks such as memory retrieval and proofreading by as much as 31 percent compared to blue' (Mehta and Zhu, 2009). The authors contend that because the colour red is perceptively associated with danger and mistakes, when red writing is identified in notes (perhaps to signify key points), this enhances attention to those words, which consequently can be stored into memory more effectively. You may want to test this out the next time you are assessing your notes.

Thin-Tip Gel Pens with Comfortable Grips

If you are dyspraxic or find it difficult or tiring to write neatly, then you may find using coloured gel pens with contoured rubber grips more comfortable to write with. These types of pens are versatile, and the ink flows smoothly without requiring much pressure. This makes writing over longer periods of time seem easier, without causing cramping and fatigue.

It may also be worth browsing through some of the stationery items at The Dyslexia Shop (www.thedyslexiashop.co.uk/), as they sell a range of carefully selected products appropriate for people with dyslexia.

Using Coloured Pens for Traffic Light System

One useful method for note taking, using three different-coloured pens, is the traffic light system. For instance, a red pen may be used for key important points. An orange pen can substantiate or provide more information on key points. A green pen could signify areas for expansion or clarification. BA Education student Stephanie would first use a highlighter to mark out important points and would then combine this with different-coloured pens that symbolised different categories of information for her:

> Well, the thing is for me I would highlight the most important things. If something was really relevant, I would highlight that in red, and I had various colours that would symbolise what it meant, you know, what was important, what was less important.

Coloured Cards

If you find it helpful to go through your notes after the lecture, condensing the information further to strengthen your learning, you may find the process of transforming your notes onto different-coloured cards effective. The act of making the cards uses kinaesthetic strengths, and abbreviating your notes into a series of bullet points that you can write on the cards using coloured pens utilises your creative and visual ability. The combination makes this method multisensory, engaging and memorable.

You can also colour-code the cards based on hierarchy of information or topic selection, and you can condense into bullet points by using the traffic light system discussed above. MSc Humanities student Alison enjoyed using this approach to her note taking:

> So, all my notes are in colour, when I would make them, so different-coloured cards and then different-coloured writing on the cards with diagrams.

3.12 Multisensory Methods

When using multisensory methods for note taking or during review of your notes, you should try to use a combination of your visual, auditory and kinaesthetic (or tactile) senses. The more senses used in learning, the easier new knowledge is to store and then retrieve from memory. As stated by the International Dyslexia Association (2000), 'multisensory teaching is simultaneously visual, auditory, and kinaesthetic-tactile to enhance memory and learning. Links are consistently made between the visual (what we see), auditory (what we hear), and kinaesthetic-tactile (what we feel) pathways.' Studies on children with specific learning difficulties have provided evidence that the teaching of multisensory phonics programmes is effective for reading remediation (Warnick and Calderella, 2016), and it has also been shown that adult learners with dyslexia can use the multisensory method and adapt this to their own ways of learning for the effective memorising and recall of information for their studies (Abbott-Jones, 2022). A few of these examples are presented below.

3.12.1   Using Different Multisensory Strategies Dependent on the Type of Information

MSc Sciences student Alan, who realised the importance of making his learning multisensory, would use different approaches depending on the nature of the knowledge on which he would be taking notes. For example, if the lecture was in relation to different foods to mitigate obesity, then he would perhaps make a spider diagram (mind map) to associate images with words. If, however, the lecture was on the main types of chemical compositions, then this type of information might be more appropriate in linear format, to see more clearly the hierarchical relationships between the different compositions:

> So, it's making it into a picture as well, not always necessarily a spider diagram, because sometimes that's really useful for certain things, but sometimes that can be more difficult to remember. I sometimes quite like linear format if I'm learning something and it's just different colours, different methods, and it becomes multisensory.

3.12.2   Verbalising the Topic, Teaching It and Explaining It to Someone

On review of your notes after the lecture, to help with placing key concepts of the lecture into memory more effectively, some students find it helpful to articulate the main points of the topic aloud as though teaching it to someone, or actually explaining it to another person such as a friend, peer or parent. The act of articulation and hearing it can be combined with using motor skills to physically write or type information. For instance, if teaching the topic, a white board can be used to write keywords. The act of translating learning into your own words, combined with hearing it aloud through your voice, whilst simultaneously using physical movement, motor skills and visualisation to write, makes this an effective multisensory strategy.

3.12.3   Hearing It Aloud

Hearing learning spoken aloud is useful for review of lecture notes, after the lecture and during the lecture itself, as expressed by two students below.

BSc Medicine student Naomi found the combination of using kin-aesthetic strengths to physically write or type things, whilst simultaneously reading aloud the words she was writing to be able to hear them, helped to assist her recall of the information:

> I have to constantly write stuff down and read stuff aloud multiple times for me to be able to recall it whenever I need to. So, it will be doing it, it will be first writing it, so it's the act of writing, it will help to get it into my memory. Then reading it, reading aloud, so getting it in different methods. I find if I physically do the writing, or physi-cally do the typing, I remember it more because it's gone through a different part.

MSc Humanities student Alison, meanwhile, would tackle note tak-ing during a lecture by using a three-stage process. As her university provided lecture materials in advance of the lecture, she would first print out the PowerPoint to show three slides per page, which allows space for notes to be made alongside each slide. Second, she would take the printout to the lecture, because she needed to associate the verbalisation of information from the lecturer to the visual of the slides whilst she jotted down key things in the space on the printout. Third, after the lecture, in the comfort of her home, she would replay a video of the lecture using the university's lecture capture services (which enables lectures to be recorded and then replayed by students on their laptops or phones). At this stage, she would expand on certain sections by adding notes, redrawing graphs or searching for terms online. The association of visual slides with audio verbalisation from the lecturer, further reinforced by the video connected to the slides, teamed with the kinaesthetic element of adding to the slides and internet searching for clarification of terms, is what makes this process useful, as it is using all learning senses.

> I'm probably just going to look at his PowerPoint and that's when I started to print the PowerPoints and write on the PowerPoints and that was more effective because actually it is better for me to listen because I'll take in a lot more.

3.13   Technology

Technology, in this context, applies to various types of specialist technology, usually allocated to the student from the Disabled Students' Allowance, that can help to support note taking and supplement the everyday technology such as Google and YouTube which the student may use to assist their learning.

3.13.1   Various Forms of Assistive Technology that Can Help with Note Taking

Note-taking technology provides an accessible alternative to pen and paper form. You can use the technologies listed below to create audio recordings, take digital notes, and sync both recordings and notes between your devices. We have seen from Section 3.3.1 on 'Using Active Learning Methods' that merely recording a lecture with a Dictaphone whilst sitting passively listening is ineffective.

If recording is, however, supplemented during the lecture by simultaneously doing something active, such as using the Q Notes method, then the use of technology can be productive, as it provides a means for reflecting on the content of the lecture when reviewing notes afterwards. Some of the devices below, when combined with other active methods of note taking, can prove to be productive.

3.13.2   Livescribe Echo Smartpen

The Livescribe pen has a microphone and speaker contained within. It also has a camera at the pen nib. You must use the pen in conjunction with the Livescribe notebook paper. Whilst easy to write on with the pen, the paper contains a series of dots that you tap with your pen after the lecture when you want to play a recording of the notes you have taken. Essentially, this is how it works. At the start of your lecture, you ensure the pen is recording, as shown on the digital display at the top of the pen. You then make notes during the lecture of key points and so on (as you would with a normal pen), in the Livescribe note pad. After the lecture, if you want to relisten to any part of the talk, you use the pen nib to press onto a keyword in the notepad, and the audio recording of the discussion around that keyword will play. The notes can also be transferred to your desktop or other electronic devices using a USB.

3.13.3   Sonocent Audio Notetaker

With Sonocent installed on your laptop or tablet, you will need to take this device with you to be able to record your lecture. The audio of the lecture is then recorded into the software using audio

111

chunks that appear as bars on your laptop screen in the audio pane. When key points are being discussed during the lecture, you can select colours to highlight the audio bars, like using a highlighter pen. In the text pane, which is displayed on your screen next to the audio pane, you may want to type in additional information. Whilst this is useful software for reviewing key areas from your notes, or for adding to your notes after the lecture, it does not enable a full transcription of the audio. To do this, you will have to type whilst listening then pausing the recording, or you may want to integrate the recording to Dragon speech-to-text software. A difficulty with this, however, is that Dragon may not be able to convert the speech-to-text accurately if unfamiliar with the speaker's voice, or if there were additional sounds and noises in the room where the lecture took place.

3.13.4   Using Technology to Supplement Learning After the Lecture

In addition to using technology such as Smartpens, Sonocent audio notetaker and speech-to-text software, you may find it useful to strengthen your learning of specific topics covered during your lectures by using internet search engines such as Google and Wikipedia. Whilst these sources should not be relied on for providing accurate evidence-based knowledge on a subject, as the information is not properly vetted, they can still help in developing background knowledge and understanding of a topic by giving the gist of something. Furthermore, difficult words can be broken down and their meanings ascertained by typing into Google.

Finally, let us consider how developing our metacognitive awareness can also help with the note-taking process.

3.14   Metacognition

As we saw from Chapter 2, metacognition is developing an awareness and an understanding of what you need to do to learn effectively. This applies to thinking about the best note-taking strategies for you, the type of environment that is suitable for you to learn in, the time of day when you are at your most productive, and other aspects that can help you to absorb and retain information more easily. For example, is your mind more relaxed and receptive to learning when you are listening to background music, or do you need distracting noises such as when working in a café to be more constructive?

In an interesting study titled 'Exploring metacognitive strategy use during note-taking for students with learning disabilities', by Boyle, Rosen and Forchelli (2016), a useful explanation of metacognition is provided. Boyle et al. cite Flavell, Miller and Miller's (2002) work to state:

According to Flavell, Miller, and Miller (2002), metacognition includes 'both what you know about cognition and how you manage your own cognition' (p. 164). These components are sometimes referred to as metacognitive knowledge and metacognitive monitoring and regulation. More specifically, metacognitive knowledge pertains to a person's knowledge about their own cognitive processes (e.g., I can remember information better that is written down), tasks (e.g., I can remember organised information better than unorganised) and strategies (e.g., if I cannot write down everything during a lecture, I will just write the vocabulary word and come back later to write out its definition) (Flavell 1979) (Boyle et al., 2016, p. 163).

Boyle et al. (2016) go on to say that 'students with good metacognitive self-regulatory skills tend to change their strategies based upon their success or failure of the task (MacLeod, Butler, and Syer 1996).

When a strategy is successful, they have a tendency to include it in their repertoire of tools for problem solving.'

Consequently, metacognition is your ability to reflect on and to become conscious of how you think and learn efficiently. When applied to note taking, it is your capacity to think about the types of methods that you have used in the past and have found to be either ineffective or effective. You then take the successful strategies and fine-tune these to work even more productively for you, so you can then add these methods to your toolbox for overcoming future difficulties in note taking.

One way to help you achieve this is to reflect on areas where you are already competent. As such, returning to Chapter 2 and the visual, auditory, kinaesthetic learning styles questionnaire, were your strengths in the visual, kinaesthetic or auditory realm? Of course, as we have seen in the 'Multisensory Methods' section, a combination of these senses when learning anything is effective; yet some students can tend to be more visual than auditory, or more auditory than kinaesthetic. Once you understand where your skills lie, you can use this knowledge to your advantage to select the most appropriate note-taking techniques for how you think.

- Are you visual?
- If so, would you benefit from using coloured pens and coloured paper?
- Do you remember images more effectively than words?
- If so, sketchnoting, drawing images to replace words, and the Mind Map method may be suitable strategies for you.
- Does the radiant thinking involved in the Mind Map method come naturally to you, or are you more of a linear thinker?
- If more of a linear thinker, the Q Notes method, the Two-Column method, the Four-Quarter method or the Outline method will be more appropriate.

114

- Are you a kinaesthetic learner who needs to be more active during note taking?
- Although it is difficult for you to physically move around the room during note taking for lectures, you may find the Q Notes method useful for helping to keep you engaged throughout the talk. You may also gain from teaching the subject to someone by moving around the room, or making coloured cards and condensing down the information into bullet points after the lecture, to use your physical and tactile skills.
- Are you an auditory learner and more receptive to information when you hear it aloud?
- If so, whilst you will find recording your lecturer's voice and then relistening to the recording after the lecture helpful, you may also profit from repeatedly hearing yourself reading out the notes.

You may be surprised to find, however, that methods less dominant in drawing upon your prime strengths, such as mind mapping for auditory learners, or the Four-Quarter method for visual learners, could be the key to solving your note-taking difficulties. If you are in the early stages of finding your most suitable note-taking approach, or you want to experiment a little and change or adapt your method, it may be a good idea to try a range of strategies to develop awareness of methods effective for you.

3.15   Summary

This chapter has:

- Outlined common difficulties with note taking encountered by students with dyslexia.

Note-Taking Strategies

- Covered techniques that can help to overcome difficulties with note taking, such as:
  - Using active learning methods.
  - Creating questions from handouts and learning objectives of the lecture.
  - The Q Notes method.
  - The Two-Column method.
  - Using shorthand and symbols to replace words.
  - Using drawing to replace words.
  - The Four-Quarter method.
  - The Outline method.
  - The Mind Map method.
- Presented useful practical materials to help with note taking, such as:
  - Using coloured pens and coloured paper.
- Discussed ways of using multisensory methods to make note taking more engaging and memorable, such as:
  - Verbalising the topic, teaching it, and explaining it to someone.
  - Hearing it aloud.
- Provided examples of how technology can be used to help with note taking.
- Discussed ways of developing metacognition in relation to note taking.

4

• • • • •

Reading Strategies

4.1 Introduction

Higher education courses generally require students to undertake enormous amounts of reading. In that sense, reading at university can often feel overwhelming, as described by MA Education student Chloe, discussing difficulties with the volume of reading required by her course:

> I would tend to read thinner books because it's more manageable. I find the reading really difficult, and I feel like it sets up a lot of anxiety about whether I can do it. I've been thinking maybe I've made a mistake with taking this course on.

It is therefore important for students with dyslexia to develop effective approaches to reading, as they may become overloaded and feel swamped with the magnitude of academic reading materials.

Or they may become frustrated by their slower reading speeds and the amount of time taken to read and comprehend the information, as explained by BSc Nursing student Tina, who had to repeatedly re-read academic texts to understand the main points:

> I'm just looking at it [the reading] and it's not having the meaning of what I'm reading. That whole process of reading it many times and trying to get the main points is what I find quite stressful, especially when you're on a time limit.

As such, this chapter, after briefly outlining common difficulties that students with dyslexia encounter when reading, will feature what the students say about how they have devised and developed effective coping strategies to tackle reading. In addition to incorporating the dyslexic learners' perspectives and views on reading, the chapter will include advice on using selected reading techniques, such as the Preview, Ask and Answer questions, Summarise, and Synthesis (PASS) strategy. The Q Notes method, already discussed in Chapter 3, is now looked at in relation to how it can be applied to reading to make the process more purposeful and selective. The Survey, Question, Read, Recite, and Review (SQ3R) technique is also outlined, as although it is similar in approach to the PASS method, from practitioner experience, students do tend to prefer one over the other. Presenting both methods provides the option to experiment. Other strategies outlined include employing skimming and scanning approaches, using selectivity to minimise the amount of unnecessary reading, utilising colour-coded highlighting, and making notes in the form of summaries of the readings.

Interestingly, students with dyslexia also benefit from employing pragmatic practical approaches to their reading (Abbott-Jones, 2022) to make the activity less challenging. These approaches will be covered in the chapter, which includes little things often overlooked – such as printing out papers rather than reading digitally, as being able to handle the material whilst highlighting and drawing on the text is beneficial for both kinaesthetic and visual learners. Practical methods to alleviate scotopic sensitivity and tracking difficulties are also discussed.

Metacognitive awareness (which, as discussed in previous chapters, is being aware of how you think and knowing appropriate strategies that you can apply effectively to your learning) is important when reading, to assist with the absorption of ideas and comprehension of the text. However, metacognition is not merely centred on your understanding of how you learn and suitable techniques for complementing your individual learning style. It also includes being mindful of things such as picking the right environment to read in, and taking breaks when feeling overwhelmed or tired. For example, MA Arts student Debra realised that using relaxing distraction techniques, such as making food or nail painting, whilst she was studying enabled her to absorb concepts more effectively:

> I'm quite good at taking in ideas when I'm distracted, preparing my lunch, or painting my nails for example. I don't know whether it's because I'm relaxed, I'm under less pressure, but I only realised that towards the end. I think that's how I learn.

As with all learning, using multisensory methods can make the process of reading more enjoyable, engaging and memorable. So this chapter also looks at how students with dyslexia say they use all senses when reading, to understand concepts in their academic texts more easily. This could be as simple as having an audio recording of the text playing to hear the words, whilst simultaneously visually following the text on a computer screen, or by having a hard copy of the paper to hand. Using technology to read can also be helpful. Consequently, various assistive technology packages and forms of technology we use in our everyday lives are discussed in terms of how they can be applied to make the task of reading less demanding.

Each of the strategies and approaches above is presented in the chapter as a clear step-by-step method. That way the reader can try out, experiment, and select a technique or combination of strategies appropriate for fulfilling their purpose in academic reading.

Let us first cover a few of the main difficulties that students with dyslexia encounter with reading before moving on to look at ways of overcoming these obstacles.

4.2 Common Difficulties with Reading

Principal difficulties that students with dyslexia have when it comes to reading include a tendency for slower reading speeds than non-dyslexic peers. This means spending longer on reading, which can be a source of frustration. Frustration is also caused by having to spend time on repeatedly re-reading to comprehend academic materials, owing to a phonological deficit (see Chapter 1). This can be a source of anger at oneself for not understanding the terminology or the meaning of the text straightaway. Furthermore, owing to phonological weakness and negative experiences at school, students with dyslexia may feel anxious if asked by their lecturer to read out loud during class, because of not wanting to be judged by peers or to feel stupid in front of others. Because of working-memory deficits, students with dyslexia may not remember what they have read and therefore may compensate by continually re-reading, which becomes time-consuming and exhausting. All these problems manifest anxiety, which causes difficulties by creating cognitive interference, and this impedes their reading ability further, leading, for example, to misreading of questions in pressurised situations such as exams. Let us now take a closer look at some of these scenarios in action.

4.2.1 Frustration Due to Slower Reading Speeds

Dyslexic students have concerns that, compared with their peers, they are spending too much time on reading. Their slower reading and processing speeds become the central focus in comparing themselves to non-dyslexic peers. These difficulties are illuminated by Locke et al. (2015) in the article 'Doctors with dyslexia: strategies and support', which involved undertaking semi-structured interviews with six clinical dyslexic doctors. The doctors' biggest concerns compared with non-dyslexic doctors related to reading: taking longer to read, misreading words, needing to re-read several times to understand text, feeling embarrassed about reading aloud, and experiencing distortion of text when reading information on charts.

4.2.2 Frustration Due to a Lot of Reading

Postgraduate student Abu stated that reading was difficult owing to the long texts he was required to go through. He also said that academic reading was problematic when the writing in texts was complicated:

> I've never had to read so much. That's partly why I chose to do it (the course), because I wanted to challenge myself with something I would find difficult. But this is reading texts every week. It's constant, and I find the lengths of the pieces I really struggle with. As soon as I know it's 30 pages, I'm thinking I don't know how I'm going to cope with this.

4.2.3   Fear of Reading Aloud due to Being Judged

Naomi, a postgraduate Veterinary Medicine student, spoke of the trauma of reading aloud in school and how this still resonated with her:

> I think when I was younger, I probably used to read out loud in school, but I always used to mess up my words and go wrong and things like that. So, I just kind of started to avoid it at all costs really.

Even though Naomi, through hard work and determination, had gained a place on an intensive postgraduate medicine course where she was coping very well, she still had an inherent fear of reading in front of others and hence chose to avoid it.

4.2.4   Getting Angry with Not Understanding Terminology or Meaning Straightaway

Charlie, an MA Humanities student, would get angry, frustrated and sad when she struggled to understand the detail in her reading materials. Yet, when taking a step back and a more holistic approach to reading, she discovered she was better able to comprehend the information:

> It's either frustrating, or angering, or makes me sad that I can't understand it [the readings]. Looking at the bigger picture and taking a step back, I am able to understand it.

4.2.5   Having to Repeatedly Re-read and Not Remembering Reading

Some students felt they had to repeatedly re-read academic texts to comprehend them or to understand the main points, as described by Nursing student Tina:

I'm just looking at it [the reading] and it's not having the meaning of what I'm reading. That whole process of reading it many times and trying to get the main points is what I find quite stressful, especially when you're on a time limit.

Tina also explained how she felt about having to repeatedly re-read text:

I can't just do big chunks of reading at once because one, if I read it, I don't remember it, so the fact that I know I have to read it like a couple of times to remember it, that's what kind of stresses me out.

4.2.6 Anxiety Causing Misreading in Situations Like Exams

Even though dyslexic students at university have generally compensated for and coped with literacy difficulties and slower reading speeds to gain entry to university, having to deal with literacy during a high-stakes and time-pressured situation such as an exam still produces high levels of worry and anxiety.

In Chapter 1, BSc Nursing student Lisa spoke frankly about how the anxiety provoked by exams could lead to misinterpreting information and misreading exam questions:

When you get into the exam, sometimes you're so anxious that you're not going to be reading the question properly.

The quote above is a prime example of cognitive interference caused by anxiety hampering cognitive processes, more so than the weaknesses caused by dyslexia itself.

Let us now move on to looking at productive methods for alleviating these obstacles.

4.3   Techniques

4.3.1   PASS Reading Strategy

For some students, a step-by-step approach like the PASS reading method is a useful way to extract important information from readings and then connect the new knowledge into what has already been learned about a topic. The PASS strategy has four steps, and these are as follows.

P – Preview, Review and Predict

- Preview by reading the Introduction of the chapter, article or report. That way, you begin to form ideas on what you expect the information to be about.
- Review what you already know about the topic by making a quick spider diagram/mind map, listing keywords connected to the topic.
- Predict what you think the chapter, article or report will be about.

A – Ask and Answer Questions
Questioning when reading is an essential strategy as it helps you to engage and interact with the text. This also helps to develop your critical thinking skills, a prerequisite for succeeding at university. Simple questions might be:

- Why did they say that?
- Is there an opposing view?
- Are the authors' points supported by evidence?

One way to start to establish the habit of questioning whilst reading is as follows.

- Turn headings and subheadings of the chapter, article or report into questions that you want answered from the reading. For example,

124

if one of the article's subheadings is 'The Phonological Theory', you may want to create questions such as: What is the phonological theory? Why is it called the phonological theory? etc. It is useful to use Who? What? When? Where? Why? How? to help to make questions.

- Go through the article, finding the answers to the questions you have made. That way, the reading becomes interactive, and the questions provide hooks into extracting relevant information.

You can also break questions down into categories dependent on the purpose you want them to serve. For example:

- Questions for understanding the *content* of the reading would use the Who? What? When? Where? Why? How? format, in addition to questions like: How does this relate to what I already know?
- Questions for *checking* your understanding of a text could be: Is my prediction correct? How is this different from what I thought it was going to be about? Does this make sense?
- Questions to resolve any *problems* you may have had with the reading may include: Do I need to re-read any part of it? Do I need to read it more slowly? Does it have too many unknown words? Can I visualise the information? Can I identify what the main points of the reading are?

After questioning, the next two steps of the strategy are as follows:

S – Summarise

- Write a brief summary in your own words on what the main points of the chapter/article/report are about.

S – Synthesise

- Say how what you learned from the reading fits in with what you already know about the topic.

125

- Making a spidergram/mind map (or adding to one already made) may be useful to show how the new knowledge gained from the reading connects with what you have previously learned on the topic.

4.3.2 Activity to Try Out Using the PASS Reading Strategy

To have a go at becoming familiar with the PASS reading strategy, or to see if this is something that may help with your reading, follow the steps below next time you do some academic reading for your course. The link below will also enable you to print out and trial the PASS strategy on your academic reading.

www.cambridge.org/abbottjones

Step 1 – Preview, Review and Predict

- Have a blank mind map to look at, titled 'What You Know About the Topic'.
- Read the heading and the Abstract/Introduction of the chapter/article to get an idea what it is about.
- Using your blank mind-map template, as in the example in Figure 4.1, put down *keywords* on the blank branches, showing what you already know about the topic.
- This will help to refresh your memory on what you have previously learned or understand about the subject of the article.
- It is also a great way to develop confidence, as you can usually fill in the branches on the blank mind map with more keywords related to the topic than you realise.
- Make a few *notes* on what you think the chapter/article will be about.

126

What do you need to find out to answer the question?

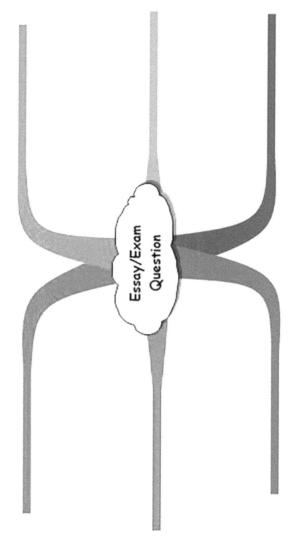

Figure 4.1 Mind map showing what you already know about the topic

Notes from Preview, Review and Predict:

_____
_____
_____
_____
_____
_____
_____
_____

_____

Step 2 – Ask and Answer Questions

- *Make up* a set of questions using Who? What? When? Where? Why? How?
- Read the text, making notes by answering the questions you have created.
- Decide if you want to ask any additional questions for the purpose of checking or problem solving.
- List these, and go through the text again answering the questions or highlighting sections of the text that you want *clarification* on.

Notes from Ask and Answer Questions:

_____
_____
_____
_____
_____
_____
_____
_____

_____

Step 3 – Summarise

- *Write* a *brief summary* on what the chapter is about.

128

Notes from Summarise:

_____

_____

_____

_____

_____

_____

_____

_____

Step 4 – Synthesise

- Make a few notes on how the chapter/article fits in with the whole book.
- Using the mind map on what you already know about the topic, add on what you have now learned from the chapter/article to see how it fits with what you previously knew (see Figure 4.2).

Notes from Synthesise:

_____

_____

_____

_____

_____

_____

_____

_____

4.3.3   SQ3R Reading Strategy

Another useful reading strategy, which also breaks the reading pro-cess down into steps, makes reading more engaging and provides

What you now know in relation to the question?

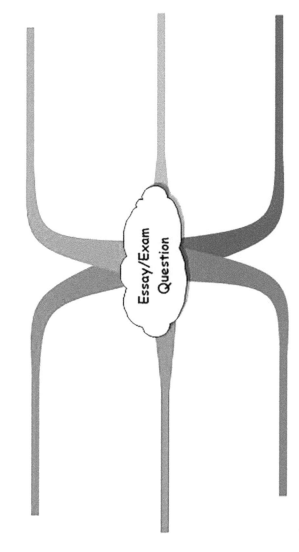

Essay/Exam Question

Figure 4.2 Mind map showing what you now know about the topic, after looking at the article

a purpose to it, is the Survey, Question, Read, Recite, and Review method, SQ3R. However, as there is a little bit more involved when applying this method, it is perhaps more suitable to use with key reading that you are required to understand for an exam, essay or seminar than for general day-to-day coursework reading. The stages of SQ3R are as follows:

Step 1 – Survey

- A *survey* is to gain a general view of the article, chapter or textbook.
- To survey the reading, you should *read the title*, which will help to pre-pare your mind for the subject. The title also lets you know what the article, chapter or textbook is about.
- Then *read the Introduction* and/or *Summary/Conclusion*. This will help you to focus on the main points discussed in the reading. These two sections of information will also help you to determine what the author wants you to understand after you have read the article.
- Always pay attention to *headings and subheadings*. These will indicate the details to come and will help you to understand the writer's method of organisation and development of the topics.
- Pay attention to any *charts, graphs, maps or diagrams*. These generally provide lots of information in an easy-to-read/understand format.
- Note whether *keywords or terms* are *italic, boldface, defined within the text* or *listed at the beginning or end of the article/chapter*. The author is signifying that these words are important for understanding the content, so you will need to become familiar with the definitions of these *terms or keywords* and how they are being used.
- Look for any discussion points at the end of sections of the article, or at the end of chapters, as these will help you to determine the *concepts the author wants you to understand*.

Step 2 – Question

- *Questioning* helps your mind engage and helps you to interact more purposefully with the reading.
- To help you to begin to make questions to apply to the reading, *turn headings and subheadings into questions.* For example, if you are reading an article on heart disease, and one of the subheadings is 'Coronary Artery Disease', your questions could be: What is coronary artery disease? Why does this disease happen? How can the disease be cured? and so on.

Step 3 – Read

- Now that you have done the *Survey* and created your *Questions*, the *Read* stage is where you carefully read through the text. In this stage, you should *read slowly and carefully*, concentrating on one section at a time. Do not worry about how long you need to take to read through the article/chapter, because at this stage, you are trying to absorb the ideas.
- *Read each section with your questions in mind*, making any notes that you feel will help to answer your questions.
- *Do not skip unfamiliar words or technical terms*. If you cannot understand their meaning from the context, then look them up.
- *Try to determine the main points of each section*. Making a brief summary of the main points in your notebook or in the margin of the text will aid your recall when you come to the Review stage.
- *Re-read* a section if it seems particularly complex. Be certain to highlight main ideas and/or *key points*.
- Writing down the author's ideas in your own words aids your recall.
- *Creating notes*, *underlining* and/or *highlighting* also helps to keep your reading active and engaging.

132

Step 4 – Recite

- Recitation can be an essential aid to memory and to comprehension of the text.
- Skim-read through the article/chapter again, and at the end of each section *try to state aloud, so you can hear yourself, the important points covered.*
- If you have trouble doing this, then you may not have understood the section and you will *need to re-read it again*.
- If the *central idea comes easily to mind*, then you can be confident that you have understood what you have read.

Step 5 – Review

- Review by skimming back over the article/chapter, looking over any notes you have made in the margins. Do they still make sense?
- Re-read any sections that you underlined or highlighted.
- Go back over the questions you made from the Questions section and see if you can still answer them. If not, refresh your memory by having a quick re-read.

4.3.4   Activity to Try Out Using the SQ3R Reading Strategy

To have a go at applying the SQ3R reading strategy, the next time you have an important paper/article or chapter that you want to understand in preparation for an exam, essay or seminar, work through the steps below to see if this can assist with deeper comprehension and memorisation of the text.

This activity can also be printed out to use on your various coursework readings by clicking on the link below.

www.cambridge.org/abbottjones

Survey

- Read the Title of the chapter.
- Read the Introduction to the chapter.
- Read the Summary/Conclusion.
- Make a few notes on what the author wants you to understand or be able to do after you have read the chapter.

_____

_____

_____

_____

- Look at major section headings and subheadings.
- Look at any charts, maps, graphs, diagrams, tables.
- Look at any keywords or terms presented in either italics or bold type, and make a few notes on the definition of these.

_____

_____

_____

_____

- Look at any points, questions or discussions at the end of the chapter, and make a few notes on which concepts the author wants you to apply.

Notes from Survey

_____

_____

_____

_____

Question

- After the _Survey_, determine whether the chapter is relevant in giving the information you need for your assignment/essay/revision notes/project.

- Review your mind map on what you need to find out to answer your question.
- Make a set of questions from this. For example, what does the chapter say about the concept of branding?
- Example of questions you could list.
- For each chapter, or each section in a chapter, ask these **four** basic questions.
  - What is the main point?
  - What evidence supports the main point?
  - What are the applications or examples?
  - How is this related to the rest of the chapter, the book, the world, my studies, my lecture notes?

List of Questions

_____

_____

_____

_____

_____

Read
Answering Your Questions

- Photocopy and enlarge the section of text you want to read in detail.
- Read slowly and carefully.
- Read each section with your questions in mind.
- If you find any unfamiliar words or technical terms, look them up in the dictionary and make a note of their meaning.
- Re-read the sentence in which the new word appears, to ensure you understand it.
- Make notes in the margin.

- Use * for key points/main ideas.
- Alternatively, use a coloured highlighter to draw attention to key points.
- Read through the section again.
- Write down the author's ideas and summarise the main points by using your own words, which will help your recall of the information.

Notes from Read:

_____
_____
_____
_____
_____
_____
_____
_____

Recite

- Talk through the ideas from the chapter out loud with someone, or record these onto your Dictaphone, or into your assistive technology.
- Recalling what you have read by stating it aloud is an essential aid to memory and comprehension.

Review

- Skim back over the chapter, looking over any notes you have made in the margins. Do they still make sense to you?
- Re-read any passages that you underlined or highlighted.
- Go back over the questions that you made, and see if you can still answer them without referring to your notes.
- If not, refresh your memory and continue.

4.3.5   Skimming and Scanning Reading Technique

Some students find using skimming and scanning approaches effective in relation to providing the general meaning and gist of a text. Skimming is to rapidly glance through a text to gain an understanding of the main point of an article or chapter, whereas scanning involves finding a keyword on a page to extract important information by reading the few sentences or paragraphs that mention the keyword.

MSc Sciences student Alan would skim materials by reading the Introduction to the text. He would then jump to the back of the text to read the Conclusion. At this stage, he would decide if the material was relevant for what he needed to know. If it was, he would then read first lines and last lines of paragraphs, and if any of the paragraphs seemed to be important, or were information he needed to learn, he would put a visual marker on the paragraph to return to for reading in more detail later. As he explained:

> I skim and scan things. I don't read things unless I have to read them. So, I will decide this is the bit that I actually need to read, and then I will re-read that. I will use the highlighter pen, or whatever I've got to hand, and I might just draw a box around the bit that I need to come back to when I'm scanning it, or something to bring to my attention visually what is the most important bit of this 10-page document.

Consequently, in addition to being useful for obtaining the main point of a text and for pinpointing important sections in reading, these skimming and scanning techniques help to speed up the reading process, enabling you to cover a vast amount of material very rapidly. The two methods, although similar in process, have a different purpose.

Skimming, the process of rapidly moving the eyes over the text to get only the *main ideas* and *general overview* of the content, is useful for the following situations:

Before reading

Use skimming to preview – establish context, purpose and content.

During reading

Use skimming to find:

- thesis
- main idea
- major supporting details
- organisational pattern
- overall style
- main characters
- plot outline.

After reading

Use skimming to review – organising, analysing, evaluating and reacting.

In contrast, *scanning* to search for a particular word is useful for:

- *Locating* a fact or piece of information.
- *Finding* a specific name, date, statistic or fact without reading the entire article.

Below is a list of steps that you may want to apply to your reading to become familiar with the approaches of skimming and scanning.

4.3.6   Steps in Skimming an Article

- *Read the title* – it is the shortest possible summary of the content.
- Read the Introduction or lead paragraph.
- Read the first paragraph completely.
- If there are *subheadings*, read each one, looking for relationships among them.

- Read the first sentence of each remaining paragraph.
  - The main idea of most paragraphs appears in the first sentence.
  - If the author's pattern is to begin with a question or anecdote, you may find the last sentence more valuable.
- Dip into the text looking for:
  - Clue words that answer who, what, when, why, how.
  - Nouns (person, place, thing or idea).
  - Unusual words, especially if capitalised.
  - Enumerations (listing of items).
  - Qualifying adjectives (best, worst, most, etc.).
  - Typographical cues, such as italics, boldface, underlining, asterisks.
- Read the final paragraph completely.

Mastering the art of *skimming* effectively requires that you use it as frequently as possible.

4.3.7   Steps in Scanning an Article

- *Keep in mind* at all times what it is you are searching for. If you hold the image of the word clearly in mind, it is likely to appear more clearly than the surrounding words.
- *Anticipate in what form* the information is likely to appear: proper nouns, etc.
- Analyse the organisation of the content before starting to scan.
  - If the material is familiar or fairly brief, you may be able to scan the entire article in a single search.
  - If the material is lengthy or difficult, a preliminary *skimming* may be necessary to determine which part of the article to scan.
- *Let your eyes run rapidly* over several lines of print at a time.
- When you *find the sentence* that has the information you seek, *read the entire sentence*.

139

In scanning, you must be willing to skip over large sections of text without reading or understanding them.

4.3.8   Ways to Improve Skimming Technique

- Read selectively for main ideas. Key parts to focus on are usually a lead/first paragraph (usually the Introduction), beginnings of key para-graphs, last paragraph (usually the Conclusion).
- Vary your rate. Read key parts carefully, and re-read them if necessary. Race past or through unimportant material.
- Read aloud when you encounter material you find difficult to understand.
- Highlight information you may want to review or find quickly later.
- Move your eyes in a wide spiral pattern. A very wide "S" curve is appropriate for most textbooks. Use the straight-down pattern when skimming academic journal articles, magazines, newspapers, or other material formatted in columns.
- Use a soft focus. Relax your eye and facial muscles, look slightly above the line of print, and let your eyes float down the page. Try to read lines and words, not individual letters.

The link below allows you to print a hard copy of the steps involved in skimming an article, so you can carry this around with you to test out on your reading materials.

www.cambridge.org/abbottjones

4.3.9   Ways to Improve Scanning Technique

- Have a think about any *key information* that you need to answer an assignment question – for instance, the definition or example of a key concept, a particular fact, a statistic, or information about a specific per-son (artist, scientist, philosopher, etc.).

- Make a note of what you want to find.

_____

_____

_____

_____

- Use your textbook or journal article to *Scan* for the information.
- Remember to use the index of a book to find out where words you are looking for are located, via page numbers in the book.
- Remember to keep in mind the shape and pattern of words you are looking for.
- Remember to let your eyes run rapidly over the text until you locate the information.
- Once you've located the information, read the sentence, then expand this to read around it by reading the paragraph.
- Now make some notes on what you have found out:

_____

_____

_____

The link below allows you to print a hard copy of the steps involved in scanning an article, so you can carry this around with you to test out on your reading materials.

www.cambridge.org/abbottjones

Below are some skimming exercises to test out, which will give you an idea of how much understanding you can gain from a text by reading specific sections.

Activity to Develop Skimming Technique

Read the first sentence of each paragraph in the following text.

THE PERSONAL QUALITIES OF A TEACHER

Here I want to try to give you an answer to the question: What personal qualities are desirable in a teacher? Probably no two people would draw up exactly similar lists, but I think the following would be generally accepted.

First, the teacher's personality should be pleasantly live and attractive. This does not rule out people who are physically plain, or even ugly, because many such have great personal charm. But it does rule out such types as the over-excitable, melancholy, frigid, sarcastic, cynical, frustrated, and over-bearing: I would say, too, that it excludes all of dull or purely negative personality. I still stick to what I said in my earlier book: that school children probably 'suffer more from bores than from brutes'.

Secondly, it is not merely desirable but essential for a teacher to have a genuine capacity for sympathy – in the literal meaning of that word; a capacity to tune in to the minds and feelings of other people, especially, since most teachers are school teachers, to the minds and feelings of children. Closely related with this is the capacity to be tolerant – not, indeed, of what is wrong, but of the frailty and immaturity of human nature which induce people, and again especially children, to make mistakes.

Thirdly, I hold it essential for a teacher to be both intellectually and morally honest. This does not mean being a plaster saint. It means that he will be aware of his intellectual strengths, and limitations, and will have thought about and decided upon the moral principles by which his life shall be guided. There is no contradiction in my going on to say that a teacher should be a bit of an actor. That is part of the technique of teaching, which demands that every now and then a teacher should be able to put on an act – to enliven a lesson, correct a fault, or award praise. Children, especially young children, live in a world that is rather larger than life.

A teacher must remain mentally alert. He will not get into the profession if of low intelligence, but it is all too easy, even for people of above-average intelligence, to stagnate intellectually – and that means to deteriorate intellectually. A teacher must be quick to adapt himself to any situation, however improbable and able to improvise, if necessary, at less than a moment's notice. (Here I should stress that I use 'he' and 'his' throughout the book simply as a matter of convention and convenience.)

On the other hand, a teacher must be capable of infinite patience. This, I may say, is largely a matter of self-discipline and self-training; we are none of us born like that. He must be pretty resilient; teaching makes great demands on nervous energy. And he should be able to take in his stride the innumerable petty irritations any adult dealing with children has to endure.

Finally, I think a teacher should have the kind of mind which always wants to go on learning. Teaching is a job at which one will never be perfect; there is always something more to learn about it. There are three principal objects of study: the subject, or subjects, which the teacher is teaching; the methods by which they can best be taught to the particular pupils in the classes he is teaching; and – by far the most important – the children, young people, or adults to whom they are to be taught. The two cardinal principles of British education today are that education is education of the whole person, and that it is best acquired through full and active co-operation between two persons, the teacher and the learner. (From *Teaching as a Career*, by H. C. Dent, Batsford, 1961)

Notice how, through reading these few sentences, you are given a good idea about the meaning of the text and will have already established an understanding of what the author claims to be the *six qualities of a teacher*.

Reading First Sentences of Paragraphs in Your Own Coursework

Now apply this technique to your own course reading.

Using a section from a chapter or a journal article, read aloud the first sentence of each paragraph.

143

Now make a few notes on what the text is about:

_____
_____
_____
_____
_____
_____

The link will allow you to print out this resource to apply to your own reading.

www.cambridge.org/abbottjones

4.3.10   Reading Using Selectivity

Another key way to get through larger quantities of academic materials in a shorter timeframe by minimising the amount of unnecessary reading, similar to the skim and scan method, is to read selectively.

Selectivity in reading is to choose which sections of a text to read. This is necessary to reduce time spent on reading superfluous information, which may lead to feeling overloaded. MA Arts student Cara would read just conclusions and introductions of texts first before deciding whether to continue. She also Googled authors' names and themes to generate a clearer understanding of the main terms used in the readings. Looking at Abstracts of articles was also useful, as they provide a summary of key information about the reading.

> I always made sure that I read the Conclusion and Introduction first. Then I Google the author and try and find out what their views were online. I Google the theme, so at least I would have an idea about what the main terms were. I will look for papers that sound relevant and I will read the abstracts. If I think the abstracts sound like the

paper might be something that I need to look at further, I will press Print and it goes into a pile to come back to do a further scan, skim through to read.

A useful method to become familiar with applying selectivity, and to make key points from your reading memorable, is to extract the specific information that you need for assignments or for revision by using the Q Notes method, as described in Chapter 3. However, rather than using this to pull out key information from lectures, you instead use it to hook out relevant data from academic articles and textbooks, as in the example below.

MSc Geology student Luke used a two-step process to make reading memorable. He would first read through an important paper, selecting and extracting key information by highlighting and making condensed notes. Secondly, he would apply the Q Notes method to test himself on the information he had read and to put his learning into memory. Similar to what we have seen in Chapter 3, the steps involved in the Q Notes process here are as follows:

- Take an A4 sheet of paper and divide it into two columns.
- In the left-hand ('Questions') column, make up and write down questions that you want to know the answers to from the reading (like the A – Ask and Answer Question stage in the PASS reading strategy).
- Once your questions are written down, find the answers in your reading, and write these down in summarised note form alongside the questions in the right-hand column of the paper – the Q Notes column.
- To place into memory, cover over the notes in the right-hand column, and see if it is possible to answer the questions without looking at the notes.
- Repeat the process, doubling the amount of time between attempts at answering the questions, until eventually it can be left for a couple of days, and answers to the questions can be given without looking at the summarised notes in the Q Notes column.

145

4.3.11   Ways of Applying Selectivity when Handling Academic Textbooks

It is usual on higher education courses for teaching staff to provide a reading list of relevant textbooks to supplement the information delivered during the lecture. Sometimes these reading lists can appear overwhelming, and students frequently wrongly believe that they must read through all the books listed. This is not the case. Instead, the books should be dipped into to determine what their content is, and when it comes to coursework essays, only those books that help with providing appropriate information for answering the essay question should be looked at in more detail. The activity below, which you can print out by clicking the link to the Resources section, will help you to understand which bits of an academic book to read to gain a comprehensive overview and summary of the information contained. This puts you in the position of knowing which textbooks to select to help with your coursework.

www.cambridge.org/abbottjones

4.3.12   Activity to Develop Reading Using Selectivity

- Select one of the books from your reading list.
- Read any information on the *back cover*.
- Browse the *Contents page*, *section headings* and *last chapter*.
- Make a few quick notes on what seem to be the main points of the book.
- Record only the gist of what you read.

At this stage, decide whether the book is relevant and necessary to read. Choose the chapter that is important and relevant for you.

- Read the introductory and concluding paragraphs of the chapter.
- When you finish reading, note any extra important information.

- Read the first line of each paragraph.
- Note any additional important information.
- At this stage you should be able to write a *summary of the book and selected chapter*.

Overview/Summary of the Book and Selected Chapter:

Reducing the Reading Load

- Which parts of the book are essential for you to read?

147

- How little could you read to grasp the main points?

4.3.13   Making Summaries

Another useful method for consolidating an understanding of your reading is to make summaries. A summary is a brief statement or account of the main points of something. Consequently, after reading through academic articles, or chapters in a textbook, you may find it helpful to write a paragraph or two of your own interpretation of the article using your own words. These written summaries not only enable you to clarify your comprehension of the reading by writing down its main points, but they can also provide helpful revision notes for future exams. MA Education student Chloe had a notebook designated for summaries of her readings:

> I have a notepad dedicated to papers that I read. I write down key things I think are interesting, words I don't quite understand, so I can check on them, and an interpretation, so if I need to refer back to anything, I can look at it and go, 'Okay, that's what I meant.'

Getting into the routine of making summaries of your readings, which is only ever a small paragraph, or three to four sentences written down, will help you to develop the skill of finding the main ideas in the text. It will also help you to think about the principal purpose of an article, chapter or textbook. That is because to summarise involves:

- Reading a text in detail.
- Finding the main ideas.

148

- Finding any supporting ideas.
- Briefly writing down those key points, concepts, main ideas in a few sentences or a paragraph.

For revision purposes, similarly to Chloe above, you may want to have a notepad of your written summaries. The notepad can then be carried around with you so that you can glance at it to refresh your memory of the information it contains, when you are travelling or are having a break. The constant jogging of the memory during relaxed moments will help with your recall of the readings when it is required during exams.

Summaries are also useful when it comes to easily being able to retrieve academic journal articles you may have filed away. If you use a couple of sentences to summarise the key ideas of the article and have these written down on the front page of the printed-out version of the paper, then when searching through hardcopies of your papers, these sentences will help you to locate the relevant text and will refresh your memory on the rest of the article's content.

If you at first struggle to make summaries of your reading, an effective method after you have read a chapter, or paper, is to verbalise the content of the text by explaining its key points to somebody else. That way, you can hear your own auditory description of the text; this will help to develop further your clarification of the material. If your friend asks additional questions (which they are likely to do) on your account of the paper, this is particularly productive for helping you to deepen your comprehension and interpretation of the information.

Next, we will have a look at ways of developing criticality when reading. This will help to develop your skills in being able to look at information analytically to evaluate strengths and weaknesses of academic texts.

4.4 Developing Criticality When Reading

You may be a little uncertain during the early stages of your university course on how to apply critical and analytical thinking to your reading, but once you get into the habit of questioning what you read and thinking of an alternative or opposing viewpoint to the text, your level of criticality will begin to develop. Let us first consider exactly what critical and analytical thinking is within the context of higher education.

4.4.1   What Is Critical and Analytical Thinking?

It is a usual scenario for first-year students to receive feedback comments such as 'not analytical enough' on early assignments. If this sounds familiar, you should not worry too much. You will find that as you progress through university, your critical and analytical skills will rapidly develop. As a definition, criticality means to question information rather than simply absorbing and then describing what you have read. For example, if you read a fact in a paper – for instance, in a medical paper, 'the Pfizer vaccine protects against the COVID-19 virus' – you should immediately begin to question and look for the 'evidence' in the paper that supports this point. Critiquing involves evaluating the information for supporting evidence, assessing whether there are limitations in the evidence, and looking for any hidden biases or hidden assumptions that the author has made. Meanwhile, analytical thinking is to break down complex information into smaller parts, to develop the ability to extract key information from data, to identify and define problems with the information, and to arrive at workable solutions for the problems identified.

As a starting point in developing these skills, you may want to apply the following steps when you next read an academic article or chapter.

4.4.2   Steps for Developing Reading Critically and Analytically

- Evaluate how far the materials are appropriate and up to date.
- Evaluate how far the evidence or examples used in the article really prove the point that the author claims.
- Weigh up opinions, arguments or solutions against appropriate criteria. For example, if you are reading an academic article in which the author argues that 'All people who live in the North of England like ice cream' owing to the results of a survey the author conducted, you have to weigh up factors such as: How reliable and valid was the survey that the author used? Did the survey allow for biases? And so on.
- Think a line of reasoning through to its logical conclusion. For instance, if you disagree with an author's point of view because you have found valid evidence to support a counterargument, you need to break down and use the facts from this evidence to form a reasoned decision as to why you have a differing opinion from the author.
- Check for hidden bias or hidden assumptions.
- Check whether the evidence and argument really support the conclusions.

You can have a try at doing these steps for any future materials that you read, particularly if the article or chapter is key to your course or is a fundamental paper for an essay or assignment you are working on.

The link will give you access to print out this list of steps which you can apply to your reading.

www.cambridge.org/abbottjones

Reading critically and analytically will also help to develop your skills in how you write. For example, you will become aware that when you cite a source of evidence for your own arguments in your assignment, you need to be sure that the evidence really does support your

151

point and is accurate and reliable. You are expected to be very critical of your sources, using evidence that has been well researched rather than just your own opinion or what you have heard from a friend.

Below is a series of activities for helping you to apply critical and analytical thinking to your academic reading materials. The link above gives you access to this activity.

4.4.3 Activity to Develop Critical Thinking When Reading

From the reading that you are doing for your assignment/essay, select a couple of paragraphs and read them.

After you've read them, provide an explanation or make some notes on:

- The hidden bias or hidden assumptions that the author has made.
- The extent to which the evidence or examples used have substantiated the point that the author has claimed.

_____

_____

_____

From the reading, can you provide an explanation or make some notes on answers to the two questions:

- What is the main argument or line of reasoning?
- Is the line of reasoning clear from the text?

_____

_____

_____

_____

From the reading, note any statements from the text that strengthen its line of reasoning or prove the argument. Provide an explanation or make some notes on these. Alternatively, also look for flaws in the argument by asking:

- What statements, if any, undermine the argument?
- Are points made in the best logical order?

_____

_____

_____

_____

From the reading, consider and provide an explanation or make some notes on:

- What hidden agendas might the writer have that might make you question the contents or conclusions of the passage?
- What information might be missing that could offer a different perspective?

_____

_____

_____

_____

Evaluating Evidence in the Text

From the reading, make notes or provide an explanation on answers to the following questions:

- What kinds of evidence or examples does the writer use?
- How reliable and useful is this evidence?
- Does it really support the argument?
- Is the evidence strong enough?
- Is the data up to date?

- Does the text use reliable sources?
- What are these?
- What makes you think they are or are not reliable?

_____

_____

_____

_____

From the reading, make notes or provide an explanation on answers to the following questions:

- Do you think there may be any bias in the text? Give reasons and examples.
- Comment on any statistics used. Do these support or weaken the author's points?
- Does the writing reflect a political viewpoint?
- Who might disagree with the writer?

_____

_____

_____

From the reading, make notes or provide an explanation on answers to the following questions:

- Does the evidence support the writer's conclusions?
- Do the arguments and evidence presented lead you to the same conclusions?

4.5 Using Practical and Favourite Things

On a different note, let us now turn to looking at practical actions and 'favourite things' that students with dyslexia have said that they use to make their reading easier and more enjoyable. Some of the things discussed below may be useful for you to apply to make your own reading less challenging and more stimulating.

'Practical', in the context of reading, relates to when a student does something to make their learning more accessible, like printing out their readings. 'Favourite things' means something a student may have personally purchased and applied to their learning, such as colourful stationery. It also refers to methods that a student may find particularly enjoyable when applied to their reading.

For example, both Alan and Ada, two postgraduate Science students, reported that when reading, they had tracking difficulties, which can be a co-occurring difficulty associated with dyslexia (Jones et al., 2008). They both alleviated the problem by simply using a ruler and blank sheet of paper directly under the sentence being read, to prevent skipping words and lines of text. Alan commented:

> I found it quite hard to follow where the next line starts, so I'd read the same line three times thinking it was the one down. I'd get a ruler and that would allow me to keep track.

Another practical activity that students would do, which you may also benefit from, would be to print out papers they had selected to read. Recognising that students with dyslexia may prefer to read from paper, the Disabled Students' Allowance provides financial support towards costs of paper, photocopying and printing. This funding enables dyslexic students to be more effective in their academic reading, because, with their own hardcopy of a paper, they can interact with the text by highlighting, drawing and making notes on sections of text. Also, printed versions of a paper are more suitable for students with tactile and kinaesthetic strengths. Consequently, if in receipt of the Disabled Students' Allowance, you may decide to make use of this provision by printing out your own copies of papers for your course. This will enable you to engage more effectively with the reading by being able to draw, colour, write, highlight and ultimately make the paper your own. Another advantage is that printing out papers allows you to practically see how difficult or easy the paper is to read. An example of this was articulated by Abu, who would print out papers to assess their length and would then timetable reading dependent upon the size of the document:

> I like to handle the material. I will print it out, I will quickly flick see how many pages it is and then figure out how much time I need to designate to it.

We have already seen an illustration of how you can use 'favourite things' to make reading pleasurable, shown by BA English student Cate. She would make her reading engaging by picking out important pages from an article and would mark them for returning to later with brightly coloured animal-shaped sticky notes:

> I have my animal markers, my little animal Post-It notes, because I just like playing with them.

Activities or stationery that make learning entertaining are important. Studies into children's education (Parker & Lepper, 1992; Rea, 2000) prove that if acquiring new knowledge is enjoyable, this makes it more memorable. This remains as necessary in adulthood as it is when educating children, particularly for students who may have cognitive deficits in memory and information processing.

4.6 Ways of Using Practical Methods to Alleviate Scotopic Sensitivity

Another reason why students with dyslexia prefer to read from printed papers could be due to difficulties in reading from a computer screen if they have scotopic sensitivity (as explained in Chapter 1, under the heading Visual Transient/Magnocellular System). The problems with screen reading are illuminated here by BSc Nursing student Tina:

> I always prefer to read on paper. I don't really like reading on the computer, and I find on the computer that it's just too much light coming into your eyes. I can keep track of where I am on paper, whereas on the computer you easily lose track, and then you get these headaches because it's so bright.

If you do have visual difficulties when reading from the screen, a few solutions you may want to consider are as follows:

- Copy and paste the text from the reading into a Word document. That way, you can change the style of the font to make it easier to read, and you can also increase the size of the font.
- On a Word document, you can also change the background colour from white to a colour you find easier to read from, such as yellow, cream, green or pale blue.
- If you have a combination of tracking difficulties and visual difficulties caused by reading from harsh backgrounds, the text-to-speech software ClaroRead has a feature called a ScreenRuler that can help to resolve these problems. The ScreenRuler allows you to use a coloured underline to highlight the sentence in the text you are currently reading. As your eyes move down the text, the ScreenRuler moves in synchronicity with your eyes, helping you to focus and stay on the line of text you are trying to read. You can personalise the colour and size of the ScreenRuler and control the shading above and below the ruler.
- When reading hard copies/printed-out versions of your academic materials, you may want to consider using a coloured overlay on top of the page you are reading. Your dyslexia support tutor should be able to help you to choose the appropriate colour from which you find the text easier to read.

157

- If your visual difficulties are considerable and affecting your ability to undertake any form of reading tasks, you may want to consider making an appointment with an optometrist who will undertake a colorimetry test (a test that helps to find the colours suitable for diminishing visual stress). The optometrist could also prescribe glasses with tinted lenses to help to eradicate light sensitivity.

This was something that helped Nursing student Lisa, who was diagnosed with dyslexia in conjunction with scotopic sensitivity whilst at school. She was sent for a colorimetry test at an optometrist, which included assessing her sensitivity to colour and identifying colours suitable for her to use during reading:

> I will often put it [the reading] on yellow paper because yellow was my reading colour when I was younger. I'm supposed to have yellow glasses, but it didn't get sorted properly when I was little. The colour does really help me a lot with the reading.

After an updated visit to the optometrist, Lisa was provided with glasses with tinted lenses which supported her reading and helped to reduce visual stress.

4.7   Using Metacognition When Reading

Metacognitive awareness when reading is not just about knowing what types of strategies are suitable for how you need to learn information. It also means being aware of your own psychological functioning during studying. This includes:

- Being conscious of ensuring the environment is suitable for absorbing reading. For example, some people can only read and comprehend the text when in total silence. Other people prefer to read when there is background noise, such as when sitting in a café or listening to music. Sitting in a park to read, surrounded by green and being outdoors, can also be effective for digesting information from readings. Issy, an MA Arts student, found that she was productive with her reading when listening to the audio of the text through her headphones, whilst simultaneously sitting in art galleries looking at paintings by the artists that her readings were about.

- Being aware of the most effective times of the day or evening to concentrate on reading, either because of external factors such the noise in shared households, or internal factors such as knowing whether cognitive functioning is more effective in the morning or afternoon.

- Knowing whether breaks are required. BA Sciences student Sue noted:

> I know I can't work in the evening, so any work done has to be done in the morning. Like if I start at 9, then that's me 9–5, done at 5, finished.

- BA English student Cate, rather than working solidly on reading throughout the day, would break it into chunks and would do something else when feeling tired:

> I portion it into specific bits, and the moment I find myself struggling, I get up and do something else for five minutes and come back to it, because my brain needs a rest.

4.8   Using Multisensory Methods

There are various ways in which you can apply multisensory methods to your reading. One technique is to combine hearing the audio of the text with seeing the words on the page, as in the example below.

4.8.1 Hearing It and Seeing It

A couple of students found it helpful to have the audio of their readings playing from their phones, so they were able to listen to the text, whilst at the same time following the words by visually reading the papers, as expressed by Dean, a BSc Nursing student:

> I actually converted a lot of my text or readings into audio and would listen to them on my iPod and read at the same time.

The auditory–visual combination not only helps to make reading more comprehensible, but also assists with increasing the speed of reading.

Another method is to use movement whilst reading.

4.8.2 Movement Whilst Reading

You could try listening to the audio of your reading whilst on the move, such as when walking, jogging or doing physical activity in the gym. Sometimes when the body is on the move and relaxed, auditory information can be easier to absorb. This is a particularly useful technique for kinaesthetic learners.

You can also use your imagination to transform the reading into something meaningful for you.

4.8.3 Visualisation and Personalising the Reading with Something Meaningful or Enjoyable

In the article 'When saying "go read it again" won't work: multisensory ideas for more inclusive teaching and learning', Newman (2019) presents a range of interesting techniques trialled by higher education students with dyslexia. Each of the methods tested was effective by complementing the way in which each individual learner processed information. One medical student, required to read factual information on patient cases for the purpose of presenting the detail to his group in seminars, enjoyed reading detective fiction, and was encouraged to use visualisation to transform academic reading materials about patient symptoms into scenarios for crime stories, as Newman describes:

> The student enjoyed crime novels and this pastime was the germ for the solution. Instead of the case presentations merely reciting a series of facts, we worked on the idea of characterising the case through a title which might have come from a crime novel and then 'unfolding' the story. Hence, "The strange case of the American tourist in London" told the story of just that, an American, who feeling ill on a trip to Europe walked into the learner's A&E department. (Newman, 2019, p. 6)

The process of transforming your reading into imaginative stories, personalised with things you enjoy, provides an element of pleasure in the task, which makes the information from readings easier to process, more fun and thus more memorable.

4.9   Using Technology to Help with Reading

Various forms of technology can be used to help with reading:

- The Internet is useful for typing in difficult words from text to obtain straightforward explanations of their meaning.
- An online thesaurus can also help in looking for synonyms of words, when trying to develop a deeper meaning of the original word in the text, or when looking for substitute words that have the same meaning.

161

- Topics in readings can also be searched for in Wikipedia. The advantage of this online encyclopaedia is that it can provide a basis for understanding a subject, as explained by postgraduate Arts student Cara:

  > Wikipedia, I know, is not very academic, but I would at least kind of know, set the base, know roughly what I'm reading about. So, I'd feel a bit more comfortable and then kind of understand the concepts more of what the paper's trying to explain.

- When the reading is converted into a PDF, the Find function is useful for helping to zoom straight into the sections of the text necessary to read. For example, MA Education student Chloe would read academic papers on her computer as PDF documents. She would also have a list of topic words/keywords written down in a separate document that she wanted to find in the readings. She would then use Control and Find functions on the keyboard to go straight to the topic/keyword in the paper. This saved time in reading that could easily be wasted by going through unnecessary information.

- Using text-to-speech software packages (such as Speechify, Nuance Dragon Naturally Speaking, ClaroRead and TextHelp Read & Write) and converting text to audio is also helpful, as it allows you to hear the material being read aloud. For instance, BA English student Cate had been provided with Read & Write literacy support software as part of her Disabled Students' Allowance package. She would use this to hear her papers read out loud. But because the computer-generated voice was monotone, she struggled with being engaged in her reading:

  > I have Read & Write, but since the voice is the same all the time, so automatic, it's not very helpful.

This was, however, going back to around 2010, and recent developments in text-to-speech software have worked to increase intonation and naturalness of the sound of voices used. Thus, future students with dyslexia can still benefit and be supported in their reading with this type of technology.

4.10   Summary

In summary, this chapter has:

- Outlined common difficulties that students with dyslexia encounter when reading.
- Presented a step-by-step approach to reading techniques that students with dyslexia may find helpful, such as the PASS strategy; the SQ3R strategy; skimming and scanning methods; reading using selectivity; making summaries of reading.
- Covered ways of developing criticality when reading.
- Looked at ways of using practical and favourite things to apply to reading, and discussed methods for reducing scotopic sensitivity.
- Listed some useful ways of being metacognitively aware when reading.
- Introduced some productive multisensory techniques to apply to reading.
- Talked about effective ways of using technology to help with reading.

5

· · · · ·

Making Learning
Memorable

5.1   Introduction

Techniques for remembering information from academic reading
materials, lecture notes and revision sources are of prime importance
for students with dyslexia, as problems with retention and retrieval
are common. As such, this chapter begins by specifying some of the
difficulties with memory that students with dyslexia can encounter
and will outline the ways in which deficits in both short-term and
working memory can affect study performance.

The chapter then focuses on cognitive strategies to assist with
overcoming these difficulties, as told from the perspectives of students with dyslexia. These techniques include using memory palaces,
saying it out loud, highlighting keywords and using image association, using sense of smell as memory activator, using multisensory

methods, mnemonics, repetition, writing things down, and using chunking, categorising and organising of information. As in previous chapters, the strategies are introduced by using a clear step-by-step approach. Some of the strategies are punctuated with student quotes emphasising the benefits of a method – as in the example below, where a student discusses how associating learning with something visual acts as a memory trigger:

> It's like the closet you open, when everything falls out, but it's sometimes finding that little thing that will open the door. It's finding the key basically.

Becoming metacognitively aware of how you remember different things is important, as you are then able to apply this knowledge to the ways you choose to study. Consequently, the chapter aims to develop your knowledge of different types of memory, so you can begin to determine your own unique memory style. For example, is your episodic memory (memory of a past event) stronger than your semantic memory (the capacity to recall facts, words, numbers and concepts effectively)? Do you remember things more productively through visualisation, by being there and experiencing an event, or through sound? The information presented in the chapter will help you to develop an understanding of how you can remember, recall and retrieve information from memory successfully. Once you are equipped with this knowledge, you will be able to dip into and pick and choose techniques covered by this and the other chapters that complement your memory style.

Furthermore, drawing from the extremely useful work of Cottrell (2008), the chapter provides some activities that illuminate the effectiveness of the rather simple processes of 'chunking' and 'categorising' information for assisting with recall. The chapter also utilises Cottrell's (2008) valuable material on memory to outline the four

165

stages of memory commonly used for any academic activity. These include *taking in information* from lectures, readings and discussions; *retaining information long enough to remember it*, for example, remembering revision and notes from readings; *encoding information*, which is interacting with the information; and *recall*, retrieving the information for exams and other forms of assessment. Useful strategies for each stage are mentioned.

The chapter concludes by outlining the ways in which technology can help to support memorisation processes.

5.2   Common Difficulties with Memory

We begin our discussion of common difficulties with memory for students with dyslexia by providing an explanation of what short-term and working memory processes are. This will help to develop a deeper understanding of how deficits in these areas can affect study performance.

5.2.1   What Is Short-Term Memory?

Short-term memory means to hold, but not to manipulate, a small amount of information in mind in an active, readily available state for a short period of time. For example, you use short-term memory to remember a phone number that has just been recited. If there are weaknesses with short-term memory, then the individual will forget information that has only just been imparted to them. For instance, they may ask the same question repeatedly as they have forgotten the answer; or they may forget where they have put something, such as keys or glasses; or they may forget recent events or something they have only just seen or read. Difficulties in this area can affect all aspects of study. It makes recalling facts and information from recent readings or remembering knowledge from yesterday's lecture particularly demanding. This has implications when it comes to coursework exams and assessments.

5.2.2   What Is Working Memory?

Working memory processes are slightly more complex than short-term memory. This cognitive system is responsible for the transient holding, processing and manipulation of linguistic and perceptual information (Baddeley, 1999). Unlike short-term memory, working memory does more than just hold information for short periods of time. Instead, it must have the capacity to hold information whilst the person is simultaneously paying attention to something else. Examples of this include conducting a long multiplication, in which working memory is required to transiently store and retrieve the numbers carried over during the calculation; keeping in mind an address whilst being given verbal directions to get there; or calculating the total bill for groceries whilst trying to find other items on the shopping list.

To break working memory down further and understand more about the components that give rise to cognitive difficulties for the student with dyslexia, we draw from Baddeley (1999). For Baddeley, working memory involves three components.

- The first component is the central executive – responsible for selecting and processing linguistic and perceptual information. This involves the tasks of encoding (which could include making written notes from auditory information received during lectures), storing (placing information into memory processes) and retrieving (bringing information back out of memory during an exam).

167

- The second component of working memory, the phonological loop, deals with spoken and written material, as was described in Chapter 1. The phonological store holds information in a speech-based form, and the articulatory process allows us to repeat verbal information in a loop. Basically, the phonological loop is responsible for converting written words into speech.
- The third component of working memory, the visual–spatial sketch-pad, is responsible for processing information in a visual or spatial form.

Students with dyslexia who have deficits with working memory will generally have weaknesses with the first component (the central executive) and the second component (the phonological loop). These two create a combination of difficulties.

Problems with the efficiency of the central executive system make academic tasks such as reading, remembering information, essay writing and taking exams more difficult; deficiencies in the system lead to challenges when note taking during lectures. Deficiencies with the phonological loop are most notable when students struggle with reading aloud and/or have particularly slow reading speeds.

5.2.3 How Some Students with Dyslexia Have Deficits in Memory and Others Don't

Whilst some students may have just a phonological deficit, others could have a combination of phonological with short-term/working memory deficits, or phonological with sensory processing difficulties (see Chapter 1). This demonstrates the spectrum nature of dyslexia: whilst there will always be common core characteristics (deficits in phonology), each student will have their own unique profile of dyslexia-related difficulties.

Taking common core characteristics into account, educational psychologist David Grant, who screens for dyslexia using the Wechsler Adult Intelligence Scale (WAIS), suggests that a typical Wechsler dyslexic profile will reveal high scores for verbal reasoning (the ability to understand and logically work through concepts and problems expressed in words) and for visual reasoning (analysing visual information and being able to solve problems based upon it), yet scores will typically be lower for short-term memory and speed of visual processing (Grant, 2010). The variations in neurocognitive function that Grant describes include 'weaknesses in visual processing speed, short-term visual memory, implicit memory processing, and short-term auditory memory, i.e., working memory' (Grant, 2010, p. 52). In his text, he goes on to present a classic profile of a dyslexic student which shows that

> …she scored above average on verbal and visual reasoning skills and below average on working memory and processing speed. Whereas her Verbal Comprehension (verbal reasoning) and Perceptual Organisation (visual reasoning) scores put her in the top 20 per cent and top 23 per cent of the population respectively, her scores for Working Memory and Processing Speed put her in the bottom 9 per cent and 32 per cent respectively.' (Grant, 2010, p. 32)

This scenario suggests that underlying deficits in working memory undermine ability when it comes to academic performance. Examples of this are specified below.

5.2.4   Difficulties in Remembering Chunks of Information for Seminar Discussion

Tasks associated with remembering large chunks of information, such as concepts in reading materials, and the memorisation of learnt processes and procedures can be particularly challenging when there are deficits in working memory. This can cause students to become frustrated and even angry at themselves. MA Arts student Debra recalled her feelings of alienation, confusion and being frozen when asked how she felt about having to remember information:

> I would say the emotion for (remembering tasks) is kind of like an alienation. I just feel like I can't take part – well, I can't take part, because I don't know what's going on. I think it affects my mood because I feel like I don't understand. I'm looking round and everyone else seems to be engaging in this process and being able to do this and I can't. I think it makes me feel stupid, makes me think maybe this isn't the right thing for me. I guess it just confuses me as to the extent that I can't do it and other people can, because in most things, there's usually ways to cope with it, but there doesn't seem to be a way to cope with it in this situation because I'm just literally kind of frozen.

Accordingly, if the student has significant difficulties with short-term/working memory processes, then reading and remembering information from the text for, say, seminar discussions will be highly problematic. In the example of Debra above, weaknesses in remembering led to her feelings of alienation and being unable to participate during group discussions.

Yet this difficulty does not just affect remembering information read for the purpose of contributing to seminar discussions. It will also interfere with recalling information from lecture materials, revision notes, academic articles and so on, in order to demonstrate knowledge and learning during exams or assessed presentations. This can affect the student's self-esteem and confidence when it comes to such tasks and can begin to foster negative emotions and anxiety in association with evaluated elements of the course.

5.2.5   Other Difficulties in Debate and Discussion

Because of the short-term memory deficits, word-finding difficulties and articulation disorders prevalent in many people with dyslexia (Shaywitz, 1996), some students need to express their ideas immediately, before the words they want to use fade from their memory. As this instant contribution may interrupt others and appear rude, it can lead to frustration and social isolation for the dyslexic individual. For instance, let us be reminded of the scenario that illuminates this difficulty, as experienced and described by MA Humanities student Charlie:

> I find it quite frustrating if I can't find the appropriate time to talk. I'm not a great believer in putting my hand up if I have something to say. If I have an idea, I'm just going to come out with it, and people have taken badly to that in the past. Last time I had to go and see the senior tutor for my year and say, I keep offending people, I keep getting these looks from people whenever I speak. I don't like it if people feel they're being interrupted, or being cut off. People strop about it quite visibly.

One reason that Charlie believed she had to blurt out her ideas was because until she heard it (or could see it visually), the concept was not coherent in her memory; it was not tangible enough. By hearing herself speaking it through, her ideas began to make more sense, as she expressed:

> If I have an idea, I need to be able to either hear it or see it for it to be a complete idea. Otherwise, it's just these images, or concepts, it's nothing coherent. Until it's being spoken, I do have a panicky feeling, because there are ideas buzzing around in my head. Suddenly my head gets quite manic, and the ideas need to come out of my head, so until I can say something, I will be on edge.

This exemplifies how students with dyslexia generally need to hear or see something to place it more effectively into memory processes.

5.2.6   How Difficulties with Memory Impede Exam Performance

As briefly mentioned above, deficits with short-term/working memory will cause obstacles to remembering learning for exams.

Yet, in many universities, the predominant form of assessment remains the traditional exam method. Many students with dyslexia, particularly those that fall within the group affected by deficits in short-term and working memory, are disadvantaged by the exam system. Additional time for examinations is provided and may to some extent compensate for slow reading speeds; but owing to the nature of exams, as essentially a test of whether sufficient information can be retrieved from memory, extra time is not always helpful. It still cannot place a student with memory difficulties on an equal footing with a student with no known learning difficulties.

These difficulties can mean that negative attitudes towards testing situations arise whilst at university. Weak test results are not usually associated with the dyslexic student not working hard enough to prepare for the exam but are generally connected more with the dyslexia. The anxiety induced by worrying about exam performance can interfere with retrieval of information from memory. When the student reflects on their hard work for the exam and does not see this demonstrated in their test results, this can become a source of frustration and anger. Additionally, students can connect their sense of self-worth to exam scores. Low grades can affect self-esteem and hinder academic motivation. This, in turn, creates further anxiety around evaluative situations. As such, for the student with dyslexia, test anxiety can be explained by the extent to which the individual is able to use their working memory capacity (Darke, 1988b; Eysenck, 1984).

5.2.7   How Difficulties in Memory Manifest as Anxiety, and Anxiety Impedes Memory Further

So, as we have noted above, difficulties in memory generate anxiety. A useful study that examined anxiety levels of dyslexic students in relation to exams is the work by Nelson, Lindstrom and Foels (2015). The study provides evidence that students with dyslexia have a higher prevalence of anxiety than their non-dyslexic peers when it comes to exams. It also pinpoints that dyslexic students with higher deficits in non-verbal ability and working memory have higher rates of anxiety during exam situations.

To arrive at these findings, 50 college students with dyslexia were compared to 50 college students without dyslexia on responses to the *Test Anxiety Inventory* (Spielberger, 1980); the *Adult Manifest Anxiety Scale – College Version (AMAS-C) Test Anxiety Scale* (Reynolds, Richmond and Lowe, 2003); and the *Wechsler Adult Intelligence Scale – Fourth Edition* (WAIS IV) (Wechsler, 2008). The WAIS IV was used as the authors wanted to explore within both the dyslexic and non-dyslexic groups the relationships of cognitive abilities (general intelligence, verbal ability, non-verbal ability, working memory, processing speed, reading skills) and their consequences for test anxiety.

Results suggested that college students with dyslexia reported higher levels of test anxiety than those without. From the cognitive constructs measured by the WAIS IV, it was found that lower scores in non-verbal ability and working memory correlated with higher levels of test anxiety.

Another reason for exam anxiety for students with dyslexia is that those with working memory deficits may have failed exams at school, so they fear exams at university. Although students with dyslexia usually do have great innovative ideas on how they can cope at university cognitively, and they have often devised their own learning strategies to overcome academic barriers, it is frequently the negative emotion that becomes a profound obstacle to successful completion of their university programmes.

Another response to the anxiety caused by evaluative situations can be panic. Panic as a stress response that blocks processing abilities was recognised by postgraduate Sciences student Alan, who noted that it not only led to unhealthy thinking but also affected his working memory capacity:

> I will panic about it, and I have now identified that that is unhelpful thinking, and I will start to think more unhealthily, which will take out more of my working memory, which will make me less able to do it, and it just gets worse.

Now that we have outlined difficulties both cognitively and emotionally, let us look at a more positive aspect. This is the proficiency in memory processes which many students with dyslexia may possess, that of strengths in visual memory.

5.3   Strengths in Visual Memory

As we saw in Chapter 3 when discussing the results of a study by Akhavan Tafti et al. (2009), students with dyslexia have strengths in visual-spatial memory and pictorial memory. Of course, there are also other forms of memory in addition to visual-spatial memory, and short-term and working memory as discussed above. Your proficiencies may lie in some of these additional types of memory. For instance, it is common for people to say they are stronger in remembering certain things over others. You might remember events and experiences more effectively than remembering something you have read, or something you have heard, for example. Let us now outline these components of memory to see if you can identify whether you remember some aspects more productively than others. This knowledge will be useful as you will be able to select activities that tap into your memory strengths when studying.

5.4   Types of Memory

5.4.1   Episodic Memory

Episodic memory is when you strongly retain memories of *personally experienced events*. For example, you may have better recall of going on an excursion or field trip with your university peers than of information you were given during a lecture. Episodic memory has a strong temporal organisation, which basically means the ability to remember events in chronological order. So, for instance, if you are recalling the field trip, you may vividly remember occurrences such as undertaking an archaeological dig before visiting the museum, and you may have strong recollection of the order in which you went around the museum. On daily outings, if you have powerful episodic memory, you are likely to remember venues and buildings, and where they are located geographically; and you will probably be able to remember the people you encountered in those places, such as what they looked like, their mannerisms and the sounds of their voices.

   If this resonates, then when learning new things, you will be able to retrieve them more effectively if you incorporate lots of physical, sensory experiences into your studying. For example, rather than just reading about an artist, historian or writer you are studying, physically visit the art galleries, the historical locations and the places featured in the writers' works. This will bring to life the information you

175

need to know, enabling you to recall the knowledge connected to your studies much more substantially than studying these things in the traditional sense. Any topic, if you use your imagination, can lend itself to being studied in a physical, sensory and tangible way.

5.4.2 Prospective Memory

Prospective memory is used to remember to do something later, such as to attend a tutorial with a lecturer in a week's time.

If you have an effective prospective memory (which, from practitioner experience, few students with dyslexia have), then you will be able to spend less time on developing colourful timetables reminding you of imminent events. If, which is more likely the case, you struggle with this type of memory, then it is advisable to invest time in making a prominent visual feature of upcoming appointments and events.

5.4.3 Semantic Memory

Semantic memory refers to the capacity to recollect words, concepts and numbers. For example, you use semantic memory when you recall the alphabet or multiplication tables. If you have a dominant semantic memory, you will be easily able to recall facts you have read, or concepts you have seen written down.

To apply this type of memory to the learning of new information, you may find it helpful to highlight key points of information from text documents. It will also be useful to reflect on strategies you used to automatise your recall of multiplication tables. Was this from seeing the numbers written down? Or did you combine this with verbalisation?

5.4.4   Procedural Memory

Procedural memory is connected to *movement* and encompasses knowing how to ride a bike, how to drive a car, how to swim, and so on. Similar to semantic memory, procedural memory remains automatised across the life course. What this means is that even if someone has not driven a car for several years, when it comes to driving, they will inevitably recall what is required as the process is consolidated in memory.

If you find it easier to combine the learning of information through movement, or by integrating cognitive thought processes with the use of your motor skills, you will find it useful to listen to recordings of your lectures while running on a treadmill or spinning on an exercise bike. You may also benefit from integrating studying with dance movements.

5.4.5   Metamemory

Metamemory relates to a type of metacognition and involves having an awareness and knowledge of one's own memory capabilities. For example, if an individual is consciously aware that they will be unable to remember text from reading passively without interacting with the material, then that individual is using metamemory. In other words, metamemory relates to how individuals monitor and control learning and memory.

5.4.6   Subjective Memory

Subjective memory, like metamemory, refers to one's perceived memory ability. Consequently, subjective memory entails *someone's perception* about his or her memory functioning.

With this knowledge of your own individual memory strengths, let us now bolster and supplement its power and ability by looking at techniques that can be used to help with overcoming difficulties with memory processes. You may want to reflect on where you feel your memory abilities lie before selecting some of these methods to test out. If you are still unsure which techniques your memory responds to more effectively, then picking a range of these strategies to analyse and compare their benefits will help to deepen your metacognitive knowledge of your memory capacity.

5.5   Techniques

5.5.1   Memory Palaces

There are various strategies that you may want to trial to determine their effectiveness for helping you to remember information. Some of the most tried and tested methods are called memory palaces, also referred to as the method of loci, or the Cicero method, as they were adopted in ancient Roman and Greek times for the purpose of retrieving knowledge from rhetorical treatise. To use this method, the learning you need to recall in sequential order is transformed into a mnemonic by becoming tied to a journey that you know, or an everyday procedure that you are familiar with. To recall the information, you simply walk through your memory journey using the places or acts that you have linked to your learning as visual and kinaesthetic memory joggers for retrieving it.

For example, if you are studying *gastroenterology*, you might use the route you take to walk to the local shops to recall the process of digestion, which includes six activities. The street outside your home could be associated with your learning around *ingestion*, the path through the woods could be *propulsion*, the top of the hill and the golf course could be linked to *mechanical or physical digestion*, the new apartment block on your right connected with *chemical digestion*, the pretty Tudor house associated with *absorption*, and the Thai restaurant attached to *defecation*. Each time you go on this walk to the shops, the visual, physical and spatial presence of the places to which you have chronologically attached your learning becomes more deeply entrenched in your memory. The journey does not have to be a walk; you could simply attach each item of information you are memorising to objects in a room. As you move around the room either touching or viewing these objects, they begin to act as your memory joggers.

If you have kinaesthetic strengths, and you want to link the items, concepts or themes you are sequentially memorising to a process or procedure you do every day, then an example of this could be making a drink. For instance, if you are studying *biology* and need to learn the *four phases of meiosis* (a process where a single cell divides twice to produce four cells), then putting the coffee grains in the cup with a teaspoon could be related to *prophase*, pouring in the hot water from the kettle connected to *metaphase*, pouring in the milk associated with *anaphase*, and stirring with the teaspoon and drinking linked to *telophase*. As you repeat each day the process of making the coffee, each act unlocks in the correct order your knowledge around the *phases of meiosis*, so when it comes to the exam, test or evaluation, the learning is so linked to the daily routine of coffee making that it is easy for you to retrieve the knowledge in the correct order.

5.5.2   Saying It Out Loud

You may want to add another layer to the journey or procedure you are using as your memory palace by initially reciting aloud the material you are learning and memorising. For instance, in the case of the walk described above, each time you get to one of the places on the route (say, the golf course), you can take out your textbook and read aloud information on mechanical or physical digestion. As the passage from your textbook becomes more ingrained in your memory and more linked to a physical place, you may in the latter stages stop relying on the textbook. Instead, each time you are at one of the locations, you may want to pause for a while to see if you can regurgitate the information, first aloud, so you can hear yourself saying it, then on later walks silently, by just being present at the location, to see how effectively the physical place now acts as memory jogger.

5.5.3 Highlighting Keywords and Image Association

Highlighting keywords from readings and associating them with images you have created either by hand drawing, or by selecting and connecting electronically, can also act as an effective memory jogger for retrieving the information linked to the image.

For example, BSc Nursing student Tina would read through an important paper, taking time to absorb the detail. On her second readthrough, she would be selective and would highlight in bright coloured pens the key important points. On her return to the paper at a later date, her eyes would instinctively be drawn only to the high-lighted sections of the paper. That way, she condensed the informa-tion down to the essential key elements to make it more memorable and less overwhelming.

Let us also be reminded from Chapter 3 of our creative MA Arts student Debra, who transformed the paper into a colourful visual indicator of main points by highlighting keywords and drawing images alongside the words in the margins of the paper. As Debra previously described, this process was a powerful way for her to unlock her memory:

> Keyword or drawing something visual, then it's like, oh there it is. It's like the closet you open, when everything falls out, but it's sometimes finding that little thing that will open the door. It's finding the key basically.

By substituting the words in the papers for images, the images became connected to the words as memory triggers, recalling the semantic meaning from the written text.

Whilst images are strong activators for our memories, as proven above, other aspects such as senses, emotions and patterns can be as equally powerful. When we taste, smell, touch or physically experience something, the memories that we may have unconsciously stored can become unleashed. We can channel this natural ability into helping us to memorise our learning.

5.5.4   Using Sense of Smell as Memory Activator

Sense of smell can be a productive way of enhancing memory. How often have you been somewhere when the cooking smells, or the scent of flowers or grass cuttings, have evoked past events such as travel, holidays or childhood memories? The strength of our sense of smell in reactivating memories can effectively be used to help with unlocking retrieval of information we have associated with a particular fragrance. In fact, in a recent study, 'How odor cues help to optimize learning during sleep in a real life-setting', authors Neumann, Oberhauser and Kornmeier (2020) divided a group of 54 pupils aged 11 and 12 years into three groups. Group 1 received no odour during learning. In Group 2, the participants received an odour cue during learning and every night whilst sleeping before a test. In Group 3, the pupils received the odour during learning, every night whilst sleeping and during the test. The authors concluded that the group that benefited most from the study was Group 3: being exposed to the odour not only throughout the night, but also during the test, helped with recall of information.

One way to experiment with whether this can be helpful for you is to associate different fragrances and perfumes with different concepts that you need to memorise for your learning. Each time you revise that particular topic in preparation for your exam, you need to ensure you are wearing, or are exposed to, the fragrance you have selected to be associated with the topic. For example, if you are learning anatomy, a rose-scented fragrance could always be used and connected to knowledge around various muscle groups. Information about the heart could become linked with a more musk or citrus-type scent. Before the test or exam, you could then apply the different smells, for instance, fragrance 1 (rose scent associated with muscles) to your left wrist, fragrance 2 (citrus smell for knowledge associated with the heart) to the right wrist, fragrance 3 to your little finger, and so on. Each time an exam question is asked on the different aspects of anatomy, sniffing the various scents linked with each topic should invoke the information and assist with recall.

5.6   Using Multisensory Methods

What we have essentially seen above are examples of how multisensory methods, such as sense, touch, visualisation and physical experience, are keys to unlocking the power of our memory. There are a multitude of ways to combine our senses for the purpose of assisting with retrieval of stored knowledge. You may want to turn your learning into a song and sing aloud or rhyme out the information you need to recall. You can combine this with acting expressively or with activities such as exercising in the gym, or swimming, or cooking. Remember from Chapter 3 how Medicine student Naomi combined her kinaesthetic strengths to physically write or type things, so that it involved the act of doing, whilst at the same time reading aloud the words she was writing, so that she could hear them. As she states below, this was the combination of senses that worked effectively for her:

> I have to constantly write stuff down and read stuff aloud multiple times for me to be able to recall it whenever I need to. So, it will be doing it, it will be first writing it, so it's the act of writing, it will help to get it into my memory. Then reading it, reading aloud, so getting it in different methods. I find if I physically do the writing, or physically do the typing, I remember it more because it's gone through a different part.

5.6.1   Using Mnemonics

Mnemonics, which are memory devices in the form of rhymes, quirky sentences, words, songs or jingles, can be useful for remembering the order of letters in the spelling of tricky words, or for retrieving core concepts of a topic. For instance, the saying 'A rat in the house may eat the ice cream' is helpful when trying to recall how to spell the word 'arithmetic', and the rhyme 'I before E except after C' assists with remembering the order of letters in words such as 'receipt', 'receive' and 'achieve'. One common form of mnemonic is to use the first letter of each keyword to make a new word that sums up the whole subject – just as MIGRAINE sums up all the main concepts in media studies.

M – Media

I – Institution

G – Genre

R – Representation

A – Audience

I – Ideology

N – Narrative

E – Economics

The word does not have to make sense. Quite often it is more memorable if it is a bizarre or unusual word.

5.6.2   Using Repetition

Whilst repetition and rote learning is not particularly suitable for students with dyslexia because of its lack of a multisensory approach, it can be a productive method for helping with memorising small aspects of learning. For example, as mind maps generally consist of succinct key information categorised under main areas, as in the example below, these lend themselves to repeated reviewing for short lengths of time without becoming overwhelmed by too much information. Brief and frequent evaluations of information such as in the form of the mind map will help to place the concepts into memory.

5.6.3   Writing Things Down

The process of writing things down by hand involves using your motor coordination skills and sensory skills combined with having to encode the information. As such, not only does the act of writing help to place the information you have written into memory, getting into the habit of writing down things like tasks to do or important dates as a visual reminder is also key to keeping you on track with your studies, as we discovered in Chapter 2 with MA Education student Chloe, who had difficulties with working memory:

> If I don't have it written down on a to-do list, or a plan, something there, I'm scared I'm going to lose it. It's going to disappear.

5.7   Using Chunking, Categorising and Organising of Information

Breaking down information that you are learning – by chunking, categorising, synthesising and organising it under headings, for example – also helps with memorisation processes, as you have interacted with the learning and done something to make it more memorable.

Stella Cottrell's tremendously valuable book, *The Study Skills Handbook, Third Edition* (Cottrell, 2008), has some useful exercises that illuminate the effectiveness of both 'chunking' and 'organising' information.

Have a go at the two activities below to see if this is something that may be productive for you and whether it would be useful to apply these techniques to your learning. The link to these activities is provided here:

www.cambridge.org/abbottjones

5.7.1   Activity – 'Chunking' Information

Cottrell states:

> Nobel-prize winner Herbert Simon found that we can generally hold five 'chunks' of information in short-term memory (1974).

However, the 'chunk' can vary enormously in size: it could be a single word or number, or a phrase, or a whole story, or how to count up to a million. Try this out for yourself. (Cottrell, 2008, p. 307).

- Read the list under 'Small Chunks' for 2 minutes.
- Cover the list, then try to remember each phrase exactly.
- Write down each phrase remembered in 1 minute.
- Do the same for the 'Bigger Chunks' list.

You should be able to remember roughly the same number of chunks, irrespective of their size – for example, five sets of two and five sets of longer sentences.

Small Chunks (Two Words)

Christmas Day	No Trespassing
Woburn Hall	Buckingham Palace
Honeydew Melon	Dressing Table
Pound Coins	Good Friday

Bigger Chunks (Six- to Ten-Word Sentences)

You're never fully dressed without a smile.
She sells seashells on the seashore.
Here's to happiness, freedom and life.
Little Miss Muffet sat on a tuffet.
Everyone deserves the chance to fly.
 A spoonful of sugar helps the medicine go down.
The wheels on the bus go round and round.
The animals went in two by two.
That's when your dreams will all come true.

Cottrell's (2008) next useful activity, emphasising how memory succeeds if organisation of information is applied, is also presented for you to try out by using the link below.

www.cambridge.org/abbottjones

5.8   Memory Thrives on Organisation

(This activity is from Cottrell, 2008, p. 395.)

5.8.1   Activity – Categorising Information

- Read List A for 15 seconds, then cover it.
- Recite the nursery rhyme, to prevent practising retrieval of the words whilst they are covered over:

  Jack and Jill went up the hill to fetch a pail of water.
  Jack fell down and bumped his crown and Jill came tumbling after.

- Write down only the words you remember.
- Check List A and write down your score.
- Now do the same with List B, including all the underlined words.

List A

Pasta	Table	Train	Bread
Shirt	Chair	Aeroplane	Camera
Trousers	Book	Banana	Boat
Beans	Skirt	Car	Hat

List B

Clothes	Objects	Food	Transport
Shirt	Table	Pasta	Car
Trousers	Chair	Bread	Train
Hat	Camera	Beans	Aeroplane
Skirt	Book	Banana	Boat

If you found it easier to recall more words under List B, it is because you are using the process of categorising the words into a distinctive group under a main word that is acting as the label. This is a useful technique during revision of your topic, for instance, in preparation

187

for exams if you are having to remember groups of concepts. For example, you may be required to remember components that make up the cardiovascular system if studying medicine, or the names of Kings and Queens from Tudor times if studying history.

When we use memory for learning or for any type of information we need to recall at a later stage, we put the memory process through four different phases or stages. Drawing again from the wonderful work of Cottrell (2008) – as, from practitioner experience, this provides effective tools for helping students with dyslexia gain a deeper understanding of how memory works and offers useful strategies to enhance it – let us now look to developing an awareness of these four stages of memory and what we should do to ensure our memory is working productively during each of them.

5.9   The Four Stages of Memory

5.9.1   Taking in Information

Many situations at university involve taking in information. These include lectures, reading coursework materials, and during discussions such as in seminar debate.

Taking in, processing and absorbing information requires that our senses – sense of hearing, seeing, touch – become stimulated, for instance by the sound (auditory output from the lecturer's voice) or by the visual information (slides presented by the lecturer, or text and images presented by the reading material). The sensory input, auditory and visual, is then transmitted to the brain, which deciphers and makes connections with the information based on previous knowledge, experiences and beliefs.

188

Strategies that can help you to take in and interpret information more effectively include the following.

Strategies

- Connect new information to what you already know about the topic. For example, if attending a lecture, you may want to take in your notes or mind map from the previous taught session. That way, you can add on new keywords and concepts by drawing arrows to connect to the new knowledge. (See Chapter 3, *Note-Taking Strategies*, for more on ways of constructively taking in information.)
- Listen to a recording of your lecture, translate into your own words, and listen to yourself verbalising your explanation aloud.

5.9.2   Retaining Information Long Enough to Remember It

You should attempt to retain key points from learning you receive during your course, whether from lectures, reading materials, practical activities, seminar discussion and debate, or presentations. As attempting to retain too much information can be overwhelming, you should be selective. (See Chapter 4 section 'Reading Using Selectivity' for more on how to develop this skill.) Use a variety of multisensory and active methods in learning situations so that you develop your ability to preserve the knowledge you have received (as discussed throughout this book; also see Cottrell, 2008, p. 300, for more suggestions on methods for retaining information).

5.9.3   Encoding Information – The Key to Memory

Situations involving encoding include any learning experience in which you are actively interacting with the information. In other words, you are not passively absorbing knowledge (which you may sometimes do during listening or reading) but instead doing something proactive with that information.

During revision, if you are using methods that enable effective interactivity, you are fostering the capacity to encode the information more productively and should find it easier to recall the learning during exams. Whilst Chapter 8, *Revision and Examination Techniques*, covers a list of useful active techniques to help you to encode your learning constructively, it is also advisable to look at Cottrell's (2008) list of inspiring methods for helping you to convert the information you have absorbed into something more memorable.

5.9.4   Recall

Recall involves retrieving the information from memory during exams, tests and other evaluative situations, when writing essays and other forms of written assignment, and during presentations and seminars.

Cottrell (2008) suggests an effective strategy to fortify information so that it becomes effortless to recall: a technique known as overlearning. If you want to have a try at overlearning, the steps below will help you to become familiar with the process. You can also access this resource from the link:

www.cambridge.org/abbottjones

5.9.5   Steps Involved in Overlearning to Help to Memorise Information

- Either create a mind map of key concepts you want to recall, or list the concepts as a set of bullet points on a large index card.

- Put the mind map or index card into a plastic folder so you can carry it around with you. Glance at it briefly in spare moments, such as when travelling or when preparing food.
- Do this several times over a few days. Just looking at the prompt from time to time, or running the information through your head, will keep the memory fresh. Little and often is more effective than simply repeating the information over and over on one occasion.
- Begin to leave longer periods of time before looking at the mind map or index card. This is helping the memory to consolidate the information.
- See if you can recite the concepts from memory.
- Work towards leaving looking at the mind map or index card for a minimum of three days. Before checking, see if you can recall all the concepts written down. This is the process of transforming the learning from your short-term to long-term memory.

Now let us turn to looking at ways in which technology and assistive technology can help to support memorisation processes.

5.10   Using Technology

5.10.1   Benefits of Using Digital Devices to Hold Information

Storing information in digital devices can be effective. If you use them to store information that you need to remember, such as tasks to do on an assignment, deadlines and exam dates, or dates for appointments, this can reassure you that the important dates are captured as visual reminders on your devices. This process reduces the anxiety of worrying that you will forget your exam date, and allows you to free your mind to concentrate on other things.

5.10.2   Using Mind-Mapping Software

Mind-mapping software (such as Inspiration) is a productive tool to help with memorising information. One of the benefits is that readings can be abbreviated into significant keywords, and the keywords can be connected to colourful images. The mind maps can then be printed out and placed face down to see if the information can be recalled.

5.10.3   Using Speech-to-Text Software

Speech-to-text software is particularly effective for students who prefer to verbalise their ideas aloud. As it enables students to capture their thoughts whilst freely moving around the room, it is a productive tool for initiating writing, especially for those who may freeze and forget what they want to write when faced with a keyboard or a pen. Once the spoken ideas are captured in the document, the student can work to shape the ideas into a more academic written format.

5.10.4   Using Power Point to Turn Learning into Visual Presentations

As we have seen in Section 5.3, 'Strengths in Visual Memory', many students with dyslexia enjoy using software that prioritises visual images over words and text. Using PowerPoint or mind mapping to transform the information into visual slides that you may want to present to an audience, or just to yourself, is an effective way of making your learning memorable.

5.10.5   Using the Dictaphone as Auditory Reminder

A recording device, on a mobile phone, or the Dictaphone (a recording device provided to students with a diagnosis of dyslexia as part of the Disabled Students' Allowance package), is also useful for students who may want to record themselves verbalising their visual presentation. That way they can frequently listen to the recording as an auditory reminder of their learning.

5.10.6   Using Portable Recording Device to Capture Ideas

Another benefit of carrying around a recording device is to capture ideas before they disappear from memory. It is common for students with dyslexia to have great ideas when off task, such as when making a cup of tea or going for a walk. However, owing to deficits in short-term memory, the ideas may instantly disappear and be hard to retrieve. Having the recording device to hand during these moments of genius will ensure that the thoughts are not lost.

5.10.7   Using Online Resources

Many useful suggestions on ways to improve memory can be found from online videos and web forums. Utilising Internet resources could lead to discovering some productive methods for enhancing your memory of your learning.

5.10.8   Using Alarms on Mobile Phones and Watches

Setting automated prompts, alarms and reminders on your mobile phone, tablet or watch can be an effective way of ensuring that you do not forget about important appointments, lecture and seminar dates, coursework deadlines and exam dates. The prompt can be set at any stage before the significant date – perhaps a day beforehand,

193

or even several weeks before – so that it is tailored to meet your needs. For example, let us be reminded, from Chapter 2, of how BSc Nursing student Lisa had an alarm set on her phone two weeks prior to coursework deadline dates, to motivate her into action and to focus her attention on her assignments.

- I make sure I've got an alarm set two weeks before on my phone. Not to freak me out, as it were, but to kind of just kick me up the bum and go, listen, remember there is a deadline.

5.10.9   Using Digital Clocks and Calendars

People with dyslexia can sometimes have trouble remembering the days of the week and may have difficulties with time perception. Furthermore, if the individual has a diagnosis of dyscalculia, reading the faces of clocks can be challenging. Digital clocks that display the date and day of the week, as well as the time, could be a productive way of remedying these problems.

5.10.10   Using Locator Devices

Locator devices, which are small electronic tags that can be attached to items you may regularly misplace, such as keys, wallets or bags, are constructive tools for helping you to find the things you lose. How they generally work is if your mobile phone has a tracker app installed, you can link the electronic tag to the app. You then place the tag into your wallet or bag, and when the electronically tagged object is left behind, you can open the app to see if the tag is within range of your phone. When you tap Find on the app, the tag will start ringing, and you simply follow the sound to where you last left the item. If the object is out of range of your phone, it will show you the last location where the object was tracked.

5.10.11 Using Virtual Assistants

Virtual assistants such as Amazon Alexa, Google Assistant, Apple Siri, Microsoft Cortana and Samsung Bixby respond to voice commands and will provide verbal answers to your questions. For example, if you ask what temperature the weather is today, the virtual assistant will provide a detailed response. If you ask for the dates of specific events (such as Easter, Christmas, Ramadan or Eid), again it will supply accurate responses, which is useful if you need a verbal reminder of important dates. Whilst virtual assistants cannot provide answers to personal questions, such as 'When is my deadline for my history essay?', they can provide factual answers to general questions. For instance, if you ask questions such as 'Who is the President of the United States? or the Prime Minister of the UK?' or 'Where is Italy located?' or 'What is the population of India?', the virtual assistant will respond, usually by drawing from sources like Wikipedia to supply its information. The virtual assistant will also give answers to calculations you may want to check, such as 'What is £75 minus £37?', which is particularly useful for people with dyscalculia who may want to check receipts from shopping or household bills. The virtual assistant can also (with additional equipment) control lights and the central heating in the home, which is useful if you forget to switch off electricity when not using the room, or forget to turn down heating when away from home, for example.

5.11   Summary

In summary, this chapter has:

- Specified some of the common difficulties with memory that students with dyslexia can encounter.

- Outlined the ways in which deficits in both short-term and working memory can affect study performance.
- Provided details of techniques to assist with overcoming memory difficulties. These included:
  - Memory palaces.
  - Saying it out loud.
  - Highlighting keywords and image association.
  - Using sense of smell as memory activator.
  - Using multisensory methods.
  - Using mnemonics.
  - Using repetition.
  - Writing things down.
  - Using chunking, categorising and organising of information.
- Specified the different types of memory, to help with developing metacognitive awareness of personal memory strengths.
- Drawn from the work of Cottrell (2008) to provide activities that highlight the productiveness of 'chunking' and 'categorising' information for effective recall.
- Drawn from the work of Cottrell (2008) to outline the four stages of memory required when undertaking any type of academic activity, which included:
  - Taking in information.
  - Retaining information long enough to remember it.
  - Encoding information.
  - Recall.
- Outlined ways in which technology and assistive technology can also help to support memorisation processes.

6

• • • • •

Essay-Writing Strategies

6.1   Introduction

Written work is a common academic task required by university programmes. However, numerous skills are necessary in putting together and submitting a well-written piece of work. These range from evaluating and breaking up the essay/assignment question to finding appropriate resources that provide evidence to support the points you want to write, to reading selectively and choosing suitable citations to interweave into your writing, to developing your essay plan, followed by the act of writing itself where you must show skills in communicating clearly, coherently and logically, whilst at the same time showing that you can analyse and critically interpret different perspectives on the topic. As such, developing competence in this area can be challenging. Furthermore, at university, academic staff will generally supply essay questions and deliver the knowledge for the questions in lecture format; yet when it comes to explaining how to actually write an essay and the list of tasks that are required from start to finish, this guidance is all too often lacking, and the student is left floundering.

This chapter then, firstly, specifies common difficulties with essay writing for the student with dyslexia, which helps to cultivate an awareness of why you may struggle with certain aspects. Secondly, it moves on to focus on overcoming these difficulties by delivering a range of cognitive learning strategies that students with dyslexia say they find useful for essay planning and techniques they find effective for writing.

Essay-planning techniques include using university resources, making plans and writing guides by using mind maps to visualise links between ideas, breaking the main question down into a series of smaller questions to provide hooks for gathering the right type of information, starting written assignments early in the term, utilising multisensory methods, developing metacognitive awareness when planning so that you use approaches suitable for how you think, and using technology.

Effective writing techniques include setting small goals by breaking up the required word length of the essay, using subheadings to help with essay structure, applying the Point, Example/Evidence, Comment/Criticism (PEC) method of writing to ensure that paragraphs are well composed, designating proofreaders to check through written work, and using assignment cover sheets on coursework submission to ensure that examiners are aware that the student is dyslexic. The PEC method is presented as a step-by-step approach to witing, and clear examples of this are provided. The chapter also provides methods for how you can demonstrate criticality in your writing.

Additionally, academic essays generally conform to a conventional style: they present an argument, they provide examples, evidence and information accurately cited from credible sources to support the argument, and they include a bibliography of materials referred to. So the chapter concludes by presenting a kind of checklist to ensure that, where necessary, you always maintain these elements in your writing.

6.2   Common Difficulties with Essay Writing

Recurrent difficulties with essay writing range from not knowing where to start (which is usually the case with first- and second-year undergraduate students) to grammatical difficulties causing anxiety and affecting confidence in writing, difficulties with spelling interrupting the writing process, not noticing mistakes when proofreading leading to stress, difficulties in identifying relevant resources and confusion using databases, structural difficulties such as producing writing with a lack of coherence and not developing ideas through logically before throwing in another idea, or having problems with putting ideas in the right order and going off on tangents rather than sticking to answering the question. Obstacles with writing could also be psychological – having a fear of writing, or being instilled with dread, particularly as writing assignments typically become longer in word length the more you advance through your course of study. These worries cause stress and anxiety, which then impedes writing ability further, in a cyclical effect. Furthermore, if you have a combination of dyslexia with dyspraxia, the dyspraxia can cause difficulties with motor coordination when writing. For example, you may struggle to make your handwriting readable, or you may be uncomfortable when typing.

Let us now take these issues and determine how students with dyslexia express their own difficulties in these areas. As we have seen earlier, Fiona, a BSc Sciences student, pinpointed that the difficulty caused by her dyslexia was with structuring writing in essays, and structuring verbal dialogue when talking:

> I suppose where I notice it [dyslexia] affecting me, is there are some things that my brain just doesn't seem to be able to work with. In an academic setting, structuring essays. I can have ideas about the subject, I can have a discussion with someone about the subject, and I find I don't even really know where to begin when I'm thinking about structure. I find my brain does not work in that way. So, I find that's something that I definitely struggle with. Also – I don't think this is necessarily a negative thing, because sometimes people find it humorous – but the way I speak. My sentences, I kind of go a bit roundabout, or some-times words kind of mix together. People know what I'm saying, but you know when you say a word and it's clearly not a word. I don't know, I think I notice, but how it affects me, definitely in structuring, sometimes I can't articulate myself in a way that other people know what I'm saying.

MA Arts student Cara recognised that her difficulty was in putting ideas in the right order in her writing, and the emotional conse-quences of her dyslexia, such as the impact on her confidence:

> I would say it [the dyslexia] has quite a significant emotional impact, mostly in my work. Occasionally, I can get sentences back to front, so I would have all the right words in, which is just something to be aware of if I've got presentations, or I'm trying to learn quotes. I have to make sure that I've got it correct. When I'm writing, I know that it never comes out right the first way. Normally I'm writing all my ideas and they're all in there, but they are in the wrong order, so then I have to rearrange it all. I think it's something that knocks my self-confidence quite a lot. Often, I try and hide it.

200

6.3   Essay-Planning Techniques

Next, we begin to look at how we can implement strategies to begin to overcome these types of difficulties. First, we discuss essay planning and the benefits of investing the time to ensure that you have an appropriate, well-developed plan in response to the essay question.

As was alluded to in Chapter 2, *Organisation Techniques and Meeting Deadlines*, preparation and planning have a consequence of alleviating negative emotion. Planning academic work, combined with applying appropriate cognitive strategies to supplement your learning style, not only helps with making learning easier, but also reduces anxiety about essay writing.

Planning your essays before you write, by listing the main points you want to cover, makes it more likely that you will produce a well-organised, reasoned and logical argument in reply to your assignment question. Planning enables you to place the key elements of your essay in an order which will make sense to your reader and allows you time to reflect and to consider an adequate conclusion for your thesis (the main idea of the essay).

In addition to planning and placing in logical order the points and issues you want to cover in the essay to make the writing more straightforward, you should also invest some time in timetabling when you will do the list of tasks involved in producing an essay. For example, the typical list of tasks in chronological order include:

- Breaking down the question to understand what is being required from you. This involves thinking about what information you need to answer the question.
- Researching to gather the information, which includes using library catalogues to search for journals and books, and using databases to retrieve academic journal articles.

201

- Reading and note taking.
- Putting your interpretation of the notes from readings into a logical structure.
- Writing using selective quotes from reading and notes, which you use to strengthen, back up and provide evidence to support your argument and the points you want to make.
- Presenting and formatting the essay, and adding a bibliography, ensuring that the essay follows your university guidelines on the style conventions.
- Checking, proofreading and reading out loud.

If you give each of the steps an appropriate timeframe, dependent on how much time you have until the essay deadline, you can at least reduce any anxiety you may have over not knowing what to do, or stress caused by leaving everything to the last minute.

Writing a plan for your essay and figuring out from your reading what you want to include to develop your argument, combined with listing and timetabling your tasks, may feel time-consuming. However, it essentially works to your benefit by making certain that during the times you are working on your essay, you are more productive and efficient, hence actually shortening the amount of time you need to put in.

6.3.1 Cognitive Learning Strategies

When we Google strategies effective for writing, we get varying advice dependent upon the aims of the website publisher. For example, the site www.indeed.com lists the following tasks as crucial for communicating successfully in writing:

- Read.
- Target your audience.

- Use an outline.
- Open strong.
- Answer Who, What, Why, When, Where and How.
- Be simple and direct.
- Choose strong verbs.
- Limit your adjectives and adverbs.

But Indeed is a website for job listings, so the advice above is targeted at writing strong applications for employment opportunities. As there are so many different forms of writing, you have to search for strategies applicable to the genre of writing you need to produce, whether that is an academic essay, a dissertation, a literature review, a report or a piece of reflective writing.

Accordingly, as we are specifically interested in techniques to help with academic writing and curious about the types of methods that students with dyslexia have found to be beneficial for both planning and writing essays, we list these strategies here. We then go into more detail below on ways you might use the techniques to support your own written work. Whilst we have already listed some of these approaches in the introduction to this chapter, which we will be unpicking more specifically, other processes that students with dyslexia find useful include:

- Researching and developing knowledge on how to write an essay.
- Writing paragraphs as contained units.
- Picking topics that are enjoyable, to keep motivated.
- Freewriting first before thinking about applying conventions.
- Writing several drafts.
- Completely investigating the topic before writing.
- Thinking about the reader and making sure it makes sense.
- Getting content down, leaving it for a few days and then editing.

203

- Using two Word documents alongside each other on the computer screen. The first document contains all ideas in a freewriting style, whereas the second one has themes and subheadings. Content from the first document can be pasted into the second one to develop structure.
- Hand-drawing mind maps to see the links.

Let us look at a couple of these ideas.

Freewriting First

MA Arts student Abu recognised that once he became knowledgeable about a topic and began to formulate ideas around it, he could, without thinking too much about sentence structure, punctuation, academic style and so on, just write endlessly, producing content, as he explained:

> If someone asks me to write freely, I could probably write endlessly. It's when that writing has to fit a certain format.

Freewriting, whereby you either type or use speech-to-text software to capture content continuously for a set period of time, without worrying about rhetorical concerns or academic convention, can be a useful method of prewriting. The process lets you record the ideas you want to discuss in the essay, whilst enabling you to overcome any writing blocks, as you are not having to think about adhering to scholarly style.

Writing Several Drafts

From this prewriting stage, you can then add another layer to the content by moving things around whilst beginning to build in the academic style, as articulated by MA student Charlie:

> When I write my first draft, it is often me just almost talking for it to come out, so it doesn't sound very intelligent when it first comes out and things need to be moved around quite a lot. So, I feel by the time I'm showing it to someone I've drafted it like two or three times.

The key with this approach is to not worry about how it sounds at first, but just concentrate on capturing the essence of what you want to say. All the academic structure and logical coherence can be interwoven from this starting point, as evidenced from Charlie's example above.

6.3.2   Utilising University Resources

Most universities have academic skills centres. These generally run programmes and workshops throughout the year, offering opportunities for students to learn a wide range of strategies including developing essay-writing skills. MA Arts student Debra would use these sessions to improve her writing ability. She also proactively looked for various writing resources provided by the university:

> Me being a person who likes to solve problems or find a way to solve things, I looked up and I found a few courses that they were giving on how to write an academic paper, and that was quite useful. I just tried to find all the resources that my university offered.

You may also want to consider the ways in which your own university's study skills or academic skills centre may be able to help you with your writing. Most centres employ writing tutors who can help you with developing academic writing knowledge, and can go through practical strategies, exercises and techniques with you.

6.3.3   Referencing Styles and Avoiding Plagiarism in Writing

Plagiarism in writing is when you use another author's words, language, thoughts, ideas and expressions by copying the text from the reading, pasting it into your own document and presenting it as your own work, without acknowledgement or reference to the original writer. This may be done unintentionally if you do not know how to cite your sources, but in the academic world plagiarism is misconduct and is usually penalised by examiners. Most university academic skills centres have booklets to help you to reference ideas in the appropriate style: this may be Harvard reference style, Chicago, Modern Language Association (MLA) or American Psychological Association (APA), dependent on your topic area. The format you are required to use for referencing should be presented in these booklets. This will help to guide you in ensuring that your in-text citations and your bibliography (the list of sources, including books, articles and websites, that you have used to obtain information for your essay) are mentioned with consistency and accuracy. Academic writing centres may also be able to provide advice on structuring an essay, writing a literature review, writing a proposal for a dissertation, and ways to write an essay during an exam.

6.3.4 Making Plans and Writing Guides

As discussed above, the key to working on written assignments is to plan both your *time spent* working on the different tasks involved in essay writing and, simultaneously, a *structure or writing guide* for how you are actually going to approach your assignment. This will make it a more productive process for you. BSc Nursing student Lisa had automatised this method for her work:

> I cross between determination and focus, like I know I have to write. Okay, I need to plan when I'm going to start writing, when I need to finish this essay by, to be able to get it spellchecked in time. I have to set up my time schedule, so I know what I'm doing. Luckily, doing BTECs at A-levels are really useful because you do lots of essay work, so like I got down to writing essay plans. It was like, right okay, so the first paragraph needs to be this, then this, then this, then Conclusion and things, so then I have that framework to go by.

Once the way you tackle writing assignments becomes systematised, having a framework to guide what you want to say in your essay becomes a necessity, as in the case of MSc Humanities student Alison:

I have to have a plan. I definitely do.

6.3.5   Example of Planning Time on Your Writing Assignment

As a useful reminder from Chapter 2, *Organisation Techniques and Meeting Deadlines*, if you are struggling to identify tasks and plan timeframes for the duties involved in essay writing, a clear example of this is set out for you below. You just need to read-just the timescale for each task dependent on how much time you have, or place the tasks in a different order if that is how you prefer to work.

The link to this resource, so you can customise your own version, is below.

www.cambridge.org/abbottjones

Steps of Written Assignment with Timeframes Set for Each Step

Break Down the Question to Understand What Is Required from You
What information do I need to answer the question? – *A few hours*

Research – to Gather the Information
Library catalogue searches for journals and books.
Database searches for journal articles.
Internet, e.g., Google Scholar. – *A couple of weeks*

Reading and Note Taking

Using preferred reading and note-taking strategies:

> Q Notes
>
> PASS
>
> SQ3R – *3 to 4 weeks*

Mind Mapping/Concept Pyramids

Using preferred method to get down the ideas from reading and note taking into a concise structure. – *A couple of days*

Organising Ideas into a Structure

Numbering branches on mind map/transforming into linear structure. – *A few hours*

Writing Using Selective Quotes from Reading and Notes

Quotes need to strengthen, back up, provide evidence of the points you make. – *3 to 4 weeks, dependent on word target set for each study session*

Presenting, Formatting, Adding Bibliography

Typing up in Word and making sure the essay follows the guidelines on style conventions. – *A couple of days*

Checking

Proofreading, reading out loud – *A couple of days*

6.3.6 Turning a Mind Map into a Linear List to Use as a Writing Guide

MSc Humanities student Alison would, firstly, read the appropriate academic materials to make notes for answering her essay question.

Secondly, she would use the mind-mapping software on her computer to type up keywords associated with her ideas on content for her writing. This enabled her to see how the ideas linked together. Thirdly, she would convert the mind map into a linear list. Most mind-mapping software has a tool to enable the initial map of ideas to be transformed into an Outline view, which is typically hierarchically organised using headings and subheadings depending on how the ideas were prioritised in the mind map. The Outline tool is particularly useful for students like Alison who like to get their thoughts down by mind mapping to see connections between concepts, yet who prefer, when starting writing, to have an ordered outline of the ideas as a linear list of subheadings which guides the structure of the writing, as explained:

> I put it onto the computer to make the plan, so that I can turn it into a list, so that becomes the basis for the essay. That's really helpful, and the subheadings kind of guide you more. That's what I learnt about why you have subheadings, whether you use them in the actual essay or not, it creates more focus and guidance.

A visual example of transforming a mind map to a linear list is provided in Figure 6.1.

6.3.7 Example of Turning Mind Map into Linear List for Essay

'An investigation into dyslexia and the co-occurring difficulties with speech, language and communication in adult learners in FE/HE'

1. Introduction
2. Memory
   2.1. P107 Baddely
3. Strategies
4. Types

Mortimore, T. (2008) Dyslexia and Learning Style: A Practitioner's Handbook. John Wiley & Sons Ltd

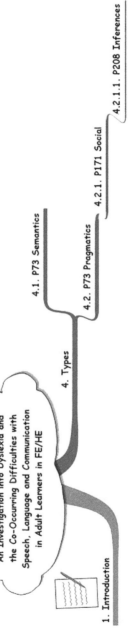

Figure 6.1 Example of turning mind map into linear list for essay

4.1. P73 Semantics

4.2. P73 Pragmatics

    4.2.1. P171 Social

        4.2.1.1. P208 Inferences

5. Phonology

The linear list is created dependent upon the order of numbers you attach in the mind map to the keywords.

The keywords on the mind map are in response to the essay title 'An investigation into dyslexia and the co-occurring difficulties with speech, language and communication in adult learners in FE/HE'.

It is using notes made by the student about the text *Dyslexia and Learning Style: A Practitioner's Handbook* (2008) by Mortimore to pull out the information for answering the question. Hence, knowledge from the book has identified that it is important to talk about the themes of memory, strategies, types of language and phonology in response to the question, in this order. Consequently, you have your essay structure on the mind map, and you also have the page numbers from the book, shown next to the keywords where these topics are discussed.

You can then create a Reading and Notes document, as in the example below, where you pull out quotes from the book that you are going to interweave into your writing to support the points you want to make. For instance, each time you find a useful quote, you capture it in the Word document, and you write underneath where in your essay structure you will use it, and what purpose it will serve in bolstering your writing.

6.3.8 Example of Notes and Quotes from Reading Being Organised into Your Essay Structure

Reading – Mortimore, T. (2008) *Dyslexia and Learning Style: A Practitioner's Handbook*. John Wiley & Sons Ltd.

p. 73. Content refers to semantics: topics, ideas, memory and meaning.

Use in 'types of language difficulties' section to (1) define semantics and (2) discuss how the adult learner may struggle to articulate their ideas in a structured way.

p. 107. The long-term memory system contains both semantic, episodic and procedural memory, thus Baddeley's latest refinement suggests integrated working between all these aspects of memory.

Use in memory as a cause of dyslexia and co-occurring speech section as evidence to support the argument that if the adult learner struggles to remember semantics, episodes and procedures, then this will affect their ability to articulate spontaneously, fluidly and fluently.

p. 73. *Human communication* involves three main overlapping components… The three overlapping circles represent the content, form and use of language. Content refers to semantics: topics, ideas, memory and meaning. Form refers to the method of communicating – spoken, written or signed. Use refers to pragmatics or the goals and social use of language.

Use in 'types of language difficulties' section to (1) define pragmatics and (2) discuss how the adult learner may struggle with social communication if they are unaware of social conventions of language, such as turn taking, appropriate use of language, etc.

So, in this example, of essay planning/producing a writing guide, what we have done is:

- Found the appropriate reading to help us respond to the question.
- Pulled out the essential key points from the reading that we have identified as important discussion points for our essay answer.
- Placed them into mind-map form to see how subtopics can link into keywords.

- Turned the mind map into a linear list which has provided the sub-headings for the essay.
- Returned to the reading to pull out useful quotes, and, in the Reading and Notes Word document, captured the quote and written underneath where in the essay structure the quote will be placed and what purpose it will serve (to provide evidence to support a point we want to make, or to define a terminology word, etc.).

A template of a Reading and Notes document for developing essay structure is available in the Resources section, so you can trial making an essay plan using this technique.

www.cambridge.org/abbottjones

Of course, there are other ways to make essay plans, and it is a case of finding a method that suits how you work. An alternative to the approach described above could be first to freewrite anything that comes to mind about the topic. Then, once you have the content, you can put the points you want to discuss in numbered order, in the way you would like to present them in your writing.

If you want to try out this method, use the link to the template, and next time you are given an essay question, have a go at freewriting on the topic.

www.cambridge.org/abbottjones

6.3.9 Freewriting Activity

Using your notebook, write anything that comes to mind about the topic, or if you prefer, say your ideas out loud, capturing them on a recording device or in summarised writing.

_____

_____

_____
_____
_____
_____
_____
_____
_____
_____
_____
_____
_____
_____
_____
_____

Put all the points in numbered order as you would like to present them in your writing.

1.
2.
3.
4.

6.3.10   Breaking the Main Question Down into A Series of Smaller Questions

Before we begin to look at ways to break the essay question down by producing additional questions that help with developing an essay structure and tell us what information we need to investigate to produce a comprehensive answer, we need to become familiar with instruction words typically used to form essay questions, and how we deal with those words in our writing.

Evaluating Instruction Words in an Essay So You Know How to Respond to the Question

Essay questions typically have instruction words (informing you on how to respond to the question) and a topic word. It is important that you understand the instruction word so that you can produce the right type of answer to the question. For example, the terms *compare* and *contrast* can often be confused. 'Compare' is asking you to discuss the similarities and differences of two or more subjects, yet putting emphasis onto the **similarities**. 'Contrast' is asking you to examine the **differences** of two or more subjects.

The link below provides access to a document that details an exhaustive list of action/instruction words generally used in essay questions. Alongside each of the action words, an explanation is supplied of the type of answer you should produce in reply to each of the instructions.

www.cambridge.org/abbottjones

Breaking Down the Question by Highlighting the Instruction and Topic Words

To break down essay questions for a deeper understanding of what exactly is being asked, an effective technique involves using two different-coloured highlighter pens:

- Firstly, highlight the Instruction/Action words in the question: words explaining what you are required to do, such as contrast, define, evaluate, outline, describe.
- In a different-coloured pen, highlight the topic words in the question.
- For example, in a question for history saying 'Compare the main features of China's modernisation efforts in the Maoist and post-Mao periods', this can be broken down to highlight the keywords that form the question:

- **Compare** [Instruction/Action: first colour] the main features of **China's modernisation** [Topic: second colour] efforts in the Maoist and post-Mao periods.
- The highlighting draws attention to the type of response required. As we discovered above, *compare* means to note dissimilarities but more importantly similarities of something, so here you are being asked to specifically focus on that. The second highlight colour gives emphasis to the importance of the topic that should be under discussion throughout the written response to the question. The highlighting is a mechanism that ensures you do not detract from the topic by making the mistake of writing about something else.

6.3.11 Developing Sub-Questions from the Main Question

Sub-questions involve breaking your main question down into a series of smaller questions. These mini questions are important because they provide the hooks for finding the relevant information to answer your main question. Below is an example of the question discussed above, broken into a series of sub-questions.

- Compare the main features of China's modernisation efforts in the Maoist and post-Mao periods.

Useful Sub-questions

- What is modernisation?
- Who is Mao?
- When was the Maoist period?
- When was the post-Mao period?
- Why was modernisation important?
- What are examples of China's modernisation in the Maoist period?

- How was modernisation being achieved in the Maoist period?
- What are examples of China's modernisation in the post-Mao period?
- How was modernisation being achieved in the post-Mao period?
- What are the dissimilarities between modernisation in the two periods?
- What are the similarities between modernisation in the two periods?

And as noted above, for the type of response demanded by the instruction word *compare*, more emphasis and weight should be given to providing answers on similarities than dissimilarities.

As can be seen from this list of sub-questions, they enable you to be guided in the type of information you need to find. They also allow you to thoroughly investigate the topic by covering all aspects of the question.

6.4   Essay-Writing Techniques

6.4.1   Starting Written Assignments Early in the Term

Starting work on your written assignments as soon as you are allocated the essay questions by teaching staff is a useful strategy to ensure that you have time to invest in the preparation and planning of your work. This will also ensure that when it comes to the writing, you are able to work in a comfortable well-paced manner, allowing enough time prior to the deadline for a reasonable word count target to be set for each of the days you have timetabled for writing. Consistently attaining a realistic and achievable word target, set suitably for the pace at which you work, allows you to build momentum in your writing and to feel more confident about your progress.

Many students with dyslexia are aware that they will need longer than their non-dyslexic peers to work on producing written assignments to a satisfactory standard. With this awareness also comes the knowledge that breaking down and timetabling the tasks involved in writing assignments as soon as essay questions are allocated eradicates the anxiety and stress caused by:

- Not knowing what to do, or not knowing what tasks are involved.
- Leaving the work until the last minute, so that it just becomes too overwhelming to deal with.

Let us return to MA Education student Chloe from Chapter 2, who would avoid the above difficulties by using the 'start early' strategy:

> From day one, I would never leave it [the assignment]. Actually, my peers at Uni, they always say, 'Oh don't be so stressed Chloe, you've got plenty of time,' and it irritated me, because I was like, 'No, you might think so, but I don't work like this, I need to start,' and a lot of them laugh at me.

Whilst this scenario demonstrates that Chloe had developed an immense level of metacognitive awareness over how she needed to work, she did have to help her non-dyslexic peers to reach a deeper level of understanding around difficulties associated with dyslexia. As she explained:

> One of my really good friends at Uni was like, 'Well, calm down.' Then one day at lunch, I really explained to her how my brain worked, and she was like, 'Well of course you do this and this.' Then she got it, she understood why I did what I did.

Through talking, Chloe thus helped to educate her non-dyslexic peers on the types of difficulties she encountered. As a result, these same peers became a support network to encourage and to motivate Chloe with her work.

218

6.4.2 Using Support Networks and Dyslexia Tutors to Help with Writing

Chloe, in the example above, not only proactively engaged her friends as support for her writing, she also productively attended regular sessions with her dyslexia tutor, who helped with breaking down her assignments. The tutor ensured that Chloe was consistently sticking to answering the essay question by demonstrating to her how easily she went off onto tangents:

> I had a disability adviser who helped me to understand. First, he was like, are you answering the question? Have you done this in the introduction? So, he helped me break it down. Then I realised very quickly that other people when they do that, they walk down the street. I don't walk down the street, I look up and then I go left, then I go right. I'll get to the destination, but I'll take lots of routes. It doesn't make sense to others. He [disability adviser] put a highlighter on the table and said, 'If you were to describe it, you would say, "It's blue, you highlight", and then you would start describing the table.' I said, 'Of course, it's on the table.' He said, 'But that was not the task, you were explaining the highlighter.'

6.5 Utilising Multisensory Methods when Planning and Writing

During the planning stage and the actual writing stage, you could have a go at handwriting the words you want to say so that you are using your fine motor skills, combined with saying aloud what you want to write so that you can hear the sentences. You may also want to consider either writing or typing specific sections of the essay in different colours. For example, the introduction to the essay could be allocated a blue pen. This is the section for:

- Explaining what the essay is going to do.
- Describing how you have interpreted the question.
- Identifying issues that you are going to explore.
- Giving a brief outline of how you will deal with each issue, and in which order.

The first sentences of your paragraphs, where you introduce to the reader the main idea of the paragraph, could for instance be written in red pen. The following sentences of each paragraph, in which you develop the topic and include relevant examples, evidence and quotations, might be assigned a green pen. That way, when it comes to developing your first draft or proofreading the writing you have produced, the vivid different colours clearly signify the various components and building blocks of the essay:

- Introduction – *Blue*
- The point/main idea of the paragraph – *Red*
- Examples, evidence, quotes – *Green*

The various colours make it easy for you to check through the essay by ensuring that all the essential elements are there and will also clearly show you if certain areas need further development. For instance, if in one of your paragraphs there is a significant lack of green, it means you have not included any examples, evidence or quotes to support the point of the paragraph, which will weaken your essay. MSc student Alan combined the act of writing, using fine motor skills, with using contrasting-coloured pens to represent various components of writing, finally teamed with hearing it read aloud whenever he was either revising or producing his own work. This multisensory process consolidated his learning.

> So, it will be doing it. It will be first writing it. It's the act of writing it will help to get it into my memory. Then reading it, reading aloud, so

220

getting it in different methods. I hate black ink. I can deal with it as a paper when I'm reading something, but if it's something I'm writing myself, I don't like putting it in black pen. I like blue or another colour, or if I've got to learn something, it will be a case of different colours to make different points and to visually break them up. Right, so there was this point, and then there was the pink point, and the red that was talking about… So, it's making it into a picture as well. Not always necessarily a spider diagram, because sometimes that's useful for certain things, but sometimes that can be more difficult to remember. I sometimes quite like linear format if I'm learning something and it's just different colours, different methods and it becomes multisensory. That's my coping mechanism.

6.6   Developing Metacognitive Awareness When Planning and Writing

As a quick reminder from previous chapters of metacognitive awareness when undertaking academic tasks, researchers suggest that 'metacognitive strategies are mental executive skills that serve to "control cognitive activities and to ensure a cognitive goal is achieved" (Xing, Wang and Spenser, 2008, p. 46). In other words, any technique that you apply to planning your writing or to your writing itself, such as mind mapping, or creating a linear structure of subheadings for planning, or using different-coloured pens combined with verbalising aloud for writing, is basically when you are using your own individual awareness and understanding of your thought processes to select personalised cognitive activities (the methods you pick and use for planning and writing). These techniques that you choose to apply – techniques which you have, over time, found useful to unlock the way your brain thinks and works – enable you to achieve your cognitive goal (in this case, writing and completing an essay).

Theorists argue that when thinking about the academic task of writing, metacognitive strategies should be applied to:

- Planning – those activities that occur before engaging in a problem and that help the writer to organise the entire upcoming processes.
- Monitoring – revising and adjusting the strategies one employs.
- Evaluation – checking the outcome of the strategic action to see whether it has been effective.

If you are still at a stage of developing or fine-tuning your metacognitive strategies and approaches to planning and writing, here are some questions you may want to ask yourself, which could help you to reflect on your own meta-awareness of the writing processes:

- Do you know how to begin, proceed and conclude the writing task?
- Are you aware of the strategies you use while writing?
- Do you have specific reasons for using them?
- If you use specific strategies, when and why do you use them?
- How do you apply strategies to your writing?

In addition to considering using suitable cognitive techniques for dealing with writing tasks that supplement the way you think and learn, it is also important to look after your psychological functioning and wellbeing when working on essays. This includes being conscious of your daily routine and ensuring that the environment is suitable for how you need to work. For example, we have all heard stories about famous authors needing to have the right conditions, or to be in inspirational places, or to stick to regimented daily routines to write. Accordingly, you need to experiment with what works best for you also: do you need to get up early to write? Do you prefer to go to the gym, or swimming, or for a run in the morning, and then to write from afternoon onwards? Do you have to be sitting at a certain place to write? Can you work effectively in a busy coffee shop, or do you need silence? Do you work best when sitting in a park or when in a library? These are all questions that you should be discovering the answers to, as the circumstances in which you write influence the way in which you think and have consequences for how effectively you can work.

6.7   Using Technology to Help with Planning and Writing Essays

As we have previously seen in this chapter, mind-mapping software that converts the mind map into a linear list that can then be used as a structure for the subheadings in the essay is a useful mechanism for some students. Other forms of technology which can be helpful include:

- The spellchecker in Word, which you can customise through altering its settings. For instance, if writing in British English, you can change the spellchecker from American English so that it will know to look for and to underline only misspelt British English spellings.
- The 'Frequently confused words' checker in Word is also a useful proofreading tool for ensuring that you have used the appropriate word for the context you are writing about. For instance, it can identify homophones (words pronounced the same but with a different meaning, such as weather and whether). To activate the checker, if you click on File, followed by Options, then Proofing, and ensure the 'Frequently confused words' box is ticked, all homophones used in the document will be underlined in blue, and you can examine them to ascertain that the correct version of the word is being used.
- Speech-to-text software, which is effective if you prefer to verbalise ideas aloud. The software also enables you to capture and record your

thoughts if they come spontaneously whilst moving around. Writer's block can be prevented, particularly when using handheld recording devices, as the feeling is that you can just talk through ideas, rather than being faced with a blank writing pad, or a blank computer screen. For example, the pad and computer screen may give rise to anxieties over academic convention, instead of, at first draft stage, just focusing on getting down content.

- There are also several online tools, such as Essay Punch and Thesis Generator, that can provide guidance in academic writing tasks. Essay Punch provides interactive writing tutorials, taking you through the various processes of writing an essay. Thesis Generator is useful when it comes to undertaking research and writing for dissertations, as the tool helps you to develop a concise, specific thesis statement on the topic you propose to investigate.

6.8   Setting Small Goals to Help with Essay Planning and Writing

Setting small goals when working on essays can involve establishing your own self-imposed deadlines during the planning stage, so you have a timeframe of when you will complete each of the tasks that make up an essay, as we saw in Section 6.3.5, 'Example of Planning Time on Your Writing Assignment'. Or you may want to set small goals to break up the required word length of the essay into smaller chunks, so for each day you want to work on writing, you have an achievable target of words to write during each study session. For example, if you have a 2500-word essay to complete, for each of the days you allocate to writing, you may want to aim to write 250 words. This indicates that in your planning, you need to have allowed at least 10 days to be allocated to writing.

MSc Sciences student Alan provides a useful example of how he created his own mini goals or deadlines for task completion to keep motivated, teamed with setting a word count for himself when writing. That way, he ensured that the assignment would be broken into a succession of small tasks, to prevent himself from feeling overwhelmed by the thought of a big project:

> It's putting artificial deadlines in. By the end of it (the course), you'd be writing 2500/3000-word essays, so you knew you'd have maybe a 100-word introduction. Then you could break up writing it. So, you'd spend today writing the introduction. Tomorrow I'd write the first paragraph. The day after the paragraph after, and then it doesn't seem as stressful.

Whilst goal setting is a practical activity, the benefits for academic and work-related tasks, such as providing greater direction, deeper focus, increased productivity and higher levels of motivation, have been proven in theory. For example, researchers Latham and Seijts argue that goal-setting theory 'is a theory that works. Its usefulness for improving performance in organisational settings has been well established (Locke & Latham, 2013)' (Latham & Seijits, 2016, p. 229). Latham and Seijts go on to distinguish between 'three types of goals: performance, behavioral, and learning' (Latham & Seijits, 2016, p. 226). All three encompass useful ways for how you can apply a holistic goal-setting approach to your academic work.

- *Performance goals* are short-term objectives that the student is expected to achieve within a set period and are determined by the task. The list of tasks provided in Section 6.3.5, where you set your own timeframe for each task, is an example of performance goals. For example:
    - Breaking down the question to understand what is being required from you – *A few hours*

225

- Research – to gather the appropriate information to answer the question – *2–3 weeks*
- Reading and pulling out suitable quotes to provide evidence or examples in the essay – *2 weeks*
- Writing using selective quotes from reading and notes – *3 weeks*

- *Behavioural goals* are not quantifiable but are goals that you set to accomplish the outcome – submission of a well-researched and written essay, in this case. Consequently, the behavioural goals you may want to set for yourself in relation to written assignment work, to maintain motivation and a proactive approach, could include:
  - To start studying at a specific time on each of the days you allocate to working on assignments.
  - To allocate 12–14 hours per week to independent study such as research, reading, note taking and writing.
  - To exercise four times a week to help with wellbeing and to release endorphins for enhanced academic productivity.
  - To have a word target of achieving X written words per study session and to gradually increase this if it becomes too effortless.

- *Learning goals* 'focus on the identification and implementation of effective strategies, processes, or procedures necessary to perform a task effectively' (Latham & Seijits, 2016, p. 229). Examples of learning goals you may want to set for yourself in the context of essay writing could include:
  - In the essay-planning stage, deciding whether a visual mind map of key concepts or an auditory verbalisation and recording of ideas for content is more useful as a starting point for your essay.
  - Identifying whether the freewriting method or the transformation of a mind map into a linear list of subheadings to act as a guide is more effective for you, in terms of helping to develop your writing.
  - During the reading and note-taking stage of your essay, pinpointing the most productive reading strategy for you from Q Notes, PASS, SQ3R (see Chapter 4).

226

○ Identifying the most effective method for you to check your writing. Is it through reading aloud your essay from the computer screen, or do you prefer to print it out and read through silently whilst high-lighting any errors?

Experiment to find the types of strategies that work in alignment with how you think and how you learn best. This is the key to mastering the task of essay writing. As you identify the techniques suitable for you, even though you will be writing about different topics, essay writing will become a series of processes that you will become accomplished in, as you progress through your academic journey.

6.8.1   Using Subheadings in Writing

Subheadings are titles underneath the main title or essay question that are used as signposts in writing. They indicate to the reader a subsection of a piece of writing. Subheadings are not only useful in an essay plan for you as a writer, helping to guide your writing and ensuring that you cover specific areas of your topic, as we saw with MSc Humanities student Alison (Section 6.3.6); they are also useful for the reader, keeping them informed about where they are in the paper.

As regards how to create your subheadings, let us return to Section 6.3.11, 'Developing Sub-Questions from the Main Question'. As we discussed, this involves breaking your main question down into a series of smaller questions, with the mini questions providing the hooks and the building blocks for finding the relevant information to answer your main question. However, not only do the mini questions supply the tools to retrieve the essential knowledge to construct your answer, they also indicate how your essay should be structured and the types of subheadings you should use to ensure you have balanced, equal coverage on all areas you want to write about. If we return to the essay title

- Compare the main features of China's modernisation efforts in the Maoist and post-Mao periods,

let us look again at the sub-questions we created to find out about:

- What is modernisation?
- Who is Mao?
- When was the Maoist period?
- When was the post-Mao period?
- Why was modernisation important?
- What are examples of China's modernisation in the Maoist period?
- How was modernisation being achieved in the Maoist period?
- What are examples of China's modernisation in the post-Mao period?
- How was modernisation being achieved in the post-Mao period?
- What are the dissimilarities between modernisation in the two periods?
- What are the similarities between modernisation in the two periods?

We can now easily transfer these into a series of subheadings to guide our writing as follows:

- Modernisation.
- Mao.
- The Maoist Period.
- The Post-Mao Period.
- Modernisation Importance in China and Examples.
- The Greater Dissimilarities Between Modernisation in the Maoist and Post-Mao Periods.
- The Limited Similarities Between Modernisation in the Maoist and Post-Mao Periods.
- Conclusion and Why There Were Greater Dissimilarities Than Similarities.

As you can see, the subheadings will form the answers we found (from our essay reading and note taking) to the set of sub-questions we used to break down the main question. Consequently, these questions are transformed into the above set of subheadings to help with structuring and guiding the content of our essay, with the words **Greater Dissimilarities** and **Limited Similarities** added in to signify our viewpoint to the reader. That is because the knowledge we have found out in response to our questions has enabled us to stamp our *thesis* statement (the writer's point of view) onto our essay. Bearing in mind that conventionally an academic essay has an argument, your perspective, that runs through all paragraphs like a thread, you will usually decide, once you have made all your notes in answering your sub-questions, whether the evidence from your reading is more substantiated on a particular perspective than another. For example, on going back to the essay title

- Compare the main features of China's modernisation efforts in the Maoist and post-Mao periods

we know that the *instruction/action* word of the essay, *compare*, is asking you to discuss the similarities and differences of two or more subjects, yet putting emphasis on the similarities. Nevertheless, if, through your research, you see evidence of more differences, you can interweave that argument through your essay. If, on the other hand, there are more similarities, you will build a justification for this throughout your writing.

Whilst the question itself does not seem to be asking you to present a thesis statement, if you just provide a descriptive essay, then this lacks in criticality and ability to show your own perspective on a subject. If, however, you are able to present an argument and to support that claim with evidence from the reading, you are demonstrating the skills and competence required for effective academic writing.

229

6.8.2 Structuring Writing Using the Point, Evidence/ Example, Comment/Criticism (PEC) Method

The PEC method is a highly effective approach for helping to structure academic writing and for ensuring that all essential components are contained within a paragraph. As the PEC method is not a technique that is generally taught at university, students may attain an understanding of how this strategy can help them through various means. For instance, BA English student Cate struggled with her writing and would frequently receive feedback from her tutors saying her ideas jumped around on the page and her points were not supported by evidence. Cate became familiar with the PEC process when her dyslexia support tutor advised that this could be a way to resolve her writing difficulties, as she explained:

> I write paragraphs as contained units as I go along. I've got the main question at the top of the essay, but for each paragraph, I ask, what is this paragraph about? What theory does this relate to? And what example?

If you want to try out this strategy, the PEC method works as follows:

- P – POINT. This is the first sentence in a paragraph and introduces its topic to the reader.
- For example, the first sentence of a paragraph in Chapter Two of the book *Unbeatable Mind* by Mark Divine (2015) states, 'Resiliency means that you can bounce back quickly from any setback, whether physical, mental or emotional.'
- This opening sentence instantly introduces the reader to the topic of resiliency. The reader is now prepared for examples of resiliency, or evidence that resilient people do bounce back. The reader is also now engaged and interested in the author's further commentary or critique (personal viewpoint of resiliency).

- The P can also be used to directly introduce the *point of your argu-ment*. For instance, the opening sentence of Chapter Five in the book *Feminism and Film* by Maggie Humm (1997) argues, 'It is striking how Hollywood cinema confines Black women to comic roles, "mammies", prostitutes and carers of whites at the very moment when Black wom-en's writing is drawing vividly on Black culture.'

- The reader is immediately made aware of the author's argument that Hollywood narrowly stereotypes representations of black women. The reader is then interested to know more about examples of these rep-resentations and to see how the author provides evidence to support their viewpoint. The reader also wants to see how the author is going to provide a counterargument to Hollywood cinema by drawing on representations from Black women's writing and Black culture.

- E – EXAMPLE or EVIDENCE. For the second sentence of your para-graph, if you introduced an idea in the first sentence, you could use an *example* to elaborate on your idea. Mark Divine, for instance, uses his second sentence to provide an example of how resiliency is a skill that can be trained.

- If, however, you used your first sentence to introduce a point of your argument, you can use the following sentence as *evidence* to support your point. This can be done by using quotes from published sources and/or peer-reviewed academic papers to substantiate the point. Maggie Humm supports the point of her argument by providing evi-dence as to why Hollywood is so out of touch with representations of Black women, compared to Black women's writing, through demon-strating the complete lack of Black women working in powerful roles in Hollywood. She states, 'The reason why cinematic representations have not matched this progressive accomplishment is self-evident. Black women are rarely the makers of movies; Julie Dash's *Daughters of the Dust* (1991) is the first full length mainstream film to be directed by an Afra-American' (Humm, 1997, p. 113).

231

- C – CRITICISM or COMMENT. For *criticism*, you may want to note weaknesses or flaws with the evidence by critiquing the quote. If you are writing about an *example*, again you may want to provide a more detailed explanation of the example, or you may want to write about its limitations. Mark Divine uses this space to supply further information on how to develop emotional resiliency, to support his point that resiliency is a skill that can be trained.
- For *comment*, this is your explanation of how your *evidence* (i.e., the quote you used) supports your point.
- Maggie Humm uses the evidence of Julie Dash's film being, at the time of writing the book, the first and only film to be directed by an Afro-American woman, to add a further comment that Black women's film theory has lacked an institutional place.

Because the PEC method provides a step-by-step approach to building written paragraphs, it is suitable for students who fear approaching academic writing. It is also useful for ensuring that points made at the start of paragraphs are supported by evidence and examples, which is essential in academic writing. The link to this resource and the template for testing out the PEC method are provided here.

www.cambridge.org/abbottjones

6.9   Designating Proofreaders to Check through Writing

It may be useful to ask a friend, parent, tutor or colleague to have a look through your work. The advantage of having a fresh pair of eyes, someone who may not be familiar with your topic, to read your writing, is that it can lead to interactive conversations over the text. Your proofreader can ask what you mean by this or that sentence, or can elicit from you what you are trying to say or convey through your written words. This process can positively help with development and can lead you to think more about the coherence of the writing itself. Your proofreaders' requests for clarification can encourage you to recognise any gaps in your reasoning or can help you to identify where your argument needs further substantiation. Furthermore, having someone you trust to act as proofreader can also provide emotional support through the writing process. The proofreader may give reassurance that you are progressing well, and/or when required, they can give you that extra push to fine-tune and complete the essay.

Additionally, owing to the concentration involved in getting down ideas, key concepts and arguments, you can become too close to the text; when you look at your own work, it may be difficult to detect errors. The proofreader, approaching your writing from a distance, will be able to detect or question any mistakes that you may have missed.

6.10 Using Assignment Submission Cover Sheets to Make Use of Reasonable Adjustments

On submission of your essay, universities will generally require you to complete a cover sheet, which is a form asking you to complete details, such as your name, name of module/course, course code and assignment title. There is usually also a space on the form for the assessor of your work to complete their feedback and grade they are allocating to your essay. Students officially registered as dyslexic at their university are typically able to complete an additional assessment/examination cover sheet for students with special allowances, which informs the marker that the student is dyslexic. These assessment forms are used by the university to reduce any disadvantage that the student may face when it comes to an evaluation of their written work and are considered by the university as a form of reasonable adjustment. For instance, some institutions have written instructions on the cover sheet to guide the examiner/marker to focus more on content and ideas in the writing, rather than penalising for structural and/or spelling and grammatical mistakes. This can vary, however, between different departments at the university and amongst individual institutions. For example, certain subject areas such as languages, which may explicitly be assessing for competence with spelling, grammar and written expression, may not be eligible for dispensation for grammatical and punctuation errors. Furthermore, some universities will apply reasonable adjustments for students with dyslexia for the marking of examination papers but not for coursework, whilst other universities will make allowances when assessing both coursework and examinations. Ultimately, it is best to check the types of reasonable adjustments your institution has in place when it comes to the assessment of written work.

6.11   Critical Writing

6.11.1   Demonstrating Critical Thinking in Writing

At university level education, it is common for essay/exam questions to ask you to 'critically discuss' a topic, concept or theme from your subject area. Students do not always understand what 'to critically discuss' means and may find it difficult to distinguish between *descriptive* and *critical* writing.

Put simply, descriptive writing is used to explain the background of a topic but does not develop an argument. Descriptive writing can be used to outline the characteristics of something, but it does not persuade your reader of your viewpoint, your perspective, with regards to the topic. For example, let us now look at a *descriptive* introduction to an essay, compared with a *critical* introduction, to determine the differences.

Descriptive Introduction

> There is a current trend amongst dyslexia practitioners to focus more on cognitive skills development than on a holistic approach to a student's support needs. The holistic approach integrates development of learning skills together with helping the student to overcome any social and emotional difficulties. This essay will outline the characteristics of the cognitive skills approach compared to the holistic approach.

As you can see, this introduction is merely telling the reader that they are going to *outline* and *describe* the features of a cognitive approach, followed by recounting any differences with the attributes of a holistic approach. The reader is not being presented with an argument and is given no indication of the author's perspective with regard to the two approaches.

Critical Introduction

> This essay outlines what a cognitive skills approach encompasses and then analyses its benefits, but predominantly focuses on its limitations when compared to a holistic approach. It argues that whilst cognitive skills development delivered from the dyslexia practitioner is necessary and benefits the learner, the holistic approach, as it deals not only with the student's learning needs but also their social and emotional needs, is a more efficacious method for supporting the student's change processes.

As can be seen here, this introduction immediately provides the reader with knowledge on what the content of the essay will do, and more importantly presents the *thesis* (the argument and the *author's point of view* on the topic) which will then run as a thread throughout the essay. To support their argument that the holistic method is more successful than the cognitive skills method, the writer will use evidence from a variety of sources and will insert quotes from those sources to legitimise the points they make within the essay.

6.11.2   Critical Appraisal

Sometimes students are asked to write critical appraisals, particularly if they are on nursing, pharmacology and medicine-related courses in which the evaluation of clinical evidence is an important skill to develop when it comes to decision making. Critical appraisal is also involved when asked to write a literature review where you are required to eval-uate research papers and then synthesise data from a range of studies.

What Does Critical Appraisal Mean?

In a useful handout created by the National Council for Osteopathic Research (2012) (https://ncor.org.uk/), a tutorial is presented with the purpose of developing critical appraisal skills. Critical appraisal is defined as:

> The process by which a reader can evaluate a piece of written material and assess whether it possesses validity (i.e., is it close to the truth) and applicability (i.e., is it clinically useful). If research is being examined, critical appraisal skills are vital to decide whether the research has been well conducted and whether, ultimately, the results of the research can be implemented into our everyday prac-tice for the benefits of our patients. Critically appraising and review-ing a paper is essentially a process to look for information that is of value. (National Council for Osteopathic Research, 2012)

Consequently, to critically appraise a published study is basically to identify the strengths and weakness of the research and to evaluate its usefulness in terms of the validity of the study's findings. If you have not carried out a critical appraisal before, it can be challenging to know how to approach this task. Identifying this difficulty in its own students, the NCOR produced a series of tools in the form of questions that can be applied to the different sections of research studies to help with developing the skills in making decisions for critical appraisal. A list of these questions, adapted from the NCOR (2012) handout, is provided below and is accessible through the link to Resources if you would like to test them out the next time you are asked to critique research papers or articles from your topic area.

www.cambridge.org/abbottjones

6.11.3 Activity on Developing Critical Appraisal Skills

Questions That May Be Applied to the Introduction and Literature Review Section of a Paper

- Do the introduction and literature review (the previously published works on the topic) adequately place the research question (what the study aims to find out) in context?
- Is the material included in the literature review relevant to the research question?
- Are the key terms in the study well defined?
- Has the research hypothesis (a proposition or predictive statement about the possible outcome of a study) been clearly stated, and is it appropriate to the research question and supporting literature?

Questions That May Be Applied to the Methods Section of a Paper

- Is the chosen research design (framework of research methods) appropriate to answer the research question?

237

- Are the methods and procedures clearly described in sufficient detail?
- If the study has used participants, sometimes referred to in clinical papers as the population or sample, are the selected participants representative and appropriate to the study?
- How was the data collected?
- Was the data collected using validated, calibrated and reliable tools/ measuring equipment?

Questions That May Be Applied to the Results Section of a Paper

- What are the results of the study?
- Are the results clearly labelled and accurately presented?
- Can a decision be made from the results?
- Are the trial results generalisable to the wider population or are they just relevant to the participants in the study?

Questions That May Be Applied to the Discussion of Findings Section of a Paper

- Does the discussion of the results relate to the research question?
- If not, why not?
- Have the results been interpreted correctly according to the results presented?
- Have the results been placed in an appropriate context?

Questions That May Be Applied to the References Section of a Paper.

- Do the references match the citations in the text?

Whilst some of these questions may not be applicable to the type of research you are being asked to critique, they still provide tools to use as a starting point in knowing what to look for when undertaking any type of critical appraisal work.

6.12 Conforming to Academic Style in Writing

Academic writing conventions and the academic style of writing expected from you will vary from one university department to another, and will depend on the type of course. For example, writing essays for law will have a different set of conventions from writing for philosophy. It is important that you check in your departmental handbook the types of style and conventions you are supposed to follow in your written work. Some of the most common conventions that generally apply across all courses are listed with examples below.

In your essays:

- Write an introduction where you tell the reader what your essay is going to do.
  - Identify the issues you are going to explore.
- State your case by confirming your argument, presenting your thesis.
- Cite authorities and sources.
  - This is using quotation to strengthen the points you make.
  - For example, in the paragraph below, taken from *Dyslexia in Higher Education: Anxiety and Coping Skills* (Abbott-Jones, 2022), it states:

People with dyslexia by the time they get to adulthood and university have usually experienced incidents of being made to feel different from their peers. Alexander-Passe's (2016) article states that 'Scott (2004), Edwards (1994) and Alexander-Passe (2010; 2012; 2015a, b) found young dyslexics commonly experience adversity as children, both educationally in school and socially through exclusion and bullying from peers due to their learning differences' (Alexander-Passe, 2016, p. 2).

- o Here, the point about people with dyslexia being made to feel different from their peers is being supported by the quote from Alexander-Passe, whose quote also cites further authorities on the topic. This works to provide the necessary evidence to strengthen the claim.
- Avoid plagiarism.
  - o Plagiarism, as previously mentioned, is to copy out another author's words and ideas and to present them as your own in your writing. Thus, you would be writing without using quotations and citations, as in the examples above, to signify you are using another writer's work. Plagiarism is heavily penalised at university and should be avoided. One way to avoid it is to put the author's ideas you want to utilise into your own words. For example, if an author has written these words: 'due to the nature of exams and the abilities they test, i.e., retrieval of information from memory and processing skills under time constraints, they place students with dyslexia at an unfair disadvantage' (Abbott-Jones, 2022), and you want to say the same thing, you could simply paraphrase, which is restating the meaning of the sentence by using other words. You could, for instance, change the sentence to: 'because exams are a test of memory under timed conditions, they are an unfair assessment method for students with dyslexia'. That way, you have said the same thing but in different words from the author.
- Present your argument.
  - o As we have discussed in this chapter, presenting and developing a coherent argument in your essay is essential to show criticality in your writing.
- Structure writing logically.
  - o You can use the ordered subheading approach and the PEC method to help with this.
- Define any key terms.
  - o When students write essays, because the tutor will be marking the essay, the student often assumes this is the person they are writing

240

for. As such, the student does not define key terms and terminology words, knowing that their lecturer is already familiar with these. Whilst it is correct that you are writing an essay for your tutor, this person is only there to ensure you have met the assessment criteria. Instead, when writing, you must write with an imaginary reader in mind and surmise that they do not know anything about your topic. Therefore, any concepts, terms or terminology words you introduce will need to be fully expanded upon and explained.

- Make appropriate use of headings and subheadings.
  - This depends on departmental conventions and whether you are writing a report, an essay or a dissertation.
- Acronyms and abbreviations.
  - When using acronyms and abbreviations formed from the initials of a term, the first time you introduce them in the text, you must put down the complete word followed by the initials in brackets. The following times, you just use the acronym: for example, 'British Dyslexia Association (BDA)'; after that, where you want to refer to this organisation, just put BDA.
- Avoid contractions.
  - Rather than writing *can't* and *don't*, which are contractions, you will more formally write *cannot* and *do not*.
- Avoid using first person.
  - Academic writing is generally both formal and objective. As such, first person (saying 'I' or 'we' in the text) should be avoided, unless you are asked to write a reflective essay.

6.13   Essay-Writing Checklist

Finally, the checklist below is helpful for ensuring that you have all the essential elements in your writing before you submit your work. You can access a hard copy of this to use before you submit each of your essays by clicking the link.

www.cambridge.org/abbottjones

Checklist for Essay Writing		Essay Titles		
Read through this checklist when you have written your essay. Check off the points at each stage.				
Stage 1: Choosing a title	Have I identified the **keywords** in the title?			
Stage 2: Research	Have I completed the **necessary** research?			
Stage 3: Planning	Have I **planned** the essay?			
Stage 4: Writing	Have I **written in the style required** (analytical or factual)?			
	Is what I've written relevant to the title?			
	Is there a **logical development** and **conclusion** to the essay?			
	Are my facts and quotations accurate?			
Stage 5: Presentation	Have I **quoted my sources** using the correct convention?			
	Have I written enough?			
	Have I listed the books I have read, and referred to, in my bibliography?			
Stage 6: Checking	Is each major idea developed in a separate paragraph?			
	Have I avoided clichés, contractions, jargon and slang?			
	Have I checked carefully for misspellings?			
	Have I left any words out?			
	Have I used punctuation properly?			
	Have I kept a copy of the essay?			

6.14   Summary

In summary, this chapter has:

- Specified common difficulties with essay writing for the student with dyslexia to help with identifying and understanding the challenges.
- Delivered a range of strategies useful for *essay planning* which included:
  - Utilising university resources.
  - Making plans and writing guides by using mind maps to visually see links between ideas.
  - Breaking the main question down into a series of smaller questions.
  - Starting written assignments early in the term to pace the work and reduce stress.
  - Utilising multisensory methods through combining writing words by hand (kinaesthetic) with saying aloud what you want to write (auditory) teamed with using different-coloured pens for different sections of the essay (visual).
  - Developing metacognitive awareness by reflecting on your meta-awareness of the writing process.
  - Using technology, such as the spell and homophone checker in Word, speech-to-text software, and online tools, such as Essay Punch and Thesis Generator.
- Presented a range of techniques to help more specifically with *essay writing* which comprised:
  - Using subheadings to help with essay structure.
  - Applying the PEC method to help with constructing written paragraphs.
  - Using assignment cover sheets on coursework submission to ensure the student is not subject to an unfair disadvantage in the marking of their work.

○ Showing differences between *descriptive* and *critical* essay introductions and presenting a range of tools/questions to help with developing **critical appraisal** of published research.

○ Listed general ways of conforming to academic style and convention in writing.

7

• • • • •

Spelling Techniques

7.1   Introduction

Phonology is the ability to map letters to sounds, which is required when spelling words. As noted in Chapter 1, phonological processing and memory is affected by dyslexia, which means that students with dyslexia can have difficulty hearing the different small sounds in words (phonemes) and struggle to break words into smaller parts to spell them. During the school years, these problems can significantly affect the developing child's ability to progress with literacy learning and can cause emotional difficulties in school. The challenges with spelling persist into adulthood, giving rise to negative emotional consequences. In Chapter 1, we saw the example of MA Humanities student Charlie being so embarrassed by her spelling that she would hide her computer screen from colleagues at her workplace and would avoid making handwritten notes during meetings:

> In work, I always put the computer at the right angle and the screen. You know, not giving hand-written notes and avoid things where my written language is visible.

This illustrates that adults with dyslexia can encounter feelings of shame, humiliation, frustration and embarrassment in connection with their spelling. Some people will go to great lengths to hide or avoid these difficulties both in the workplace and in daily situations that may expose their writing.

This chapter will firstly continue this theme by specifying, at a deeper level, the common obstacles with spelling for the student with dyslexia and the impacts they have on academic work within the higher education context, both cognitively and emotionally. This explanation will help the student to identify with the challenges outlined and will also foster a deeper understanding of why these barriers with spelling exist.

Secondly, the chapter moves forward to provide productive guidance on a range of general strategies to assist with spelling difficulties. These techniques can, to an extent, help with overcoming problems connected with spelling. They include: using mnemonics involving memorable phrases or rhymes to help with spelling of difficult words; using the process of sounding out words, not phonetically, but as the word is spelt; the Look, Say, Cover, Write, Check method of repetition; copying words down from academic papers, or dictionaries and thesauruses, to become familiar with the visualisation of the word; using multisensory methods which are fun, engaging and effective, use all senses and are memorable ways of becoming aware of the spelling of certain words; developing metacognitive knowledge in relation to spelling and being able to determine which strategy is most appropriate to use dependent on the word and situation; and using technology, such as Grammarly, the spelling and grammar checker on word processing software, and/or Google dictionary. Clear examples of the techniques are provided, and guidance is presented on the steps involved in using the Look, Say, Cover, Write, Check strategy, together with samples of templates that can be used to support this method.

7.2   Common Difficulties with Spelling for Students with Dyslexia

Students with dyslexia are often all too aware that they encounter difficulties when it comes to spelling, but they often do not understand why this obstacle exists. This is demonstrated by the quote below from BSc Nursing student Lisa, who stated:

> So, I don't really know why my spelling is so bad, I mean it probably says in my dyslexia report in my bag, I will probably look through it and go 'Oh well this is here.'

Lisa is correct here in identifying that her educational psychologist report, written to convey the results of her dyslexia screening, will contain information about her spelling. In the report, this is called phonological awareness, and tests are usually carried out to assess for ability in phonemic decoding efficiency, which measures how effectively the student can look at made up words, or nonwords, and accurately pronounce (decode) them. Sight word efficiency is also usually evaluated, which tests the individual's skill at accurately identifying real words. Some psychologists will also use an assessment tool referred to as the *Comprehensive Test of Phonological Processing* (CTOPP). The CTOPP measures for phonological awareness (the

247

ability to correctly pronounce a range of words and to recognise different speech sounds in written language) and phonological memory (the capacity to hold in memory recognition of the sounds of parts of words and to accurately recall the correct pronunciation of sequences of words). Phonological memory is also assessed through digit span, whereby the psychologist will say a series of numbers and will ask the individual to repeat the numbers in the exact order. The final test in CTOPP is the rapid naming test, which involves the psychologist giving the individual a list of words, which could be colours, objects or numbers. The individual is then required to verbally repeat the words as quickly as possible. The test is looking for any difficulties with visual processing speed, which affects the ability to recognise shapes, letters or words during reading. This in turn causes problems with developing spelling competence.

Accordingly, the psychologists' tests in relation to the types of measures carried out tell us that how they assess for spelling and literacy ability is through competence in phonology (the ability to map sounds to letters; see Chapter 1 for further information), memory aptitude and processing speed (time needed to process visual information connected to word patterns).

If the reported percentiles (a number which represents a percentage position on a range) are low for any of the tests, it indicates that there are problems in that particular area. For example, say your reported percentile number is 95: this signifies that out of a group of 100 people who have been used as the norm to standardise the test, 95% of those people scored lower than you, and thus the number represents high ability in that area. If 50, however, denotes average performance on the test, then any number below this will signal a below-average score.

Sometimes the percentile number is placed alongside the standard score. In psychologists' reports, 'standard score' is another

descriptor of how far away you rank from the average in that competence. Scores below 85 or above 115 are outside what would be
considered the normal average range.

Whilst this is a simplistic explanation, and whilst dyslexia assessments will vary dependent on the psychologist and the types of
assessment tools being used, it should still provide a basic understanding of what you are being evaluated for in a dyslexia screening and how low scores in any of the three areas mentioned above
(phonology, memory, visual processing speed) can cause significant
difficulties with your spelling ability.

If the phonological difficulty is present, perhaps, as an adult having gained access to higher education, it may now be less severe
than during the school years. Phonological deficits, though, however
mild, can still influence the ability to read quickly, can cause problems with the efficiency of decoding text and pronouncing words
accurately when reading aloud, and can continue to cause difficulties when trying to spell. The British Dyslexia Association argue that:

> Spelling is one of the biggest, and most widely experienced difficul-
> ties for the dyslexic child and adult. Most dyslexic people can learn
> to read well with the right support, however, spelling appears to be
> a difficulty that persists throughout life. (British Dyslexia Association)

This is evidenced by the significant number of adult students who
comment during support sessions on the difficulties that continue
with their spelling. For instance, MA student Charlie commented in
connection with her spelling:

> I will see letters on a page, but won't notice the order of them, so
> then when it comes to writing out a name, I have to copy it out,
> because I've never absorbed the spelling of it.

MA Arts student Debra talked about how her challenges with spelling interfered with the flow of her writing when working on essays:

249

I think spelling for me is part of being able to write fluently. When you have problems with spelling it sort of slows that momentum down. I have to stop and then look what the word is, or how it's spelt, and then continue. That can be a long process, sometimes, if I'm trying to find a word and trying to find the meaning and how it's spelt, instead of having that fluent flow. I shall have to stop and then try and find the meaning, or try and find the spelling, so for me personally I just feel like it slows me down.

Now let us turn to some useful strategies that may be helpful to overcome some of these difficulties as discussed above.

7.3   Techniques to Assist with Spelling Difficulties

There are numerous strategies that can be used to support spelling, such as chunking (breaking the word down to between two and four chunks and memorising each section separately), rhyming (rhyming words that are spelt like each other, such as dog, fog, log; or using rhymes to help with remembering spelling rules, e.g., I before E except after C), phonetic spelling (spelling words the way they sound), using visual spelling strategies (writing the word down in different ways to see which version looks correct), and spelling by morphemes (learning the prefixes, suffixes, bases and roots of words).

There are also countless studies that have been carried out by linguistic and spelling theorists analysing the types of spelling techniques that children with dyslexia, and other developing children, use as methods for remembering the exact spellings of words. For example, a study by Ruberto, Daigle and Ammar (2016), titled 'The spelling strategies of francophone dyslexic students', found that the students were using phonological strategies, visuo-orthographic methods (checking to see if the written word seems correct visually), analogy (when the writer uses another word to help with writing the word to be spelled, e.g., writing 'four' first to help with remembering how to write fourteen) and finally backup (applying personal mnemonic devices to help with spelling specific words, e.g., the saying '*big elephants can always understand small elephants*' to help to spell *because*).

A similarly useful study, titled 'Comparing the verbal self-reports of spelling strategies used by children with and without dyslexia', by Donovan and Marshall (2016) discovered that a range of techniques were being employed to help with spelling. These included retrieval – automatic (just remembering the word), retrieval – using strategy (remembering combined with using a mnemonic or a memory trigger), sounding out the word by saying the word aloud, retrieval sound out (whereby part of the word is automatically remembered and the rest is sounded out), drawing on analogies (referring to other words with similar patterns, or identifying words within words), relying on rules, visual checking, and relying on semantic knowledge by identifying the differences between homophones (e.g., spelling patience rather than patients).

The authors arrived at these findings through interviewing the children and asking them to explain what they were doing when attempting to spell. Via this productive approach, Donovan and Marshall identified 'that children with dyslexia are less likely to use the same range of strategies as typically developing children and more likely to use a sounding out (i.e., phonetic strategy) when approaching the task of spelling identification' (Donovan & Marshall, 2016, p. 27). The authors advocate the fruitful process of interviewing the children to gain an understanding of what they are doing to spell, suggesting 'we conclude that an assessment protocol for spelling that incorporates self-report seems a promising way forward in providing in-depth qualitative information for targeted support' (Donovan & Marshall, 2016, p. 27). Consequently, the valuable interview data gathered by the authors has led to the understanding that 'it may be useful to explicitly teach a range of strategies to children with dyslexia when supporting their spelling' (Donovan & Marshall, 2016, p. 27).

Using the same approach as Donovan and Marshall, with the knowledge that students with dyslexia learn more productively from each other than from theoreticians telling them how to spell, we now move on to look at spelling strategies gathered from interviewing university students with dyslexia. These strategies tap into methods that the students say they find beneficial when struggling with the spellings of certain words. As Donovan and Marshall found, using self-report data from people with dyslexia to determine what they find helpful and not so helpful is a key to providing the appropriate support to impart to other students with dyslexia.

7.3.1   General Strategies that Students with Dyslexia Say They Use to Support Their Spelling

Strategies that the interview participants discussed as being helpful for overcoming difficulties with spelling included using mnemonics, sounding it out, repetition, copying down words, designating problematic words to colleagues and friends to spell, and avoidance. Students would also use the technique of writing down the word in two different ways to check visually which version appeared to be more accurate, as explained by MA Arts student Cara:

> It helps if I write it down. I hate spelling tests where you have to say it out audibly because I can't picture it for very long in my mind, if that

252

makes sense. Then usually I will try and write it down. If it doesn't look right, I will write it out again. Usually I've got all the letters, but not always in the right order.

Spelling games, if they had been effectively taught at school, provided a memorable way to remember the spelling of difficult words, as described by BSc Nursing student Lisa:

My learning disability teacher at school, my first one, she was dyslexic herself, and we did a lot of board games. She created board games for kids with dyslexia to improve spelling, and we did that practical aspect. I learned a lot of things off her. I think when you talk to other people with dyslexia you do learn a lot.

Yet spelling games are not just for children. If the games are fun, accessible and memorable, adults can productively use this method to improve their spelling, as recounted by MA Education student Chloe:

There's these board games where you do different things. It's super fun, it's definitely for dyslexic people as well. It's Cranium, something like that. Cranium, super fun, and it's for everybody. Everybody will be good at something. Spelling words backwards, I'm super at it if I know how the word is spelt. I'm really good at it because I close my eyes and then I can just look at it back. I always win more than the others, but if I don't know the word I'm lost.

7.3.2   Using Mnemonics

Mnemonics also provided a memorable and engaging way to recall how certain words are spelt.

A mnemonic is a learning device that aids information retention and retrieval. Spelling mnemonics usually involve using memorable phrases or rhymes to help to remember the spelling of difficult words.

For example, to help with spelling ARITHMETIC, the phrase 'A Rat In The House May Eat The Ice Cream' can be used, as the first letter of each word in the memorable phrase spells arithmetic. The spelling of GEOGRAPHY could use the phrase 'George's Elderly Old Grandfather Rode A Pig Home Yesterday'. The quirkier and more bizarre the phrase, the better, as this helps to make it more memorable.

Rhyme can also be used to assist with remembering the order of letters in words. For instance, the saying I before E except after C is a mnemonic rhyme to help if unsure whether a word is spelled using the order IE or EI. Thus, the rhyme suggests that the correct order of the word is often IE unless the preceding letter is C, as in the case of RECEIPT.

BSc Sciences student Helen used mnemonics to help with remembering spellings of words. She also created her own mnemonic words to help with memorisation of lists of concepts for exams. For her Anatomy module, to remember the main organs of the body – stomach, heart, intestines, bladder, brain, liver, lungs, kidneys – she created the mnemonic SHIBBLK and the phrase 'Stay Home In Bed Before Lemons Leave Kingdoms', as she explained:

> If I can learn it mnemonically, I can get it, I will be fine, or if I practise it over and over again, I will get it.

The benefits of mnemonics are supported by empirical evidence in research papers that have investigated their effectiveness in education as a technique for recalling important information. Putnam's (2015) paper 'Mnemonics in education: current research and applications' discussed the results of one study by Carney and Levin (2011) in which students were split into two groups. The first group took a 14-week course focusing on mnemonic training, and the second group undertook a course of the same length developing traditional study skills, such as note taking and identifying main ideas. Putnam reported that the findings of Carney and Levin's study showed that 'students in the mnemonic training group recalled twice as much information from a 2200-word passage as the control group' (Putnam, 2015, p. 133).

7.3.3   Using Sounding Out Words

For students who are adequate readers and have satisfactory phonetic skills, a useful technique is to sound out difficult-to-remember words by saying the sound of each letter whilst writing it. For instance, if you can say aloud the individual sounds of w-e-d-n-e-s-d-a-y (Wed-nes-day) but find this word challenging to spell on hearing it, it may improve your accuracy if you say the sounds of the syllables whilst simultaneously writing the letters down.

As with the mnemonics method, the sounding out strategy is also supported by empirical evidence confirming that the technique is effective for helping with spelling. A study by Mann, Bushell and Morris (2010), titled 'Use of sounding out to improve spelling in young children', trained five typically developing elementary students to sound out the spelling of words whilst writing them using the Cover, Copy, Compare (CCC) method (discussed below). After practice with sounding out, each student's post-test performance was compared to the post-test of spelling words with no sounding out. On analysing the results, the authors concluded that 'for every student, post-test accuracy was higher following practice with sounding out, indicating that it is an effective and easily implemented strategy to improve spelling instruction' (Mann, Bushell and Morris, 2010, p. 89). Although the study was done using a sample of children, the sounding out method is just as productive when used by adults with dyslexia. This is because it is a multisensory strategy which combines hearing the sounds of the letters by sounding them out, with kinaesthetic strengths by using motor-sensory skills to write down the letters, teamed finally with the visual aspect of looking at and checking the word once it is written down.

One of the problems, though, with sounding out words is that it is a difficult technique to use with irregular words (words with sounds that do not match their spelling, such as yacht, father, etc.). Irregular words in English language can cause a lot of confusion. For instance, the letter combination /ch/ has three very different pronunciations in the words 'chef', 'choir' and 'cheese'. One strategy to overcome this difficulty is to say the word aloud, not phonetically, but how it is spelt (as for Wed-nes-day above).

7.3.4 Saying the Word Not Phonetically but How It Is Spelt

BA English student Cate used a combination of remembering spellings from mnemonics she had learned at school teamed with the process of sounding out words, not as they were supposed to sound phonetically, but saying the word exactly as it is spelt. This process helped Cate to ensure her spelling of more difficult irregular words was accurate:

> There are certain words that I still use the mnemonics for from when I was younger. Also, I had a teacher once, who always used to pronounce keywords as they were spelt, so if I need to write the word Parliament, in my head, the word is said par li a ment.

The verbalisation of longer words broken down into how their syllable parts would sound, as in Cate's example above, or irregular words said exactly as they are spelt, is a process that can support the spelling of more difficult words. Furthermore, the mispronunciation phonetically of tricky irregular words, as it may make them sound bizarre, unusual or fun, can provide an effective memory jogger. For example, the word *business* would be said aloud as 'bus (as in the transport) – i – ness'.

7.3.5   Using Visualisation of Objects to Help with Spelling

As seen in the example above, because *bus* can easily be remembered as an object visually, visualisation of objects in a particular order can also be used to help to recall the spelling of a word. The word 'diarrhoea' can be difficult to spell, and people are easily confused as to whether the word has one letter /r/ or two. A useful way to remember this is to 'chunk' the word into *dia rr hoe a* so that it is sounded out rhythmically and to visualise garden tools combined with the saying *'two rakes and a hoe'*. The phrase 'two rakes and a hoe' ensures that the word is always spelt with two /r/s

7.3.6   Cover, Copy, Compare (CCC) Combined with Sounding It Out

CCC is a productive method for helping with memorising spellings. Firstly, the word is copied down; secondly, it is covered up; thirdly, it is written down from memory; and finally, it is uncovered and evaluated for accuracy. When this is combined with sounding out the word in the copying down and writing from memory stages, it helps to consolidate the spelling of the word into memory more effectively.

A template together with the steps to guide you through the trialling of this technique is provided below, containing random words that are regularly used throughout this book. The link takes you to blank templates for CCC which you may want to complete with

257

terminology words from your course, or words commonly used in your subject area that you are currently struggling with spelling.

www.cambridge.org/abbottjones

7.3.7   Activity – Testing Out CCC Spelling Method with Sounding Out

business		
diarrhoea		
phonology		
multisensory		
metacognition		
technology		
visualisation		

Steps of CCC Spelling Technique

Step 1

Look at the words in the left-hand column and write each word down in the next column whilst saying the word aloud.

Step 2

Cover up all the words and from memory write each word down in the right-hand column whilst saying the word aloud.

Step 3

Uncover the words and check how accurate the words in the right-hand column that you wrote from memory are when compared with the original words in the left-hand column.

Step 4

Leave for a few days, then repeat the whole process again. Repetition will proactively help to place the spelling into memory more productively.

7.3.8   Using Repetition and Look, Say, Cover, Write, Check Method

MSc Geology student Luke would use rote learning (memorisation technique based on repetition) to remember the spelling of specific words. Whilst rote learning is not particularly suitable for students with dyslexia due to its lack of a multisensory approach, it can be a satisfactory method for learning certain things, such as spellings, the alphabet, numbers and multiplication tables. However, whilst constantly repeating the writing down of words to learn the pattern and order of letters may be appropriate for developing visual memory of spellings, especially if using the Look, Say, Cover, Write, Check method for learning spelling, the rote learning process does not develop the student's understanding of the contextual meaning of the word, which is important for establishing accurate spelling ability. Consequently, Luke supplemented the repetition process with reading extensively, developing his spelling ability through word recognition and an understanding of the semantic meaning of the word through seeing it in context, as he explained when asked what strategies he used for spelling:

> Just rote learning, just repeating and repeating and repeating. Reading also does wonders for your vocabulary.

7.3.9   Look, Say, Cover, Write, Check Method

A very similar approach to the CCC technique discussed above is Look, Say, Cover, Write, Check. This is another productive method for helping with the memorisation of spelling of difficult words. In fact, it is much the same as CCC when this strategy is combined with sounding out the word. Firstly, you look at the word you want to learn, which is written down in the Look, Say, Cover, Write and Check template. Secondly, you say the word aloud a few times. Thirdly, you cover the word up with a piece of paper. Fourthly, you write the spelling next to the original word, and finally, you check the version you have written down, comparing it to the original word.

A template together with the steps to guide you through the testing out of this strategy is provided below, containing the same set of random words used in the CCC template. That way, if you wish, you may compare CCC with Look, Say, Cover, Write, Check to see which is the more effective method for you. The link takes you to blank templates for Look, Say, Cover, Write, and Check which you may want to complete with terminology words from your course, or words commonly used in your subject area that you are currently struggling to spell.

www.cambridge.org/abbottjones

7.3.10   Activity – Testing Out Look, Say, Cover, Write, Check

	Look	Say	Cover	Write	Check	Correction
business						
diarrhoea						
phonology						
multisensory						
metacognition						
technology						
visualisation						

Steps of Look, Say, Cover, Write, Check Spelling Technique

Step 1
- Look at the words in the left-hand column.

Step 2
- Say the word aloud a few times whilst looking at it.

Step 3

- Cover up the word with a piece of paper.

Step 4

- From memory, write the word down, saying the word aloud as you do so.

Step 5

- Uncover the word, and check how accurate the word that you wrote from memory is when compared with the original word in the left-hand column.

Step 6

- Write any correction in the right-hand column, identifying where the mistake was made.

Step 7

- Leave for a few days, then repeat the whole process again. Repetition will proactively help to place the spelling into memory more productively.

7.3.11   Combining Repetition Technique with Replacing Difficult Words with Synonyms

PhD Sciences student Ada would avoid the spelling of particularly difficult words by replacing them with an easier-to-spell synonym (a word that has the same meaning as the difficult-to-spell word). That way, her written language was conveying the same message as what she intended to say through using the difficult word, but she had wisely substituted the hard-to-spell words with words she found easier to write down. If, however, there were words she needed to use, she would apply the repetition technique as described:

261

There are some words that… There's like a little batch of them like weird, wired, scared, scarred, which is annoying because I work in regeneration, so I have to spell scarred quite a lot and I have to get someone else to check it, or I will use a different word completely to avoid using it over and over again. I will replace it with a different word that means the same that I can spell which is good because it's enhanced my vocabulary, but at the same time, I'm like, I think I've used that one too many times, wait what other word? Quick, find a thesaurus. But also, I was just taught if I find a word I don't know and I'm really struggling with, is just write it out as many times as possible, because that's how I tend to learn really well. Utter repetition, it's so boring, but it works. If they are ones that are used commonly all the time, like just really good linking words, then I just have to repeat them over and over again.

7.3.12 Copying Down Words to Become Familiar with Visualisation

In the paper 'Does testing with feedback improve adult spelling skills relative to copying and reading?', Pan, Rubin and Rickard (2015) define copying as 'written transcription of a visually and aurally presented spelling word', and reading is defined as 'simultaneous viewing and vocal pronunciation of a visually and aurally presented spelling word' (Pan et al., 2015, p. 2). They go on to suggest that *copying* and *reading* as spelling techniques 'are among the most commonly used for spelling acquisition across a wide range of age levels (for the cases of copying and reading, see Cronnell & Humes, 1980; Ormrod & Jenkins, 1989)' (Pan et al., 2015, p. 2).

In the study, Pan et al. (2015) aimed to discover whether testing when applied to spelling development was more effective than copying of words. They hypothesised that testing may 'promote superior spelling acquisition than repeated copying of spelling words

(Grskovic & Belfiore, 1996; McGuffin, Martz & Heron, 1997; Wirtz, Gardner, Weber & Bullara, 1996)' (Pan et al., 2015, p. 2). This theory was influenced after reviewing similar studies conducted on children (Jones, Wardlow, Pan et al., 2015), which discovered that 'testing with feedback produced substantially more learning among normally developing first-and second-grade students than did a copying technique known as rainbow writing, in which children repeatedly write spelling words in different colors in an effort to maintain engagement' (Pan et al., 2015, p. 2).

Pan et al. (2015) wanted to see if they gained the same results when spelling experiments were conducted with adults, so they recruited a large sample of University of California San Diego undergraduate students for the study. Interestingly, and unlike the results of the study with children, findings revealed that there were no differences in spelling acquisition between the techniques of testing and copying. Both showed good results in spelling development for adults.

The authors conclude that copying is an effective spelling method for adults, because, unlike children, adults have 'extensive spelling expertise'. Also dissimilar to children, the copying technique fosters focused study as the adults intently concentrate on duplicating the grapheme of each letter from the original word, which helps to place how they have copied down the word into memory. As stated by Pan et al. (2015):

> As the adult subjects wrote each letter of a presented word, they are likely to have subvocally pronounced the word (cf. Zago, Poletti, Corbo, Adobbati & Silani, 2008) or to have compared the visual presentation of the word to their copying of it. Based on their spelling expertise, incongruous phoneme-to-grapheme sequence mappings are likely to become salient during that process, providing an opportunity to focus attention on learning those mappings while

263

copying. Less attention would be needed to sections of a word that have standard and highly familiar phoneme-to-grapheme mappings. (Pan et al., 2015, p. 9)

7.3.13   Using Copying Technique for Medical Terms and Terminology Words

The copying technique, as empirically evidenced by Pan et al. (2015) as being effective for adults, should productively be employed when coming across difficult spellings that are regularly used in your subject area. Words can be copied from academic papers or from physical/online dictionaries and thesauruses – or, in the case of MSc Sciences student Alan, whose course involved being on placements in hospitals, to accurately spell medical terms, he would copy words from electronic charts and doctors' notes:

> There are medication words, my coping mechanism for this is, a lot of hospitals now have electronic charts, so I copy it off their electronic chart. If it's not correct on there, well then that's it. Or if it's a medical term I've never heard of, it will be how the doctor spelt it and the letters I can make out, and that will be how I will spell it.

7.3.14   Other Ways of Using Copying

To deepen the use of all senses when copying out words, you could be creative and trace over the word, saying it aloud as you do. You can then replicate the tracing by writing the word again next to the original word. That way, you are using motor memory from when you traced the shape of the letters, combined with auditory memory from hearing the word pronounced aloud. You may then want to cover the word (like in the CCC and Look, Say, Cover, Write, Check methods) to write it out again, before checking that you have written it down correctly.

7.3.15   Copying Combined with Developing Understanding of Semantic Meaning of the Word

If the word you are learning is a terminology word from your topic area, or, like in the example of Alan above, a medical word, deepening your understanding of its semantic meaning (basically the definition of the word and how it is used in language) will help to consolidate your knowledge of how it is spelt. This can be achieved through finding an article which uses the word frequently and reading around all the sentences in which the word is mentioned. This will help you to recognise the word visually in terms of the order of letters and will confirm to you how the word is used in context. Another technique is to create written sentences in which you are using the word. This will develop your vocabulary around the use of the word and will help when it comes to writing essays or responding to exam questions that require you to discuss the terminology.

7.4   Multisensory Methods

There are numerous studies and strong empirical evidence to show that the multisensory approach to learning and remembering spelling of words is more effective than the traditional teaching approach. For example, a study from Malaysia by Ahmad et al. (2012), titled 'Applying phonic reading and multisensory approach with interactive multimedia for dyslexic children', argues that 'There are two ways to teach dyslexics, either by using traditional teaching approach or Multisensory Teaching Approach' (Ahmad et al., 2012, p. 555). They go onto argue that:

> the traditional method is not effective for dyslexic children as they need to stay focused on the information that is being given

to them (Ismail, Mahidin, Umar & Yusoff, 2010). Unable to stay focused for long durations (Singleton, 2003) and having short term memory problems (Ismail et al., 2010; Ahmad et al., 2012) are major contributors to the ineffectiveness of traditional methods. A better approach to teach dyslexics is by applying the Multisensory Method in the teaching and learning process by teachers (Ismail et al., 2010) as it consists of strings of multisensory strategies (linking of eyes, ears, voice, and hand movements). (Ahmad et al., 2012, p. 555).

The strength of the multisensory approach lies in its ability to attract dyslexic people's attention, as they usually have problems staying focused during the learning process (Ismail et al., 2010). Whilst Ahmad et al. (2012) are advocating this approach for children, it is just as useful for adults with dyslexia.

7.4.1   The Orton–Gillingham Approach

The Orton–Gillingham approach developed in the 1930s by Orton, a neuropsychiatrist and pathologist, and Gillingham, an educator and psychologist, to remediate what was referred to as 'word blindness' was one of the first early methods that identified, utilised and combined multisensory instruction, characterised by visual, auditory and kinaesthetic/tactile learning, with an instructional approach that provided systematic and cumulative overlearning of information. As demonstrated in a study by Dr Shamim Ali (2012) titled 'Teaching reading and spelling to adult learners: the multisensory structured language approach', Orton–Gillingham was regarded as a productive technique, because:

> using auditory, visual, and kinaesthetic elements, all language skills taught are reinforced by having the student listen, speak, read and write. For example, a dyslexic learner is taught to see the letter A,

say its name and sound and write it in the air – all at the same time. The approach requires intense instruction with ample practice. The use of multiple input channels is thought to enhance memory storage and retrieval by providing multiple 'triggers' for memory. (Ali, 2012, p. 41).

To have a go at using the Orton–Gillingham technique to apply to difficult words from your course or to help with remembering the spelling of words you have always struggled with, try out and/or adapt to your way of learning the steps below. You may also want to pair up with a study buddy, someone you trust in the role of teacher, or a mentor to make the process more interactive, hence more memorable. The link provides access to the hard copy of this technique.

www.cambridge.org/abbottjones

Steps of Using the Orton–Gillingham Spelling Technique

Step 1

Review any difficult combination of letters with sound cards which you can create and make yourself. For example, if you struggle with the letter combination *psy* used in words like *psychology*, *psychiatry* and *psychometrics*, you may want to create a sound card for *psy*. You may then want to create a different-coloured sound card for other challenging letter combinations, such as *ch* for *church*, *chair*, *cheese*. Or you may want to create sound cards showing vowels using one colour, say pink, consonants on white cards, and suffixes on orange cards. That way, you can play around with the cards making up individual words.

Step 2

Once you are comfortable with the *psy* and/or *ch* sounds, introduce a new concept by learning a new sound, syllable type or letter pattern.

For instance, you may want to develop your knowledge of letter patterns used with *psy*, or you may want to try out pronouncing the different sounds of *ch*, such as *church*, how this sounds different from *chef*, and how this also varies from *chemistry*.

This is where it is useful to have a study buddy to work with. That way, each new concept to be introduced can be discussed in the previous session in terms of how it is supposed to sound, and your study buddy can present the coloured cards with the new word on for you to absorb visually. You can then both pronounce the word aloud to hear its sound, using auditory skills, and then you can move using motor skills to replicate the shapes of the letters in the new word, kinaesthetically, either by tracing as discussed above, or by skywriting and moving the hands and arms in the shape of the letters whilst simultaneously saying the sounds aloud so they become rhythmic.

Step 3

With the various coloured cards that you have created, play a game where you shuffle the pack, select random cards and place them alongside each other to make a word, or nonsense word (it does not have to be a word used in the English language). Once you have made a word or nonsense word, have a go at pronouncing the sounds of the letters. In the Orton–Gillingham method, this is called blending and helps to develop the skills of decoding.

Step 4

If you want to learn how to identify irregular words, words that cannot be sounded out phonetically, then write these words onto red coloured cards (the Orton–Gillingham approach calls these *red words*). Get your study buddy to introduce the red word by presenting the card, as in step 1, so you can both see it, then, using rhythmic tapping on the arm, hand movements and/or finger tracing, say aloud the word. The combination of visualising the word on red card with rhythmic tapping of the arm, and hearing yourself verbalising the sounds, should help to place the irregular words into memory.

Step 5

Using the concepts and words you have learned, find them in your course reading either in an academic article and/or textbook, and read aloud the sentences they are presented in.

Step 6

Get your study buddy to say each new word you have learned in a random order. With each word, have a go at writing it in a sentence you have created, so you are placing the words into context. As you are writing the word, say it rhythmically as you did when you were learning it, and/or move your hands in the way in which you memorised it.

7.5   Metacognitive Awareness

In a 2010 study by Vanderswalmen, Vrijders and Desoete, the authors claim that 'metacognitive experiences, metacognitive knowledge, and metacognitive skills are all involved in proficient spelling' (Vanderswalmen et al., 2010, p. 4). Another study, by Kernaghan and Woloshyn (1995), provided empirical evidence to support how metacognitive awareness influences improved spelling performance. They divided students into three groups, the first group receiving instruction in the use of phonetics, imagery and analogy to help with spelling. The second group received the same instruction combined with metacognitive information about when and where to use each spelling strategy, and the third group completed traditional language arts activities. After assessing student spelling performance, it was shown that pupils 'who received multiple strategy instruction with metacognitive information outperformed those who received strategy instruction alone or completed language arts activities' (Kernaghan & Woloshyn, 1995, p. 157).

Consequently, developing your metacognitive knowledge, skills and experiences in relation to spelling will help to make the task of spelling less of an obstacle. Ways of helping you to develop this awareness of your thought processes in connection to spelling are evaluated below.

7.5.1 Metacognition and How to Develop Your Awareness of This in Relation to Your Spelling

Whilst metacognition as a concept has many elements (Vanderswalmen et al., 2010), the two we are concerned about here are: metacognitive knowledge, and metacognitive strategy-knowledge. Let us take each in turn.

7.5.2 Metacognitive Knowledge

Metacognitive knowledge is described as the 'knowledge and deeper understanding of cognitive processes and products' (Vanderswalmen et al., 2010, p. 6). In fact, Vanderswalmen et al. use the example of children knowing they must check their spelling after writing a text or email.

Thus, questions you may ask yourself to develop your metacognitive knowledge of your spelling are:

- Are you relying too much on phonetics when writing words, which is causing misspellings (spair rather than spare, tipe rather than type, etc.)?
- Do you have visual-sequential difficulties (two letters within a word confused, for example aviod rather than avoid)?

- Are you unaware of spelling rules or acceptable letter combinations (for instance, babys rather than babies, apointed rather than appointed)?
- Do you mishear sounds and so miss them out in spelling (seet rather than street, thee rather than three)?
- Do you have motor handwriting difficulties when spelling which can lead to repetition (for instance, rememember for remember), or can lead to omitting letters unintentionally (for instance, rember for remember)?

Once you become more aware of something you are doing repeatedly with various words, you are in the advantageous position of knowing where your spelling difficulties lie and why this happens. You are then able to check for this and to select and use appropriate strategies to help with overcoming the problem.

7.5.3   Metacognitive Strategy-Knowledge

According to Vanderswalmen et al., 'Metacognitive strategy-knowledge involves knowledge of multiple strategies as well as the conditions for their use (e.g., when why and how a strategy should be used)' (Vanderswalmen et al., 2010, p. 6).

Applying this to spelling, the range of strategies presented in this chapter provides some knowledge of different methods you can try to use when it comes to dealing with challenging words. If you combine strategy-knowledge with the above recognition of where your main difficulties with spelling lie and why you encounter those obstacles, you are able to be more aware of the appropriate techniques to assist with overcoming the problem.

For instance, if you have visual-sequential difficulties, as discussed above, you may want to try out the Look, Say, Cover, Write, Check method combined with using different-coloured pens to highlight the various syllables of the word. That way, the repetition involved in the method teamed with consistently looking at the different-coloured parts of the word and hearing yourself saying it aloud may place the sequence of letters more meaningfully into memory.

If you have a tendency to spell words phonetically, you may want to break the word up into different sounds and try the strategy of 'saying the word not phonetically but how it is spelt', as in the example of BA English student Cate above with the word 'par li a ment'.

The key is to utilise and apply different strategies appropriate to each difficulty you encounter, but also to develop knowledge around the most suitable technique to employ in any given situation.

7.6   Using Technology

7.6.1   Spellchecker in Word

The spellchecker in Word can be a useful device for automatically checking your spellings as you type. Any errors in the document will be signified by coloured underlining, dependent on how you have customised the spellchecker. For example, blue may highlight spelling errors, and green may represent grammatical errors. One of the problems, however, with the autocorrect feature of spell-checker is that if it recognises commonly misspelt words, such as words you may have typed with the incorrect letter order, it will automatically change this to the correct version. Frequently, this happens without you even noticing how you originally typed the word, and consequently, because you are relying on spellchecker to do the work for you, you are not learning or developing from your mistakes. If, though, you do spend some time reviewing the words that the autocorrect changes, or analysing the words that the spellchecker underlines in colour, then the spellchecker can be a productive way to gain an understanding of why you are making inaccuracies with your spelling.

7.6.2 Assistive Technology Software

In addition to spellchecker, Dragon speech recognition software, Read & Write software, and Grammarly, a software package that assists with spelling and grammar, are all forms of technologies that contain features for helping with spelling and grammar development.

7.6.3 Google Dictionary

Google Dictionary is also useful for looking up definitions and synonyms of words. Furthermore, if you know how the word is spelt but are unsure of how to pronounce it, the Google Dictionary has the helpful added feature of a sound icon, which when clicked will say the word aloud and pronounce it accurately. BSc Medicine student Naomi benefited from this device:

> Google is amazing because if you type in a word, it tells you what it is phonetically, so that's really useful.

7.7 Summary

In summary, this chapter has:

- Specified common obstacles with spelling for the student with dyslexia.
- Provided guidance on using a range of general spelling strategies to assist with overcoming difficulties, such as:
  - Using mnemonics.

Spelling Techniques

- ○ Using the process of sounding out words.
- ○ Using Cover, Copy, Compare technique combined with sounding out.
- ○ Using repetition in the form of Look, Say, Cover, Write, Check method.
- ○ Copying words down to become familiar with visualisation of the word.
- ○ Utilising multisensory methods in the form of an adaptation of the Orton–Gillingham technique.
- Outlined ways of developing metacognitive knowledge in relation to spelling.
- Discussed forms of technology that can be useful to assist with spelling development.

8

• • • • •

Revision and Examination Techniques

8.1   Introduction

As previously noted, working memory difficulties mean that many students with dyslexia struggle with the retention and retrieval of their learning, yet because exams are such a widespread assessment method for university courses, such students not only need to be structured in their approach to revision, but they also need to use revision methods that make their learning memorable and easy to retrieve. Additionally, because of the time-constrained conditions of exams, which make them more difficult for a dyslexic student, students with dyslexia need to be supplied with strategies for tackling exam papers to enable time to be used efficiently.

This chapter, firstly, explores common difficulties with revision and exams for the student with dyslexia which will help to develop an understanding of reasons for the obstacles related to this academic activity. Secondly, it introduces effective revision methods. These include: creating questions; practising past papers; repetition through a process of re-reading information; covering over information to see what can be remembered, followed by leaving it for longer periods of time to transfer learning from short-term to long-term memory processes; making summaries of information and carrying them around; and utilising multisensory methods such as creating colourful wall posters. Thirdly, guidance on exam technique is delivered, which includes advice on timetabling exams, breaking down questions, selecting appropriate questions, verbalising exam questions, and using practical and favourite things to make taking exams a more comfortable experience.

8.2   Common Difficulties with Revision for Students with Dyslexia

As mentioned above and in previous chapters, for students with memory deficits (a common characteristic of dyslexia), the main barrier to revision is the difficulty in remembering, recalling and retrieving what they have read and learned. This makes revising for exams extremely arduous.

These challenges can be a trigger for anxiety, and, in a cyclical effect, the anxiety can further impede working memory processes, hindering the ability to remember learning even more extensively. Some students struggle to identify revision techniques that may be more suitable for how they retain information. If taught through traditional methods of learning during their school years, for instance, students could still be inclined to use cramming techniques (working intensively to absorb large amounts of

276

information) which are counterproductive and likely to generate stress and anxiety.

Consequently, inappropriate study techniques in preparation for tests and exams can lead to fearing this type of evaluative learning experience, as explored by researchers Mealey and Host (1992). Looking at causes of test anxiety, Mealey and Host (1992) suggest that there are two main sources for this: 'first, researchers believe that some highly test-anxious students have deficits in the organisational stage of test preparation, primarily inadequate learning or study skills (Culler & Holahan 1980; Hodapp & Henneberger 1983; Wittmaier 1972)' (Mealey & Host, 1992, p. 147). For students with dyslexia, unless they have used strategies appropriate for their learning style to interact with and memorise large amounts of information, they can struggle with processing and organising their learning effectively for recall. They will then have high levels of anxiety going into the testing situation. The second major cause of test anxiety 'stems from habitual, irrelevant, negative thoughts that some students have during a testing situation (McKeachie et al., 1986; Sarason 1984; Wine 1971). These negative thoughts distract students from the task of taking the test and cause them to focus on their fears, inadequacies, and past failures' (Mealey & Host, 1992, p. 147). The effect of this is creation of an attitude of 'learned helplessness' (Dweck 1975; Dweck & Licht 1980; Schwarzer, Jerusalem & Schwarzer 1983; Schwarzer, Jerusalem & Stiksrud 1984; Seligman 1975). Mealey and Host suggest that

> learned helplessness occurs when students who have failed or done poorly in the past develop negative self-images, causing irrelevant thought patterns during the test. 'I can't do this,' 'I'm not smart enough,' 'The teacher is watching me,' and 'Everyone is finishing before me' are common thoughts this type of test anxious student has reported during testing situations (Ganz & Ganz 1988; Stipek 1988). (Mealey & Host, 1992, p. 147).

Students with dyslexia are prone to having such thoughts, possibly due to being made to feel different, slower to learn, inferior to their peers during their earlier education. Although, by the time the student has arrived at university, they may have adopted effective coping strategies to deal with revision and recall of information, these types of distracting thoughts during exams can still interfere cognitively and cause poor performance.

8.3   Common Difficulties with Exams for Students with Dyslexia

In the book *Dyslexia in Higher Education: Anxiety and Coping Skills* (2022), Abbott-Jones investigated, through 20 one-to-one interviews with students diagnosed with dyslexia, the types of academic tasks that generated greater levels of negative emotion for the students. Out of the tasks, which included reading, remembering reading, spelling, note taking in lectures, organisation, exams, meeting deadlines, presentations, seminar discussion, and writing, exams were shown to manifest greater feelings of anxiety, stress and fear due to retention and retrieval difficulties than the other tasks discussed. This high level of negative emotion connected to exams was ultimately because students were unable to remember information they had previously absorbed from readings and lectures. The anxiety caused by the exam would further worsen the ability to recapture the information required. Consequently, students found they could not retrieve the relevant knowledge during the tests, leading to frustration. This frustration is captured by BSc Medicine student Naomi:

> I get really frustrated that I don't remember. It's not that I never read it. I know there's something I know, but I can't recall it.

Although exams are less exposed in terms of working in front of others, the feelings of embarrassment and humiliation so frequently felt by students with dyslexia in relation to spelling and reading aloud in front of peers become replaced by the emotions of stress, anxiety and terror in connection to exams. Fear of failure becomes heightened for the student with dyslexia in association with exams because the exam, within the university environment, is usually presented as the main opportunity to perform and to demonstrate the knowledge learned and consolidated from lectures throughout the academic year.

This fear is validated from the Abbott-Jones (2022) research which showed that 16 out of the 20 students linked exams with emotion words of stress, anxiety, terror, and panic about failure. BSc Nursing student Lisa spoke frankly about how the anxiety provoked by undertaking exams could lead to misinterpreting or misreading the exam paper:

> When you get into the exam, sometimes you're so anxious that you're not going to be reading the question properly.This quote illustrates that cognitive interference caused by anxiety can hamper cognitive processes more than the weaknesses caused by dyslexia itself. Whilst traditional research on dyslexia has attributed poor academic performance to merely cognitive deficits associated with dyslexia (Bruck & Parke 1992; Lefly & Pennington 1991; Smith-Spark & Fisk 2007; Wiseheart et al., 2009), quotes such as the one above more appropriately suggest that poor academic performance in students with dyslexia is due to the interaction between anxiety and the central executive and phonological components of working memory.

8.4   Revision Strategies

Strategies that students find effective when revising for exams include: using to-do lists and setting a purpose; creating questions;

condensing the information into bullet points and word triggers; practising past papers; repetition through a process of re-reading information; covering over information to see what can be remembered followed by leaving for longer periods of time to place learning into long-term memory; making summaries of information and carrying them around; and having an awareness of the best times of the day or evening to allocate to revision. Some of these techniques, as articulated by students with dyslexia, are detailed below.

8.4.1 Being Creative and Making Own Revision Books and Colourful Posters

Two students, BSc Nurse trainee Tina and MA Arts student Debra, believed that because of their dyslexia, they had to be more creative, to devise revision methods that worked for them and went against traditional styles of learning. For example, Tina, who could not revise for exams through rote learning, would create her own interactive revision books:

> I find it's the only way I can cope with it [revision], and I feel because of my dyslexia, I kind of was forced to create something that would work for me, rather than struggle reading loads and loads of black and white textbooks. So, I feel like it's kind of forced me to do it but in a good way because it works for me.

Debra also innovated and would create revision techniques that would suit her learning style:

> I don't know if other people feel like this, other people with dyslexia feel like this, but I would always come up with a very different solution and I do think slightly outside of the box because my mind works in a different way. I'd have all these posters which may appear

childish to some, using colourful pens, whatever, but I know that works for me and I know that's how I remember things, so I would stick to that, and thinking of different ways of converting my readings to audio, listen to them on the train.

One of the advantages of creating a revision strategy that aligns with how you naturally process, remember and recall information is that it can help to reduce the anxiety generated by fearing that ineffective revision techniques will make you unable to retrieve the relevant information during the exam. This was articulated by BSc Nursing student Tina:

> The only thing that helps me reduce the anxiety is where I create my own revision book, if that makes sense. So, if I've organised myself well enough, I know I need to know this topic, this topic and this topic. Then I will take the information and put it in one booklet. When I'm on the bus or when I'm in the library, I just read that. I don't read any of the other resources because that will confuse me, and I've already highlighted what I need to know. It's in my own language, and whereas they may have like a big diagram, I've kind of just scribbled something that I understand. I can take that literally up until I'm going into the exam and just be skimming, like flipping through it, so that kind of helps reduce my anxiety.

Consequently, for Tina, this became her personalised revision technique: she would organise herself early in the revision period by identifying what she would need to know on each of her topics, usually pinpointed by going through the learning objectives of lectures, which generally specify what students should know about the subject (see Chapter 3 section 'Creating Questions from Handouts or from Learning Objectives of the Lecture'), followed by condensing the information from various resources into one booklet to carry around at all times, with relevant information transcribed in her own words to be more meaningful. This not only helped to reduce her anxiety in the lead up to the exam but was also her way of being able to retrieve the learning during the exam itself.

Let us now consider a range of other useful strategies you may want to try out and have a go at applying to the learning you need to remember in preparation for your exam.

8.5   Implementing Revision Strategies

8.5.1   Mind Maps

Select one of your revision topics and use the mind-map templates provided:

www.cambridge.org/abbottjones

- On the first mind map, put down everything you **know** about the subject using **keywords** only.
- On the second mind map, put down everything you either **need to find out** or need to have a **further re-cap on**, using **keywords** only.
- Use your second mind map as your guide to help to create a **list of topics** on which you need to have a further re-cap from your revision notes.

8.5.2   Sticky Notes

Using different-coloured sticky notes (such as Post-It notes):

- Select one colour for **each topic**.
- Decide **what object (or room)** you're going to stick each sticky note on.
- Create sticky notes for each topic using bullet points, keywords, symbols, diagrams, headings, etc.

8.5.3   Flash Cards

Go to the link: www.wikihow.com/Make-Flash-Cards to review how to make *flash cards*.

Using the different-coloured flash cards:

- Select one colour of card for each topic.
- Create flash cards for each topic using bullet points, keywords, symbols, diagrams, headings, etc.
- Create **questions** for your flash cards, either on the reverse side of each card or on a separate card.
- Create your questions by placing yourself in your examiner's shoes. If you had taught the module/topic, what would you now expect your students to know?
- Also use the **Learning Outcomes** of the module, as they provide a clear idea as to what you are expected to know by the end of the module.
- Once you have created your flash cards, you can test yourself.

8.5.4   Recording Revision Notes

Using your revision/lecture notes, either **read them aloud** or explain them to somebody and record this by using either a Dictaphone or the voice recorder on your mobile.

- Listen to the recording when doing something relaxing like sitting in the bath; sitting in the park; travelling on public transport.

8.5.5   Creating Visual Diagrams/Flow Charts on A3 Paper

If you're revising **processes or procedures** such as those learnt in medicine or biology, get an A3 sketch pad and a selection of coloured pens. Break the process or procedure up into a step-by-step method and, using your coloured pens, draw out each step, labelling your visual diagrams.

- Using the templates from mind-mapping software as examples of flow charts, choose your preferred layout and draw out onto your A3 sketch pad (or create using the computer software) your own flow charts for your topics.
- Create the flow charts by breaking your revision information up into **keywords** which make **links** to other keywords.
- Once the flow charts have been created, put these onto your bedroom wall and use as your posters to look at each day.

8.5.6   Making Questions and Searching for Answers

Create a **list of topics** that you know you are likely to be tested on by reviewing the Learning Outcomes of the Module, by going through your lecture notes to see where the emphasis was placed, or by reviewing past examination papers.

- Using the Q Notes template (www.cambridge.org/abbottjones), create some **questions** to test yourself on by writing these down into the Questions column.
- To help you to create questions, place yourself into the examiner's shoes and think what you would expect a student to know if you had taught that topic.
- Use past examination papers to also help you to create questions. Reviewing past questions will help to familiarise yourself with the types of questions asked and the way the questions are structured.
- Once your Questions column is completed, search for the answers by using your lecture notes or your course textbooks/journal articles.

- Write down your answers to the questions in abbreviated format using bullet points and symbols in the Q-uiz Answers column.
- Repeat the process until you can complete the Q Notes template without using your lecture notes, textbooks or journal articles to find the answers.

8.5.7   Interpret Material into Own Language

If you must revise some very complex material or remember information that uses lots of scientific or medical terminology, **translate** this so that it makes sense to you.

- Read through the complex lecture notes, paper, or section of a book slowly, highlighting any words you don't understand.
- Look up the complex words or phrases by using an online subject-specific dictionary or by using Wikipedia (just do not reference it in your essays), which will give you a clear definition of the complex words or phrases.
- With scientific or medical terminology, once you are clear on the definitions, you can begin to create your own Dictionary of Terms which you will be able to refer to throughout your academic and professional career.
- Once you have broken up the complex information into a way that you can understand it, rewrite it in your own words, or in layman's terms (easy-to-understand language for the normal person) as though you are explaining it to someone who is not an expert in your field of knowledge.

Compare Revision Notes with Someone

Team up with someone on your course or module and arrange a suitable time to meet somewhere each week to spend a few hours revising together.

285

- Go through lecture notes and take it in turns to explain to each other your understanding and interpretation of the topic.
- You can also take it in turns to **test each other** on the material by asking each other questions about the topic.

8.5.8 Talk to Someone about the Material

Verbalising complex information aloud will help you to understand it better.

- Find someone such as your study support tutor to explain the information to.
- Talk your support tutor through your lecture notes, revision notes, diagrams, processes, procedures, etc.
- If you can **explain** the information so that somebody outside of your subject understands it, it usually means that you understand it also.
- Sometimes by explaining your topic to someone outside of your own subject, you can get questions from the novice that you may not have thought about. Explaining the answers to the questions helps to give you a **deeper understanding** of your topic.

8.5.9 Turn into a Rhythm or a Rap

This may sound strange, but if you must remember for your exam lots of formulas or scientific and terminology words, then sometimes associating these with a rhythm or transforming them into a rap will help when you are trying to recall the information in your exam.

- **Chant aloud** the information you must recall by applying a favourite tune or by breaking it up into a rap.
- In the exam, once the tune or rap has come to mind, it will be easier for you to recall the information.

286

8.5.10   Use Memory Joggers/Mnemonics

The word MIGRAINE (see Section 5.6.1, 'Using Mnemonics') is an example of a mnemonic as each letter that makes up the word stands for a key concept in media studies, and all the key concepts are needed in the media exam to break up and analyse a media text, such as a film clip, poster or photograph.

- Think of **key concepts** that you need to remember for your exam. Write these down and turn the first letters of the concepts into a memorable word for you. The word you make up can be anything to help to trigger your memory. It doesn't have to make sense – it can be a nonsense word such as jingo.
- During the exam, when a question is asked about the key concepts, write your **memorable word** down on the preparation part of your exam paper, and this should act as a trigger to help to retrieve the knowledge from your memory on your topic.

8.5.11   Use Review Cycle

Use **mind maps** (or **concept pyramids**) for each of your topics to put down keywords from your subject. (A concept pyramid is a diagram of a pyramid in which information is placed in hierarchical order by using keywords, structured in the same way as Maslow's hierarchy of needs.)

- Once you've created your mind maps (or concept pyramids), review these and then place them face down.
- Get a blank mind map and try to complete this with all the keywords and information from your first face-down mind map.
- Repeat this process, but leave it for an hour before you complete your third mind map.

- Each time you repeat the process, double the amount of time that you leave it for before completing a new blank mind map: e.g., 2 hours; 4 hours; 8 hours; 16 hours.
- You should aim to be able to leave it for 3 days before completing a new blank mind map replicating the keywords and information from your first face-down version.
- The aim is to get the keywords and information from your first face-down mind map (or concept pyramid, if preferred) from your short-term memory to your long-term memory. Once information is in your long-term memory, it stays.

Now we have covered a range of revision strategies, let us now turn to looking at ways that students maintained motivation and kept organised during their revision and exam preparation periods.

8.6   Using To-Do Lists and Setting a Purpose

Making a revision timetable, using a daily to-do list (see Chapter 2) and setting a purpose for your revision is key for preventing procrastination, for helping with remembering the list of topics you need to go through, and for ensuring you are giving equal coverage to all subjects that may come up in the exam.

BSc Nursing student Lisa explained that she had to have a to-do list for each day dedicated to revision, to help with keeping motivated and to prevent distraction, distraction frequently being a co-occurring difficulty of dyslexia (Brosnan et al., 2002). The to-do list would consist of a list of topics that she would want to go through during a revision session. The topics would be allocated a specific timeframe to prevent spending too long on some subjects at the expense and neglect of others. Consequently, her revision would be effectively timetabled over the period of weeks allocated to revising before exams began, with each topic allocated an equal amount of time to go through over the duration of the revision period.

> I'm a to-do list person because my mind is so 'All right I'll just go over here and do this and don't focus.' My friends think I'm nuts, or I have OCD [obsessive compulsive disorder] because I'm like, 'Okay I've got a list, leave, get on with it.' I have to have a purpose or otherwise I will just procrastinate all day.

Below is a series of steps for helping you to plan your revision, which you can also access from the list of Resources.

www.cambridge.org/abbottjones

8.6.1   Steps to Planning the Revision

Step 1

Consider how much time you have until your exams to revise and then divide the time you have, allocating it equally to the number of topics/subjects you need to study.

Step 2

Analyse your list of subjects and evaluate whether there are particular topics within those subjects that you need to spend more time on. For instance, perhaps a mock test brought up areas that you now feel you need to pay more attention to, or some areas may be more complex than others and warrant spending a little extra time on.

Step 3

Adjust your designation of time accordingly to reflect the above step.

Step 4

Next to your list of topics, plan and write down the type of strategy you will apply to revise that area. For example, some topics such as World Wonders in history or the cardiovascular system in medicine may be remembered better by transforming into visual diagrams and flow charts. Other topics like asteroids in science could be memorised more easily by applying memory joggers and mnemonics; and epistemology in philosophy, for instance, could lend itself to being recalled if some time is spent talking with someone about the material. Sometimes, you may want to apply more than one technique to a topic to consolidate the learning.

Below is a helpful template for listing topics and revision strategies, which you can then go through and tick off once completed. Also below is a template of a revision timetable to help with plotting when you will revise each topic. The numbers in the left column of the timetable reflect the number of weeks you have available. Both resources can be accessed via the link.

www.cambridge.org/abbottjones

8.6.2   Revision List

Date	Topic	Strategy	Completed

8.6.3   **Revision Timetable**

Week number	Monday	Tuesday	Wednesday	Thursday	Friday	Saturday	Sunday
1							
2							
3							
4							
5							
6							
7							
8							

Whilst the above is an example of a revision timetable, what you may also find helpful is the link below which takes you to a useful site for creating your own revision planner.

https://getrevising.co.uk/planner

8.7   Creating Questions

From the list of strategies above, making questions from your revision material and searching for answers can be an effective method of enhancing recall of information during the exam, so we will expand on it a little here. Asking yourself questions to test yourself on your learning can be done in many forms, and some of these are listed below.

- You may want to practise past exam papers to get an idea of the types of questions that have been previously asked on the topic.
- You could be creative and develop quizzes to test out with a group of peers from your course.
- You can make some multiple-choice questions or use the Internet to check for multiple-choice questions in your subject area. For example,

these types of questions are often freely available on the Internet for topics in medicine and science-based courses.

- You could team up with a revision partner and verbally ask each other questions.

8.7.1   The Advantages of Creating Questions

Having to think of and create productive questions so you can test yourself on your topic area encourages you to revisit material and to think about it on a more intense level. Being required to then retrieve the information to answer your questions, even when feedback from your tutors is not available, can lead to better long-term recall than simply revising by passively going through your notes. This type of activity also helps you to identify what you do and do not know in connection with your subject which helps to guide your revision.

In fact, a paper by Jobs, Twesten, Göbel et al. (2013) titled 'Question-writing as a learning tool for students' provides empirical evidence to support the effectiveness of this particular revision strategy for assisting with student retrieval of information. As the authors say, 'it has been reported that constructing questions enhances recall for a studied text (Frase & Schwartz, 1975). It may also foster a more active self-determined way of learning (Brown, 1991) which is more likely to promote a deeper understanding of the subject (Rash, 1997)' (Jobs et al., 2013, p. 1).

8.7.2   Example of Creating Questions Used as Effective Revision Strategy by Student

To help with setting a purpose in preparation for exams, some students with dyslexia interviewed by Abbott-Jones in *Dyslexia in*

Higher Education: Anxiety and Coping Skills (2022) said they would make their own exam questions by putting themselves into their lecturer's shoes and by thinking, if they had taught that subject, what would they ask their students? What would they want them to know about the topic?

If learning objectives are provided at the start of taught sessions, these statements usually provide an indicator on specific areas of a topic that students will be tested on during exams to ascertain whether the student has met the learning objective (see Chapter 3 'Activity on Creating Questions from Learning Objectives').

BSc Medicine student Naomi would transform the learning objective statements into her own exam questions and would test her knowledge by ensuring she knew the answers to these questions by extracting relevant information from her lecture notes as part of her revision process.

Naomi also used her kinaesthetic and visual strengths by putting each individual question onto a coloured card, which she would laminate by using the university's laminator. Answers to the questions condensed to keywords would also be placed on individual laminated cards.

Working with a study buddy, friend, colleague or dyslexia tutor, she would place the laminated questions and answers in two separate piles and would randomly pick up question cards. She would then connect the question to the relevant keyword answer and would provide a detailed verbal explanation of the answer to her study buddy, as though teaching her study buddy new information.

Whilst she provided the verbal explanation, she would move and walk around the room like a teacher in a classroom.

The process of creating questions and condensing answers to word triggers, combined with the practical activity of making and laminating cards, followed by matching questions to answers, and verbally explaining answers to a study buddy whilst moving around, was highly effective for Naomi as it used all learning senses and made revision memorable, as she explained:

> Yeah, so the lamination technique was definitely worth it with the question and answers. That definitely helped with the bigger topics I was struggling with. I'm having to think, I'm also moving around and picking up things and touching things, and then I can try and remember. When I picked up that word, what answer was that affiliated with, and try and do links in my brain, so that was quite handy.

8.8   Practising Past Papers

If you are in a position where you can access and practise past papers on your topic as part of your revision, you will benefit from this process. For example, past examination questions will enable you to target your studying, by allowing you to figure out through looking at older questions what aspects of the topic were previously asked about. This gives an indication as to what is important in connection to your subject and shows where your lecturers are placing emphasis in testing your knowledge.

Practising past papers under timed conditions also permits you to become familiar with exam circumstances in relation to how much time you will have for each question. This will allow you to fine-tune and develop your time-management skills in preparation for the exam. Furthermore, if your exam is going to be composed of problem-solving questions, rehearsing answering these types of questions, and becoming used to their format, grants you the time for developing your skills in tackling this kind of question.

For example, if the questions are multiple-choice, you can work on progressing your skills in analysis, followed by improving your ability to evaluate and to go through the process of logically eliminating potentially wrong answers. Or, if your exam requires essay responses, you can rehearse to become comfortable with developing the strategy of firstly mind-mapping ideas, secondly putting ideas in order using numbering or bullet pointing, and thirdly expanding on ideas by elaborating in writing. By the time you take the exam, as you have done the process previously on numerous occasions under timed conditions, even though you may be responding to different questions, the steps you need to take will have become automatic.

The activity sheet below, which can be accessed via the link, covers crucial things to consider for achieving success when undertaking any kind of exam paper.

www.cambridge.org/abbottjones

8.8.1   Important Things to Consider for an Exam

- Dividing your time amongst the questions.
- Dividing your time when the allocation of marks is weighted differently amongst the various questions.
- Breaking up questions using two different-coloured highlighter pens (please see 'Breaking Down the Question by Highlighting the Instruction and Topic Words' in Chapter 6).
- Allocating time to planning responses for essay exams.
- Planning responses, either through using mind maps or bullet points, followed by putting your ideas in the order you want to write and present them.
- Allocating time to check through your answers.

8.8.2 Activity Sheet in Preparing to Tackle Exam Papers

- Your examination is 1 hour and you have three questions to answer. How much time will you allocate for answering each question?
  Answer:

  _____
  _____
  _____

- If one question is worth 60% of the marks, one question 30% and one question 10%, how much time will you allocate for answering each question?
  Answer:

  _____
  _____
  _____

- Look at the questions below.
  (1) Outline the advantages to the customer of offering an online shopping service.
  (2) Analyse Maslow's hierarchy of needs.

- How will you make sure that you know exactly what you are being asked to do?
  Answer:

  _____
  _____
  _____

- Choose one of the questions.
- How will you prepare for answering the question?
  Answer:

296

_____

_____

_____

- How will you put your ideas into a logical ordered structure to help to provide you with a coherent answer?

  Answer:

_____

_____

_____

- What will you finally do after you have answered all the questions, or answered the questions that you have selected?

  Answer:

_____

_____

_____

8.9   Repetition through a Process of Condensing and Re-reading Information

Another useful revision technique involves condensing down information on a topic area to a few keywords, which can then act as memory joggers for retrieving the relevant knowledge connected to the subject. As most students with dyslexia cannot remember information from just looking at it once, it may be useful to carry a notepad containing the keywords/memory joggers and/or the more elaborated revision information around with you, so you can look at it when travelling, taking a break, or sitting in the park, and so on. These repeated visual reminders will help to strengthen your ability for active recall during the exam when a question is asked on the topic or contains a word you have used as a memory jogger.

In fact, this type of revision activity, whereby you examine your notes intermittently and at specific intervals over a period of time, is referred to as spaced repetition.

8.9.1   Spaced Repetition

Spaced repetition, originally conceptualised by psychologist Hermann Ebbinghaus, involves, as noted above, occasionally reviewing your topics and the compressed abbreviated form of your topics – your memory triggers (see Chapter 5 *Making Learning Memorable*) – after having left ever-increasing lengths of time between viewings.

Ebbinghaus suggested that information becomes lost from memory over time following a 'forgetting curve', with the idea being that we forget things initially at a gradual rate, progressively becoming exponential. However, he argued that to break the pathway of the forgetting curve, the information should repeatedly be examined with the time intervals between reviews continuously increasing, which encourages active recall (the review cycle revision strategy above is a technique based on this theory).

Accordingly, the idea behind spaced revision is that as time passes, you are likely to forget some aspects of your learning. Following the forgetting curve, as you leave your evaluation of your revision for longer durations of time, when you come to look at your memory joggers, abbreviated information and condensed notes, you must force the brain to work harder to retrieve the knowledge. As such, if the process of active recall is mentally challenging, then it is more likely to be memorable, and this helps with placing learning from short-term memory into long-term memory.

Additionally, the idea behind spaced repetition is that it should not be a passive activity whereby you merely just re-read the notes (which is passive learning). You instead think about what you can do with the notes to make the task more active.

If you have already condensed, abbreviated and created keywords from the notes, you have done something active, so doing something additionally active with this contracted information works to consolidate learning even more effectively into memory. Some ideas are listed below.

- Sort through and highlight what is essential.
- Make notes on notes to help recall.
- Make flash cards with key points and memory triggers.
- Reduce notes to key headings, points and references.
- Focus on your notes each time you review them and keep engaged by asking, 'What does this mean? How does it relate to X? What is important about this theory/point?'

If you choose to do any of these methods, your highlighted notes, notes of notes, flashcards and reduced notes can be the new form of notes you carry around with you to review. Each time you do an evaluation, remembering that with spaced repetition you are doubling or tripling the amount of time between your review, you can continuously repeat one of the methods above, so that your notes with each review become more and more condensed and hence perpetually reinforce active recall.

8.10   Multisensory Methods

There are numerous ideas that you can experiment with if you want to make your revision techniques more multisensory. Quite a few

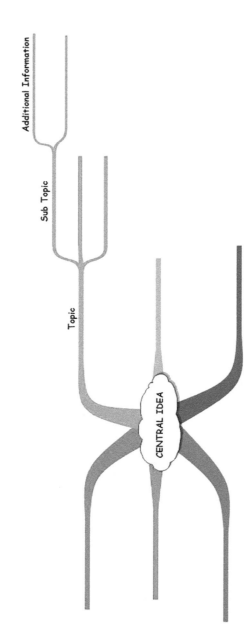

Figure 8.1 Example of blank mind map

of the methods already discussed during this chapter, such as mind maps, sticky notes, flash cards, recording revision notes and creating visual diagrams/flow charts on A3 paper, all lend themselves to having multisensory elements.

Filling in mind maps, as in the example – or creating your own bright, colourful mind map – and completing the branches with keywords and terms from your topic area provides a good starting point for recalling and retrieving relevant information on your topic.

In fact, the blank mind map exemplifies and encourages what is referred to as a Gestalt principle, the principle of closure from the area of Gestalt psychology (see Figure 8.1). Gestalt psychology, conceptualised by Wilhelm Wundt and Edward Titchener in the early twentieth century, argued that in relation to the principle of closure, the human brain has an innate desire and need to fill in and complete the missing gaps in information. Consequently, when incomplete branches are seen on a mind map, concept map or spider diagram, this motivates and inspires the person to write terms on these branches, completing the missing pieces in the quest for closure. This can be helpful as the blank mind map stimulates concentration on the topic in the pursuit of a finalised diagram. This method can develop confidence in your knowledge levels of the subject, as it will confirm how much you actually do know in relation to the area you are revising.

Once you have a completed mind map, you can take this a step further, chopping the map into pieces with scissors to separate out each branch and keyword, which adds a kinaesthetic aspect to the process. You can then have a go at reassembling the branches of the mind map, putting them into a logical order. This will strengthen your memory of the individual key terms on each of the branches.

Finally, to add a stronger visual/audio element to the process, you can make a video of the mind map which features yourself talking about each branch. The video can then be carried around on your phone and played back during your spare moments to recall information on your topic through a visual–auditory process.

Other examples of students benefiting from using multisensory approaches to revision include the case below from MA Humanities student Charlie. Charlie had to revise and remember a list of historical authors and the historical topics or concepts that each author was linked to for her exam. To remember the information, she transformed the topics into colourful wall posters. On the posters, historical concepts were converted into her own hand-drawn images. Arrows from the images would link to the authors' names. She placed the posters on the walls of each room around her home so that they were always there as visual reminders. During times of the day when she was cooking, or in the bathroom brushing her teeth, she would look at the posters and describe aloud what they showed. The combination of the visual with the auditory, whereby she could hear herself linking her knowledge to the images, helped to strengthen the information in memory in preparation for the exam:

> My room was covered in big colourful posters. I'd also stick them around the house. Each subject had its own colour, and I would use images to remember certain authors or certain concepts and draw arrows to link ideas together. If I was having a shower or just brushing my teeth, I'd talk about the topic out loud as well.

8.11   Making Summaries of Information

In Chapter 4, we discussed the usefulness of making summaries from your reading by selecting key points and writing in your own words an abbreviated paragraph to help to consolidate your understanding of an article or chapter. This technique is also useful as a revision strategy, as it helps to bring your lecture notes and resources on a topic together, so they are in one place in condensed form.

8.11.1   Reducing Summaries to One Side of A4

For instance, to effectively abbreviate your notes on a subject from the various sources you have accumulated, you could:

- Determine what the main points from these notes are.
- Reduce these main points even further by using bullet points and categorising under headings and keywords.
- Try to contract this information by one more step, to one side of A4 paper, which you can then carry around with you to glance through frequently.

8.11.2   Using a Blank Mind-Map Format to Help to Make Summaries

BSc Medicine student Naomi would use mind-map templates to help with extracting keywords from her topic, hence summarising during the process of completing the mind map. She combined this with saying aloud answers to learning objectives from her lecture notes. As we have seen, she also integrated this auditory aspect with the kinaesthetic by creating her own questions on cards, condensing answers to keywords on separate cards, and laminating these in a machine, followed by matching questions with answers with a peer from her course using a quiz game format, as she describes below.

The mind maps are always good for summaries, but I think it was talking as we talked through all those learning objectives, talking through the learning objectives, and those lamination questions and answers were very good. It was very helpful; I definitely will be continuing that next year, I think.

The above quote demonstrates that once students have found a combination of techniques that are working effectively for memorising the types of information they need to recall during the exam, these strategies become applied each year as the students' own unique way of tackling their revision.

8.11.3   Using Tables to Help with Summarising Work

Summarising your studies by condensing important aspects of your topic into useful tables:

- Forces you to comprehend the subject matter, as you are having to decide what are the essential components of your topic.
- Enables you to evaluate, compare and contrast the various parts of topics in the table, which gives you a deeper understanding of how they interrelate.
- Allows you to carry around for regular review a semester's worth of material relating to the module you are to be examined on, in one amalgamated table.

You can use a table like the ones shown below and just change the number of columns, rows, and aspects of the topic you want to memorise, whether it is themes, concepts, issues or interventions, and so on, from your subject.

	Topic 1	Topic 2	Topic 3
Theme 1			
Theme 2			
Theme 3			

	Strengths	Weaknesses	Comments
Theory 1			
Theory 2			
Theory 3			
Theory 4			

8.12   Timetabling Exams

We should not underestimate the importance of time management during the exam period. This is crucial as it helps to reduce your anxiety and stress both in relation to the run up to exams and throughout the assessment interval, by enabling you to feel organised and in control of what you are to do and when you are to do it. Important questions to know answers to are as follows:

- When are your exams?
- How many exams have you?
- How long is each exam?
- What is the order that the exams will come in?

Using a timetable like the one below, which you can access via the link, and placing it on the wall as a poster near where you study, will help you to keep a record of the topic or module you are to be examined on, the type of exam (multiple-choice questions, open-book exam, etc.), and the date, time and location of each of your exams.

www.cambridge.org/abbottjones

8.12.1   Exam Timetable

Name of Exam	Type of Exam	Day	Date	Time	Location

8.13   Exam Techniques

In relation to constructive strategies for tackling the exam paper on the day of the exam, students with dyslexia spoke about effectively using a range of techniques. As well as timetabling exams (Section 8.12), these included breaking down exam questions, selecting appropriate questions to answer, drawing diagrams, verbalising exam questions, using metacognitive awareness by having breaks when tired or overwhelmed to regroup thoughts, using exam concessions by requesting a more suitable environment for the exam such as a small room, and taking in comforting things to feel reassured during the exam, for instance, by wearing a favourite jumper or writing with a preferred pen. Some students also used mindfulness and attempted to remain calm through breathing exercises, which helped to prevent distracting thoughts and bolstered focus and concentration on answering the questions. As time can be problematic for students with dyslexia, some students would take into the exam a clear-to-read watch or digital timer (if the university allowed this) and would pre-plan by writing down timings for each question before proceeding with their answers. To maximise marks, other students would read through the whole exam paper first and would then put in order questions to answer, starting with responding to questions that they knew most about first. Or they would allocate time according to the question value, so if one question was worth 20% of the marks and another 10%, the 20% question would be given more time and answered before the 10% question, in the attempt to generate a higher score.

Students also use a range of methods specific for tackling each type of exam: for example, particular techniques can be applied for dealing with essay exams, problem-solving exams and open-book exams.

Some of these strategies are elaborated on below.

8.13.1   How to Tackle Essay-Style Exams

In the Preparation Stage

- Read through the entire exam paper and set up a **time schedule** to answer each question.
- Make sure that when you set up your time schedule, you have deducted time to allocate to reviewing and checking through your answers.
- Start with your first question and break down the question by highlighting the **action words** in one colour and the **topic words** in a different colour (please see 'Breaking Down the Question by Highlighting the Instruction and Topic Words' in Chapter 6).
- Using a blank mind map or a drawn-out spidergram, write down **key terms**, **concepts** and/or **themes** in connection to the question. List these as they are fresh in your mind.
- If you prefer to work from a linear plan, using **bullet points** write down your ideas in connection to the question in abbreviated form.
- Have a quick review of your ideas on the mind map/spidergram or linear plan and add **numbers** to the branches or bullet points depending on

the order in which you want to write and present each of the themes, concepts, etc. in the essay (see example of the numbered mind map and linear plan below).

In the Writing Stage

- Use your **first paragraph** to provide an overview of your essay.
- Use the rest of your essay to **discuss these points** in more detail.

To make sure you have all the necessary components in each of your written paragraphs, use the **PEC method** (see 'Structuring Writing Using the Point, Evidence/Example, Comment/Criticism (PEC) Method' in Chapter 6).

- This will ensure that you state your **main point** in the first sentence of each paragraph and that you back up your main points with **examples, evidence, quotations**, etc. Using this method will also make sure that you round off each of your paragraphs by **commenting or critiquing** your examples or evidence.
- Summarise what you have argued or discussed in your last paragraph.
- When the time is up for the first question you have tackled, stop writing, leave space, and begin the next question. The incomplete answers can be completed during the review time.
- Several incomplete answers, one for each of the questions you are expected to answer, will usually receive more marks than complete answers with a few questions left completely unanswered because you have run out of time.

In the Review Stage

- Read through your answers and add to any response you feel you need to clarify.
- If time, add further to any incomplete answers.

8.14   Time Management During the Exam

In addition to managing time by making sure you are keeping a record of when your exams are to take place (Section 8.12), time management during the exam, which has already been discussed a little in this chapter, is also important to oversee.

Students with a formal dyslexia diagnosis evidenced by an Educational Psychologist assessment report qualify for special examination arrangements whilst at university, such as being allowed extra time to complete examinations and timed tests. This is usually in the form of an extra 25% of time (i.e., an additional 15 mins per hour). Consequently, productive planning on how to use the additional allocated time for the exam by dividing time between the number of questions that need to be answered in a paper (see above), whilst also allowing time per question to check and go over responses, was successfully used by BSc Nursing student Lisa:

> I always made sure I had my watch. I always had a watch, and I wrote down timings on a piece of paper which I was allowed to take in with me. This is when your exam starts, this is when it finishes, you need to try and get these bits done and then give yourself this amount of time to go back through it, and I set myself time. I made sure that I wrote everything I need to do within that hour and used those extra 15 minutes to identify all my mistakes, and that's always what I did. I made sure that those 15 minutes was spent reading through really slowly initially and then just a quick skim over in case I missed anything.

For Lisa, the additional 15 minutes per hour was productively used to proofread written responses and to amend any noticeable errors. (Note that universities vary in their reasonable adjustment policies when it comes to exam arrangements for students with dyslexia, and you should check whether a watch is allowed.)

It is also common for Nursing courses like the one being studied by Lisa here to assess students through what is referred to as the open-book exam. Below are some useful strategies for dealing with open-book exams.

8.15   How to Tackle Open-Book Exams

Open-book exams can prove to be a useful evaluation method, as, rather than merely testing your ability to remember information as with the traditional exam, the open-book exam is appraising your skills in understanding, finding and applying relevant information from your sources, notes and textbooks in relation to the exam questions. Yes, as the name 'open book' suggests, with this type of assessment you can take your study materials along with you to the exam. This does not mean, though, that you can just extract the appropriate information from your textbook and copy it down verbatim in response to the question. Instead, you are being asked to demonstrate your capacity to **constructively critique, synthesise and analyse** the information through your written responses to the questions.

In the Preparation Stage

- Find out from your tutor the types of materials you will be allowed to take into the exam.
- Make a list of these.
- Find out from your tutor the topic areas the exam will cover.
- Make a list of these, which will help to form your revision guide/timetable, and will show the emphasis that you should place on ensuring you can easily find these topics when it comes to preparing your resources.

- Find out from your tutor the types of responses you will need to give to the questions – essays, short answers etc.

Preparing Your Resources

- Gather the materials you know you can take in with you to the exam.
- With textbooks, use the **contents** and **index pages** and place colourful **bookmarks** or sticky notes to make it easy in the exam to locate the relevant topics.
- Write **brief summaries** and your **own interpretations** in the **margins of texts** alongside the topics, and again place colourful or colour-coded bookmarks onto these so they are easy to find.
- To ensure that you are using **criticality and synthesis** in your exam responses, either in the margins of texts, or on sticky notes placed where you can easily find with colourful bookmarks, write in abbreviated form and in your own words:
  - Your understanding of what the topic is.
  - The topic's strengths and weakness.
  - A reference, if applicable, to another topic, author, source which may have expanded further or critiqued the topic.
  - This linking to other topics, authors, sources will enable you to demonstrate your synthesis of materials easily during the exam without having to waste time searching through your sources.
- Using one colour-coded index card per book or resource, **condense the content** of the textbook down onto the card by listing key topics and relevant page numbers. The cards can then help you to identify the information quickly.

In the Answering Stage

- Read through the entire exam paper and set up a **time schedule** to answer each question.

311

- Make sure you have deducted time to allow for reviewing and checking through your answers.
- Break down each question you are answering first by highlighting the **action words** in one colour and the **topic words** in a different colour.
- Use a blank drawn-out spidergram, or linear plan using bullet points, and write down the key terms, concepts and/or themes in connection to the question.
- Find the topic and key terms/concepts in your sources using your index cards and bookmarks, and respond to the question using your notes from the margins/sticky notes.
- You can use the **PEC method** (see Chapter 6 *Essay-Writing Strategies*) to help to construct your answers and ensure in your answer you are linking by referring to other topics and ideas to show your criticality and synthesis of your materials.

In the Review Stage

- Read through your answers and add any **further clarification** or **references to other materials** that will demonstrate your knowledge on the topic more substantially.
- If time, add further to any incomplete answers.

8.16   Selecting Questions

Whilst we briefly mentioned above the technique of reading through the whole exam paper during the preparation stage, to select the questions that you know most about to respond to first, the importance of this strategy for maximising your marks cannot be underestimated. For example, in her early exams, BA Education student Sam would work through the paper tackling the questions in the order they were presented. Disappointed by exam results, Sam came to realise that in doing this she would often come to questions later in the paper that tapped into her knowledge more effectively, but because of her inefficiencies in time management, she would regularly run out of time before being able to demonstrate her understanding of the question.

In later exams, however, she learned to strategically read through the entire paper at the start of the exam and would place marks against questions she knew she was able to answer. She would then progress through the exam, not in chronological order of the paper, but in the order of the questions where she knew she was most able to demonstrate her knowledge. That way, if all questions were equally weighted in terms of marks, she knew she was maximising the number of marks allocated by answering questions in order of what she was most knowledgeable about:

> It's just being calm. What I shall do is read the questions thoroughly. If I see a question that I know more about, then I will answer that first. I won't necessarily start at question 1. If question 1 is the one that I know the information about, then I will quickly write that down, but if it's question 10, I will start there and then go back, or go forward, so it works variously for me.

Another type of exam that you may be asked to do could include a multiple-choice exam. Some techniques listed below may be helpful for dealing with this type of exam:

8.17   How to Tackle Multiple-Choice Exams

With multiple-choice exams, you are usually given questions with each question having four options/answers to choose from, one of which will be the correct answer. These types of questions usually look like the example below:

What is the capital of France?

- Paris.
- Rome.
- Marseille.
- Perth

With multiple-choice questions, you will always have:

- **A definite yes answer**, which in this case is Paris.
- **A definite no answer**, which is Rome, the capital of Italy, a separate country entirely.
- **A perhaps, maybe, could be answer**, which is Marseille as it is the second biggest city in France, so could be confused with its capital.
- **A trick answer**, which could be similar to the correct answer, but is there to distract you. In this case, the trick is Perth, as it is the capital of Western Australia, and the word looks similar in appearance to the correct answer Paris. With trick questions, your tutor is not trying to deceive or outwit you, they are just examining your decision-making skills.

A useful technique for dealing with these questions is through the process of elimination as follows:

- Read the question, cover up the answers and see if you can retrieve the correct answer before looking at the options.
- Read all the answers slowly and carefully.
- Get rid of the answer you perceive as the definite no.
- Then rule out the answer that you would say is the perhaps, maybe, could be answer.
- Identify the trick answer and decide why this is the trick answer and rule it out.
- You should then be left with your answer.

To help to make the process of elimination clearer when working on identifying the correct option for a question, you could create your own set of symbols that you quickly draw next to each type of answer. That way you will be prevented from being confused in having to re-read through answers to the question, as you may have forgotten the type of answer you originally allocated it as. For example, you could have a symbol like a cross assigned to answers you have decided are the **no**, a different symbol such as an arrow for **perhaps** answers, an alternative symbol like a lightning sign for **trick,** and a final symbol to represent the **yes** and correct answers. **Process of elimination** teamed with **symbol allocation** should help avoid indecision and accelerate your progress through the paper, leaving you with enough time to check your responses. The table below, accessible through the Resources link, will help you to create the type of symbols you would like to use.

www.cambridge.org/abbottjones

8.17.1   Table for Making Symbols to Allocate to Different Types of Answer

Definite Yes	
Definite No	
Perhaps: Maybe: Could Be	
Trick	

8.18   Verbalising Exam Questions

During an exam, it is conventional for students to be required to read the questions on the exam paper silently to themselves. However, this can cause difficulties for students with dyslexia who when reading silently may struggle to decode words accurately or could easily skip words in the question, consequently misinterpreting the question. Some students with dyslexia can gain a deeper and more accurate meaning of a question if they associate what they visually see in writing on an exam paper with hearing it aloud. Thus, PhD student Ada would use the strategy of mouthing the words in the question to herself so she could hear them, to ensure she had the correct semantic sense of what was being asked:

> I also would always talk it through in my head. As well as reading it, I would slightly mouth the words, because for some reason, mouthing it, or talking it, would show where I've missed something. But because you're in an exam condition, it's more like whisper, whisper. It's like an ever so tiny whisper, so as not to disturb anyone else.

Whilst students with a formal diagnosis of dyslexia undertaking exams at university should have the option of being able to work in a smaller quieter room, if you feel that you would be at a lesser disadvantage by being able to verbalise your exam questions so you can accurately decode the question, you should have a word with the tutor setting the exam, or with the exam invigilator, to see if they are able to accommodate this.

8.19   Practical and Favourite Things

A technique to lessen anxiety during the exam, which may help you to feel more relaxed, is to take in a favourite object which you identify with security, or to wear something familiar to help you to feel comfortable during the test. For example, MA Humanities student Charlie, when preparing for an exam, would practise past papers in her room at home under timed conditions. She would frequently put herself through this experience to develop her ability to tackle the exam paper under time pressure and to lessen the anxiety she had in connection to exams. She believed that, as with most things, the more times you do something, the less overwhelming it becomes. On taking the exams at home, she would always use her favourite pen and would wear her favourite jumper. On the day of the official exam, she took the pen and wore the jumper, which, being associated with her home and with comfort, helped to erad-icate her nerves:

> I had the same pen and I used to wear the same jumper, so when I was in the exam, I would be writing with the same pen in the same jumper, and it would just feel like I would be writing in my bedroom.

Any object or item of clothing, if associated with safety or providing a homely feel, can help to alleviate nerves and anxiety during the exam, which in turn allows cognitive functioning to work more effec-tively in tackling the exam paper.

8.20   Summary

In summary, this chapter has:

- Specified common difficulties with revision for the student with dyslexia.
- Outlined obstacles with exams for students with dyslexia.
- Presented a range of effective revision methods, which included:
  - Being creative and making own revision books and colourful posters.
  - Using mind maps, sticky notes, flash cards.
  - Recording revision notes.
  - Creating visual diagrams and flow charts on A3 paper.

- Making questions and searching for answers.
- Interpreting material into own language.
- Comparing revision notes with someone.
- Talking to someone about the material.
- Turning revision into a rhythm or a rap.
- Using memory joggers/mnemonics.
- Using review cycle.
- Identified ways of staying motivated during revision by:
  - Using to-do lists, setting a purpose and planning the revision.
- Detailed ways of using other proven productive revision methods, such as:
  - Setting out ways of creating questions from your revision and the advantages of this.
  - Practising past papers.
  - Using repetition through a process of condensing and re-reading information.
  - Applying spaced repetition.
  - Utilising multisensory methods.
  - Making summaries of information.
- Listed a range of constructive methods for tackling the exam, which included:
  - Timetabling exams and time management during the exam.
  - Strategies for tackling essay-style exams.
  - Techniques for tackling open-book exams.
  - Selecting appropriate questions to answer.
  - Ways of tackling multiple-choice exams.
  - Verbalising exam questions aloud.
  - Taking favourite things into the exam to help to eradicate anxiety.

9

• • • • •

Presentation
Techniques

9.1   Introduction

This chapter begins by describing difficulties with presentations faced by the student with dyslexia. Whilst these obstacles are in both the cognitive and emotional realm, the reader will identify that the larger challenge for the dyslexic learner is in overcoming barriers such as the fear and anxiety connected with presentations. Specifying these impediments leads to practical methods for helping to alleviate these problems, as described from the voices of students with dyslexia. These strategies include: making a plan; using visual images; preparation by continuous rehearsal and timing; using activities for audience participation to take the spotlight off oneself; and ensuring the topic selected for presentation is interesting and enjoyable, to assist with motivation, planning and delivery, and also to ensure that audience questions can be answered through the student's wider interest in the topic. Advice on techniques is punctuated by quotes from students with dyslexia who use the methods presented. For example, below, Charlie uses marks on her presentation script to help with alleviating nervousness:

> If I do panic and start to talk too fast, I can see from the slashes where I can pause and breathe and then restart.

These quotes from students not only help to illuminate appropriate methods, but also provide the reader with identification hooks for recognising the emotional aspects of learning. For instance, the quote above illustrates how worry about panicking during the presentation is combatted by a pragmatic solution applied to the script.

9.2 Common Difficulties with Presentations for Students with Dyslexia

What was most noticeable during interviews in Abbott-Jones (2022) was when students with dyslexia were asked what challenges they faced with presentations, the response of identifying an emotional difficulty before specifying any type of cognitive difficulty was commonplace. For example, MA Arts student Debra spoke about fear and anxiety generated from presenting in front of people who do not particularly understand difficulties associated with dyslexia, and the feeling of being judged by her audience. She stated:

> So now I feel a hundred per cent comfortable with you here. I'm talking, I feel really relaxed, and I feel that my answers are really articulate, but that's because you know I have dyslexia and you're a specialist in dyslexia. It's almost like you're understanding and you're not judging

me. If I was in a job interview hoping to get a job, or in an academic situation, I would feel that people are judging my academic ability, or my professional ability, and it comes back to that kind of stupid, stupidity feeling as a child, or not being good enough, and I would really stutter, repeat. I repeat myself quite a lot. As I get older, I am learning to deal with it, I think as you become more mature, so it's more of a relief now, but no, it's still there. It's still there.

The awareness of caring too much about what others think, self-doubt due to negative school experiences and feeling negatively evaluated by others are unfavourable emotions encountered all too often by students with dyslexia in association with tasks such as presentations. This detrimental emotion was felt so intensely by MA Education student and full-time teacher Chloe that although she could confidently stand up to speak in front of a class full of pupils at her school, when it came to presenting in front of her peers at university, she would refuse to undertake the assignment.

It's really weird, because I do it every day, six times a day, all the time. It's adults, I don't know, I feel judged. I feel I will block, and I feel I will forget everything, and this awkward silence will appear, and I have no idea where I'm going next. Or that I'm talking, if I'm just talking at least, it helps a little bit, but also that I'm talking and suddenly I realise nobody has a clue what I'm saying because I lost them.

This fear of exposure and being critically assessed disparagingly by an audience is very well documented in an early (1971) paper by Howard Rome titled 'The psychiatric aspects of dyslexia'. Rome highlights the associated emotional problems of dyslexia by questioning, 'is it not conceivable that in attempting to adapt to a handicap that continually makes progressively more demands from age six on, a person afflicted will likely develop anxiety, frustration, resentment, and bitterness when normal social circumstances constantly threaten to expose the handicap to the world?' (Rome, 1971, p. 64).

Rome's focus here is on the nature of dyslexia as an invisible disability, and consequently, the affected person's manifestation of anxiety is caused by the fear of being revealed as someone struggling to meet typical social norms and expectations, particularly in learning development. Rome suggests that this fear of exposure is a source for the anxiety: 'the chronic anxiety that this provokes is a variant of the phobic state, one in which a realistic fear of exposure is implicit in all situations and explicit in certain ones in particular' (Rome, 1971, p. 69).

In practitioner experience, this terror of being judged is witnessed all too often when capable students with dyslexia refuse to do presentations, as in the example of Chloe above, because they feel vulnerable when displaying perceived weaknesses. Rome goes on to suggest that 'visible or invisible, one's sense of personal worth (self-esteem) is constantly being valued and revalued in accordance with the myriad of tasks he is called upon to perform in social milieu that are constantly changing' (Rome, 1971, p. 66). Thus, as the dyslexia impinges upon the increasing complexity of academic tasks from childhood through to adolescence, the person's sense of self-esteem is continuously being damaged. As a consequence, presentations involving a high level of display to an appraising audience are a task that students with already damaged self-esteem will attempt to avoid, to protect their self-esteem from further harm.

Let us now look more positively at a set of strategies that may help to alleviate the nervousness associated with presentations.

9.3   Techniques for Dealing with Presentations

Techniques to alleviate anxiety over thoughts of the presentation and to ensure that the talk goes well on the day essentially include the processes of preparation, rehearsal and practice. These strategies are dealt with in more detail below.

9.3.1 Making a Plan

In addition to creating a draft of points you would like to say, you may find it useful in the initial stages of the work to devise an overall plan for the project by listing the types of tasks involved, placing these in order of priority, and working out an achievable timeframe for each step. This will help you to identify the activities included in putting together a well-researched and engaging presentation, and will also break down what may feel like an overwhelming task into a series of more manageable parts. The plan can be similar to the example presented in the *Essay-Writing Strategies* chapter. Below is an illustration of how this can be done.

9.3.2 Example of Planning the Tasks and Time for Your Presentation

If you are struggling to identify tasks and plan timeframes for the steps involved in preparing for a presentation, a clear example of this is provided here and accessible via the link to Resources. You just need to readjust the timescale for each task depending on how much time you have in the run up to the presentation.

www.cambridge.org/abbottjones

Steps Involved in Preparing for a Presentation, with Timeframes

Read, Interpret and Understand the Assessment Brief – A Few Hours
Consider the criteria and the aims of the presentation. This will inform the research for your topic and will give you an idea of the

main points you want to deliver to your audience. For example, if your assignment states that the objective of your presentation is to show your knowledge of a particular subject, then you know that in preparation for your talk, you will need to learn about all aspects of that area. If, however, your brief is centred around assessing your communication skills and ability to engage with the audience, then you will need to concentrate more on practising the delivery of your talk.

Research Your Topic – A Couple of Weeks
Like the way in which you researched a topic for essay writing, to be able to talk knowledgeably on the subject and deal effectively with audience questions, you will have to gather the relevant information on the area you are presenting. This can be achieved by using library catalogues to search for appropriate journals and books, databases to find suitable peer-reviewed articles, and internet search engines to find additional knowledge connected to the topic.

Read through the Information You Have Gathered, and Take Notes – 2 to 3 Weeks
Again, in the same way you prepare to make an essay plan, you will firstly need to select from the information the pertinent material that fits with the aspects of the topic you have been asked to talk about. Secondly, you should go through the reading applying a suitable note-taking strategy to pull out the relevant points to put into your presentation.

Write an Outline of Your Talk – A Few Hours
From the notes you made on going through your reading materials, you will now be able to either mind map, or list in bullet point form, the main things you want to say during your talk. The questions below may also help you to make a suitable outline.

- What is your topic?
- What do you know about the topic?
- What do you want your audience to know?

Create Your Visual Slides to Complement Your Verbal Message – 1 to 2 Weeks

Begin to make your slides by using a mixture of abbreviated bullet points signifying ideas and thoughts which you can expand upon during the talk, together with any images or diagrams which can be used to enhance and illustrate your message. The key when creating the slides is to not overwhelm the audience by putting too much written text on, but to keep visuals simple, limiting the number of words used. The minimal text should be there to enhance what you are trying to say and should not detract from it.

Develop the Presentation Script – 2 to 3 Weeks

The presentation script, like the essay, should have an Introduction, a middle (where you expand on points) and a Conclusion. Similar to the essay, the body/middle of the presentation, where you deliver your main points in logical order, should be backed up with evidence from your research to support your argument, examples and, if appropriate, statistics. More detail on developing the content for the script is provided below.

Practise Your Presentation – The Remaining Time

If you are given a set length of time to deliver your talk, you can rehearse the presentation by verbalising your script out loud, in conjunction with showing your slides, whilst timing yourself. If your talk exceeds the time, you can edit out some of the content. If it is too short, you know you have leeway either to expand on some of the points or to add more information. You should then practise the talk repeatedly to feel more confident, knowledgeable and comfortable when it comes to the actual presentation.

9.4   Developing a Presentation Script

Before looking at ways of structuring content for the presentation, let us first go through some practicalities that will help to make the script work effectively for you. As presentations in front of a live audience can often generate nerves and anxiety, which can have the effect of causing mental blocks and can easily lead to the misreading/misinterpretation of text in a document, it is advisable to avoid convoluted language and words that are difficult to pronounce. Try to use words that you would use in general conversation with friends, or to use lay terms when talking about your topic. That way, your audience will be able to engage more thoroughly with the presentation, and your anxiety will be lessened by knowing you do not have to attempt to articulate complex language. This technique was used by MA Humanities student Charlie, described below:

> The way that I prepare presentations is very similar to exams in that I will have a script written, and it will be written as similar to my essay, but it will be all words that I know I can pronounce well. I kind of write as I speak, and I think that sort of comes across.

Another reassuring function of the script is that it can be used to display signs, symbols or marks for things to remember, such as places to display visual/audio images to highlight the talk, or, as in the case of Charlie in the introduction, to indicate places to pause and to take a minute for the purpose of easing panic:

> I will read it out loud and I will put little slashes, little like forward slashes in pencil on my script, so I know that if I do panic and start

to talk too fast, I can see from the slashes where I can pause and breathe and then restart.

Rather than using a big A4 sheet of paper for the script, which can easily be used to hide behind if nervous, thus creating a barrier with the audience, it is preferrable to use smaller, handheld, coloured presentation or record cards, or a small (A5) notepad. That way, interaction and eye contact with the listeners can be maintained, and your talk should retain its natural delivery without sounding too scripted.

Let us now move on to discuss some ideas for ordering the content of your speech.

9.4.1 Structuring Content

As with essays, your presentation script should have an Introduction, a main body, and a Conclusion. Let us take each of the elements separately to discuss the type of material we could include in each.

The Introduction

The Introduction of your presentation is where you engage your audience's attention. Depending on the nature and context of your talk, you can either begin by using an attention-grabbing technique or use a more formal introduction. Here are some ideas for both.

Attention-Grabbing Introduction

- You could start your talk by *asking a stimulating question* to act as a hook for capturing your audience's attention. For example, if you were doing a presentation on climate change, you may ask, 'How many degrees has the Earth warmed since 2000?' That way, you have begun your speech by engaging the audience, and you can maintain their attentiveness until you reveal the answer in the main body of your talk.

327

- Your presentation could begin by *showing a disturbing statistic* or by *displaying a thought-provoking image*. Your audience then immediately wants to know more about what has led to the statistic, or what the story is behind the image, which you deliver through your key points.

Formal Introduction

- For a more formal introduction, you should begin by:
- Introducing yourself.
- Outlining what you will be talking about – for example, the title of the presentation, the topic, and the aspects of the topic you will be focusing on.

The Main Body

- The main body of your script is used to discuss your key points in a logical order, using evidence and examples from your research to support your ideas.
- The evidence could take the form of factual data, quotes from peer-reviewed articles or academic books, statistics and diagrams.
- You can present the evidence in imaginative and creative ways by using visual slides or video segments, which will add clarity and colour to your talk.

The Conclusion

- The Conclusion is where you will remind the audience of your main points by summarising what you have discussed. For example, you could begin your Conclusion with the statement, 'In this presentation we discussed the following points….'
- You will then come to an end by thanking the audience for listening and will invite any questions.
- You could also conclude with a parting stimulating sentence to encourage your audience to reflect on the content of what you previously discussed.

Next, we will have a look at ways of using visual images to enhance the substance of our speech.

9.5   Using Visual Images

Fortunately, students with dyslexia generally have strengths in transforming words into pictures. Furthermore, the use of images in presentations is particularly helpful for students with dyslexia, because, as we have seen in previous chapters, visualisation can be used as an effective memory jogger for unlocking speech if the mind goes blank during the talk. This was exemplified in Chapter 3, when MA Arts student Debra spoke about how she placed information she was learning into memory:

> Keyword or drawing something visual, then it's like, oh there it is. It's like the closet you open, when everything falls out, but it's sometimes finding that little thing that will open the door. It's finding the key basically.

Another positive aspect of images is that words that are difficult to spell can be replaced by drawings, as explained by BSc Nursing student Tina:

> I will draw pictures of certain aspects that I can't spell, and people still get what it is. If I can't spell a word like thermometer or something – why on earth would I be able to spell thermometer? I will just draw a thermometer.

Additionally, in Abbott-Jones (2022) when students were asked about how they felt about undertaking presentations, it was discovered that as students with dyslexia believed they had visual strengths, they enjoyed using PowerPoint and mind-mapping software to create slides. Visuals were also used as a resourceful device

329

to help to take audience attention away from the self, as discussed by MSc Humanities student Alison and Nursing student Lisa:

> Because I'm quite good at visual stuff, I always spend too much time making my PowerPoint presentation look nice to be impressive and to take some of the attention away from me. (Alison)

> I will mind map, I love mind mapping, if I have to present my work. (Lisa)

When it comes to creating the slides for your talk, the main things to consider are the layout, the images, the fonts and the colour. In an interesting article by Alley and Neeley (2005) titled 'Rethinking the design of presentation slides', the authors gathered a series of criticisms regarding the default styles provided by PowerPoint. They state:

> The default styles of PowerPoint limit the amount of detail that can reasonably be presented and often obscure logical connections (or the lack thereof) among facts used to make an argument. In a similar vein, Shaw and colleagues (1998) point out that bullet points 'leave critical assumptions unstated' and 'critical relationships unspecified.' Perhaps the most common criticism is that presentations using PowerPoint have become overly predictable and generic. John Schwartz (2003) characterised this phenomenon as "PowerPoint's tendency to turn any information into a dull recitation of look-alike factoids" (Alley and Neeley, 2005, p. 418).

Consequently, Alley and Neeley (2005) have created a series of guidelines, providing an alternative design from the default styles supplied by the software, yet still using PowerPoint. They say their design helps to orient the audience better so they can comprehend the presentation more easily, and as the slides are more memorable the audience retains information from the speech for longer. Some of the ideas from Alley and Neeley's substitute plan are delivered below, so you may want to have a go at these the next time you prepare for a PowerPoint presentation, to see if they make your slides appear more powerful.

9.5.1   The Layout

Alley and Neeley suggest:

- For every slide other than the title slide, use a single-sentence head-line that states the slide's main assertion. For example, rather than using 'Results' as a headline, Alley and Neeley propose you should use something more explanatory, such as 'Dyslexic students had higher level of anxiety than their non-dyslexic peers'. That way, the audience are explicitly told the findings of a study immediately by the headline.
- Left-justify the headline in the slide's upper left corner, which fits naturally with the Western convention of reading from left to right.
- Avoid bulleted lists where possible, because, as Alley and Neeley argue, such lists do not show the connections among the listed items.
- However, if you do need to use bullet-pointed lists, try to keep these to two, three or four items.
- Limit the number of slides so that at least one minute can be spent on each slide (preferably more time in a longer presentation of up to, say, one hour).

9.5.2   The Images

- On the title slide, include an image that orients the audience to the talk's main subject or purpose.
- In the body of each slide, present supporting evidence in a visual way with images, graphs or visual arrangements, such as tables or prefera-bly drawings, connected by arrows, which is useful for showing pro-cesses and how separate elements link together.
- End with a conclusion slide and an appropriate image for summarising the talk.

9.5.3   The Fonts

- Use sans-serif fonts such as Arial and Verdana, which are easier for your audience to read. Make them bold.
- On a typical slide, use 28-point type for the headline and 18- to 24-point type for the body text.
- Larger type is appropriate for the title on the title slide.
- Avoid setting the text using all capital letters.

9.5.4   The Colour

- Use simple colours and avoid using multiple clashing colours that can cause distraction and eye fatigue.
- Bright white backgrounds, which make text look harsh and difficult to read, are unsuitable for people with dyslexia. Non-dyslexics can also get visual stress if colours are too contrasting. Off-white or cream backgrounds can help to make the text appear softer to read.

Next, we move on to looking at ways of feeling prepared and confident with the presentation.

9.6   Preparation, Rehearsal and Timing

In Abbott-Jones (2022), when students with dyslexia were asked how they ensured they were feeling comfortable with performing their talk on the day, preparation by rehearsing proved to be a consistent theme for alleviating nervousness and anxiety. Twelve out of the 20 students with dyslexia said they would plan and repeatedly perform the presentation. This would be done whilst timing the speech to indicate whether it needed to be edited down or expanded upon to meet the allocated time. The advantages of rehearsing your presentation, in addition to helping you to build confidence, are that you will become more familiar with the information you are delivering, and during your practice sessions, you will be able to make the content flow more productively by cutting out anything unnecessary or illogical. Below are some ideas you may want to trial during your rehearsals:

9.6.1   Time Your Presentation

As emphasised in Section 9.3.1 'Making a Plan', timing your talk when you are rehearsing is key to ensure you can cover everything you want to say within the specified time limit and that you do not exceed this on the day. If you are concentrating on your content delivery at the same time as estimating the length of your speech, it could be advisable to ask a friend or relative to time you. That way, you can focus on the structure and organisation of the information, and your friend can observe and provide feedback on your talk whilst simultaneously checking you are adhering to the time limit. This was a strategy used by MA Humanities student Charlie, who would ask her mum to help:

> Usually there is a time limit. I make sure that it is to the time limit, so I will practise it with my mum, and she will time me and then I will cut it if it needs to be shorter.

9.6.2   Rehearse in Front of an Audience

On expansion of the point above, delivering your presentation to a small group of your peers, a couple of friends, or a single relative like in Charlie's case above, is particularly useful. This is because you are placed under pressure to perform in front of an audience, who can provide you with constructive commentary, which can then be implemented as ways of improving your speech.

9.6.3   Get Your Audience to Ask You Questions on Your Presentation

This is a great strategy for helping you to feel more confident and prepared in dealing with audience questions at the end of your presentation. It also enables you to develop a more comprehensive knowledge of your material, as you have had opportunities to clarify your thinking in practising responding to inquiries on your topic. The types of questions your rehearsal audience ask also give you an insight into the types of things you are likely to be asked on the day of your presentation.

9.6.4   Rehearse Out Loud and Video Record the Presentation

If you are unable to recruit an audience to give you feedback and questions, or if you would just like an additional method of practising, then recording your presentation and watching it back to see points for improvement can be an advantageous technique for instilling more confidence in your performance and delivery. For example, watching the recording will give you instant insight into areas of your speech you may need to simplify or explain more cohesively. The recording will also allow you to check if you need to improve your body language, eye contact and voice intonation. You can then work on these areas and make a second recording to see how your presentation has advanced from the earlier version, which is a great strategy for generating assurance over how you are going to perform on the day of your speech.

Next, we look at some activities to help with audience interaction, which you may want to consider including to accompany your speech.

9.7 Activities for Audience Participation

As mentioned in the introduction, providing the audience with activities so that they can participate more in the presentation is a constructive strategy for taking oneself out of the spotlight, as the spectator instead turns their attention to the task offered, as articulated by MSc Science student Alan:

> The strategy I learnt years ago was taking the focus off me at the beginning of the presentation. If you do that you feel so much better, and as soon as you start talking, you're fine. I generally get people to do an activity, 'What do you think about this?'

9.7.1 Having Access to Wi-Fi during Presentations

In an engaging study by Golub (2005), titled 'On audience activities during presentations', the author conducted an experiment looking at the consequences of keeping Wi-Fi access enabled during students' assessed talks. Results were generally positive for both presenter and audience. For instance, presenters were able to show screenshots of websites they referred to during their speeches. They were also able to browse a search engine during or at the end of a presentation to bring up details of an article or database used as resources for their information gathering. By accessing the Internet on the presentation screen, presenters were able to share materials with the audience, which led to interactive discussions between speaker and spectator.

9.7.2 Use of a Chat Room during the Presentation

The study mentioned above also analysed effects of using a chat room during presentations. Again, productive results were discovered for both speaker and audience, leading to a more interactive and communal experience for all, as the author states:

> The result of this chat room included a mixture of back-channel chatting, sharing of references and resources, and micro-discussions on the topic of the current talk. Although it was not without a learning curve, the students involved claimed it as a great success and an important part of their workshop experience.

Furthermore, the author found that the chat room provided a source of constructive social support amongst the students:

> One particularly interesting anecdote is that a student who had a question they did not feel confident about asking the speaker basically asked it in the chat room. The other members of the chat room had a discussion around it and encouraged the student to ask their question. After the student asked their question, she told me that there was no way she would have done so without the encouragement of the chat room members, and that she was very happy that they convinced her to do so.

Consequently, if you feel that both you and audience would benefit from these technological supplements, and it would lead to enhancing your speech as a more shared experience, then you should enable internet access and the chat feature to your PowerPoint.

9.7.3 Use of Props

Use of physical, tangible props is another technique for increasing audience participation while you present. You can either use hand-held objects during your talk to demonstrate ideas, or you can pass them around the audience so they have something tactile to engage with. For example, if your talk is in medical sciences, you may want to illustrate processes through using a model of a heart, lung or kidney; or if you are doing a speech on art, you could encourage your audience to have a more kinaesthetic experience by handling an artwork such as a ceramic or sculpture.

9.7.4   Use of Activities

You could incorporate activities into your speech to make it more engaging. For instance, you could ask your audience members to work in pairs, and you could provide them with a short activity to complete. The activity could be anything from icebreakers, quizzes, puzzles or word games to having a few minutes of conversation with each other on a selected topic. This could be done just to generate more alertness and energy amongst the audience or could illustrate the context of the speech.

In addition to coming up with ways of heightening the interactiveness of your talk, you need to ensure you pick an enjoyable topic to speak about. This will maintain your motivation in researching, planning, preparing, rehearsing, conducting and answering audience questions on your presentation.

9.8   Picking the Right Topic

Sometimes topics for presentation are pre-set for you in the assignment brief and you must adhere to delivering a talk on a subject selected by your tutor. If this is the case, you are likely to still have scope to pick a specific aspect of the topic that you have particular interest in, so that you can tailor the talk around a concise theme, which will help to make it more absorbing for your audience. On occasion, however, you may be given freedom to select from a diverse range of topics in your subject area. If that is the case, you should choose something that appeals to you, as you will find it easier to research and to talk about something you enjoy, as in the case of trainee Nurse Lisa below. She believed that if she chose an engaging topic to present, it would maintain her motivation in the planning and delivery of the presentation. It would also ensure that she would be able to answer audience questions on the topic:

> Pick something that you enjoy, because for me, if they ask a question, I can answer it no problem because I enjoy it.As demonstrated by Lisa, the more interest you have in the topic selected for presentation, the easier it will be to remain driven to develop further knowledge on the area, which will help you effectively deal with audience questions. Some tips for ensuring that you pick something absorbing for your talk are as follows.

Pick an Area in Which You Have Received Positive Feedback on Previous Assessed Work

Choosing a topic that you know you are good at and knowledgeable about will help you to feel more confident in delivering your presentation. You will also be able to demonstrate the extent of your understanding on the subject when it comes to answering any questions.

Pick Something You Are Passionate About

If you are free to select a topic of your choice, you should take the opportunity to present on a subject you are passionate about. The intensity of your enthusiasm in relation to the area you are discussing will help to keep your audience alert and engaged. Furthermore, presenting a topic you feel impassioned about will help you to be in a strong position to defend your viewpoint if challenged during audience questions.

As mentioned above, effectively dealing with audience questions is an important aspect of presentations. As such, below are a few techniques for tackling queries on your talk professionally and productively.

9.9   Dealing with Audience Questions

The first and foremost thing to remember with questions asked by audience members in connection with your presentation is that they are positive forms of feedback. Your audience is inquiring further into your topic because they have been stimulated by something you have said, they want further information on a particular issue, or they are interested to hear more on your opinion about a certain aspect. So, when it comes to dealing with questions, do not be defensive, but treat the queries as opportunities to develop open discussion and interaction with the audience on your subject. Furthermore, if you handle the questions directly and honestly and in a manner that helps your listener to be more informed about the specific points you have raised during the presentation, then you will earn the audience's respect as someone who wants others to understand their area.

State at the Start of the Presentation That You Will Take Questions at the End

The norm for presentations is that questions are generally asked at the end of the speech. However, audience members may not always be aware of this. If you are easily distracted by being interrupted mid-flow and having your train of thought disrupted by questions, then as it is your presentation and you are in control of it, you should inform your audience before you begin your talk that you will take questions at the end. That way, the audience knows to make notes on any areas they may want to look at in more detail. They can then explore these further with you after your presentation has concluded.

Repeat or Paraphrase the Question
If you are uncertain as to what you have been asked, an effective technique is, firstly, to ask for clarification from your questioner by simply saying, 'Could you please repeat the question?' In most cases, the audience member will ensure they rephrase the question to ask it clearly, simply or in a more straightforward way, to make certain that you understand and can provide the answer they are seeking. However, if you are still struggling with interpreting the question, then you can repeat or paraphrase what they have asked. Your questioner will then, most likely, assist you in clarifying what they are saying to avoid any misunderstandings.

Pause and Reflect Before Answering the Question
Once asked a question, take a pause, which enables you to process what has been asked and gives you the time to reflect on an appropriate answer. After you have considered a suitable response, take your time to deliver this to your questioner rather than rushing your answer, which may then come across as confused or uncertain.

Chunk Your Answer or Put It into Threes
If an answer to an audience member's question is going to be long and you are struggling to think of ways to make it more concise, then a constructive strategy is to either chunk the answer into sections so

that it is delivered clearly or provide the answer by distinctly stating it as three points, which makes the explanation easier for the listener to retain. Say, for example, your presentation has been in medicine, focusing on processes involved in the heart's pumping cycle, and your listener asks, 'How does the heart function?', then you can return to a diagram used for your speech and can break up your response into segments by explaining, firstly, how the systole phase (the heart pushing blood out) works, before moving on to clarification of how, secondly, the diastole (blood filling the heart chambers) functions. As your answer is in segments, your questioner can digest the information more effectively. If you have delivered a speech on climate change and the spectator asks, 'What are the causes of climate change?', even though your presentation may have been more complex, the specification of three of the larger influencing factors, such as fossil fuels, deforestation, and farming livestock, enables your audience to process and retain the information more productively, so you can be satisfied they have taken something memorable away from the talk.

If You Do Not Know the Answer to the Question, Be Honest and Say So

Never try to make up a response to a question and bluff your way through. Your audience will be able to detect that you are not sure what you are talking about. Instead, to retain your audience's respect, you should openly admit that you do not know the answer. You can also explain that although you are unaware of the appropriate information, this, however, is what you do know about the topic. That way, you are coming across as wanting to help your listeners by offering the knowledge that you do have in relation to the subject. Another effective method is to ask if any of your audience members can supply the answer. As such, you constructively transform your question-and-answer session into an interactive discussion.

9.10   Summary

In summary, this chapter has:

- Presented difficulties with presentations faced by the student with dyslexia.
- Discussed strategies for overcoming the barriers connected with presentations as described from the voices of students with dyslexia, which included:
  - Making plans.
  - Using visual images.
  - Preparation by continuous rehearsal and timing.
  - Using activities for audience participation for the purpose of taking the spotlight off oneself.
  - Ensuring the topic selected for presentation is interesting and enjoyable to assist with motivation.
  - Effectively dealing with audience questions.

10

· · · · ·

Public Speaking, Interviews, Seminar Discussion and Debate Techniques

10.1   Introduction

If students have phonological difficulties combined with deficits in short-term/working memory, this causes anxieties around academic tasks such as delivering presentations and verbally contributing to seminar discussion and debate. That is because these deficits impair the acquisition and production of spoken language, and manifest as word-finding difficulties. If the student has any form of social anxiety connected with fear of being exposed and judged by others, this also leads to problems when required to interact verbally with a group of peers. Consequently, this chapter firstly specifies the types of obstacles that students with dyslexia may face when asked to

343

take part in class discussion, which will help to develop a deeper understanding as to why these problems exist.

Secondly, ways of overcoming these barriers are provided by looking at techniques used by students with dyslexia who have the difficulties noted above. These strategies will help to deal with anxiety connected to expressing ideas verbally and can also help to combat any issues around speech production. The methods include: preparation for class discussion by taking brief notes into the seminar, written in an ordered structure to guide verbalisation; asking questions to demonstrate critical thinking and to develop debate; and using the multisensory technique of hearing ideas spoken aloud during preparation stage, recording these, playing them back to hear, then jotting down keywords from the recording to take along to the seminar to act as visual memory joggers. Illustrative examples of each strategy are provided, with clear step-by-step guidance on using the techniques.

Thirdly, public speaking is an undertaking that most people, whether dyslexic or not, find daunting. As such, a range of strategies is offered to develop confidence when participating in any form of public speaking, whether a seminar discussion, a formal presentation, interaction with colleagues at networking events, or just general informal conversation amongst a group of friends. This section therefore not only helps to provide various tools for developing self-assurance with public speaking but also assists with providing appropriate techniques depending on whether you are having to speak to inform, to persuade, to actuate or to entertain.

Finally, interviews, whether for part-time work whilst at university or for graduate posts, can be an anxiety-provoking situation for students with dyslexia. The anxiety may be heightened as the student may not know what to expect or what questions they will be asked. For example, there are so many different types of interviews, ranging from behavioural, to case interviews, to panel interviews, unstructured interviews and competency-based interviews. They can be a minefield to navigate and to know how to prepare for. Consequently, clarification is delivered here on what the different kinds of interview require from the candidate, and advice is supplied on how to plan for and feel more assured when tackling each kind of interview.

10.2　Common Difficulties with Seminars for Students with Dyslexia

As noted in Chapter 1 when discussing the McDougall et al. (1994) study, there is empirical evidence to suggest that if a phonological difficulty exists, this may be related to 'an underlying problem with speech production mechanisms that also results in impaired speech rate' (Hulme & Snowling, 2009, p. 62). When looking at what students with dyslexia said when describing how they felt about seminar discussion at university, this impediment becomes apparent (Abbott-Jones, 2022). For example, BSc Sciences student Fiona said she felt awkward contributing to seminar discussion because of her worry that she would be unable to articulate herself clearly:

> If it's in an academic seminar, I'd definitely feel uncomfortable with it. Probably because I wouldn't say I'm the most efficient speaker, probably stumbling on my words.

Consequently, problems with speech articulation and word-finding difficulties can lead to self-consciousness and embarrassment in front of peers and tutors, as experienced by MA Education student Chloe:

Again, it's that the words don't come out. Almost like blocking words. It doesn't make sense. It makes me feel nervous. It makes me feel like blushing, and I blush really easily, but then I shall blush even more, or at least I will be aware of it because I can feel it. I shall feel everything shaking a little bit.

The humiliation of showing embarrassment, teamed with worry over the student's speaking problems being exposed in front of others, can lead to avoidance, whereby the student does not participate verbally throughout the seminar. This form of disengagement was being used by BA Philosophy student Henry and BSc Nursing student Dean:

But in the seminar groups I would be silent. (Henry)

No, I never contribute anything. I like to sit back and, like, just get on with it. (Dean)

Withdrawal from contributing orally for students with dyslexia is also associated with their difficulties in processing convoluted auditory language during the seminar, as explained by BA English student Cate:

There's definitely been seminars in the past that I just have not really spoken much, and then when you don't speak, then you never speak kind of thing. This year I've definitely spoken in them, but sometimes it's over my head. I'm reasonably okay in groups with speaking, but I definitely sometimes struggle when people say stuff, like complicated stuff and I'm like, 'Oh, I just don't really know what they mean,' and it takes me a second. Or maybe the GTA, the person who is leading the seminar, says something in a convoluted way. I have to ask them to repeat it, you know what I mean.

As seminar discussion is generally based around student viewpoints of an article they have previously read, the retention and retrieval difficulties that students with dyslexia have with their reading can also lead to obstacles in participating verbally. This particularly happens if they feel they have been put on the spot, as described by BA Education student Sam:

Sometimes I feel like I can read something and retain very little of it, or not get a sense. Unless I've been very structured about how I've read it, I might not have any sense of what it said. Then if somebody asks me about it, which obviously in the seminars, I will get asked, 'Is there something that came up for you in the reading?' Then I know, I've got to be put on the spot and I know I've got to have a clear understanding of it, and I don't want to say something that is completely irrelevant.

A further difficulty with seminar discussion could arise if the student has social anxiety. Social anxiety connected to the academic environment can become exacerbated in situations such as seminar debates and presentations that not only involve interaction with academic peers, but also have an element of being observed and judged by an audience. People with dyslexia may be more vulnerable to social anxiety as, firstly, there is the fear that weaknesses with verbal language can be exposed during social interaction. Secondly, social anxiety may be derived from memories of negative experiences during childhood. If reactivated during learning situations at university, these could cause the student to withdraw from the social activity.

These negative experiences during the school years are documented in Sako's (2016) article 'The social and emotional effects of dyslexia'. Sako states that dyslexia can affect children's social life for five main reasons. Firstly, the child finds it difficult to understand jokes or sarcasm. Secondly, the child can have trouble with finding the right words to articulate, particularly if they are required to respond quickly or must think on their feet. Thirdly, the child may miss or misinterpret social cues. Fourthly, the child could withdraw from sending messages either through text or email to their friends owing to the embarrassment caused by having their written language on display. Finally, the child may remember things inaccurately, owing to difficulties with short-term memory, which others could perhaps interpret as the child being vague, misleading or untrustworthy (Sako, 2016).

Whilst these difficulties with social interaction still exist in adulthood, what is more damaging for the adult dyslexic learner is when the negative experiences leave a lasting impairment (Ingesson, 2007; Nalavany, Carawan & Rennick, 2011). MA Arts student Abu's response to the question of how dyslexia affected him illustrates this scenario:

> Socialising, it goes back to the improvising thing, thinking on my feet is always difficult to relate to. I mean the thing that always frightens me is at the beginning of a course, everyone stands up and gives a brief bio about themselves. That always scares me, and I think, everyone's saying exactly the same thing, there's no point.

The response here not only reveals the student's worry with rapid verbal articulation when put on the spot, it also highlights anxiety at being placed in the limelight in front of others, driven by the fear of feeling inadequate. The feeling of not enjoying being in the spotlight becomes a common occurrence for students with dyslexia, as explained by MA Education student Chloe:

> The attention, I don't like to be centre of attention. I like when I forget I'm there and I like when everybody forgets as well, and we are discussing about something. For example, like now, I'm not very conscious of myself because we're kind of sharing this topic, so I'm not conscious about myself. In the beginning I can be, I feel everybody looking.

Furthermore, worries of reactivation of negative memories from harmful social experiences at school, teamed with the student's current concern of being unable to articulate coherently during seminar discussion, can become the essence of withdrawal for the student with dyslexia, as exemplified by BSc Nursing student Tina:

My point wasn't coming out clearly, and some people weren't able to understand what I was trying to say. I wasn't confused, but not being able to kind of articulate myself in the way I wanted worries me and then I just feel shy.

Let us now consider some techniques for helping with overcoming the above difficulties.

10.3   Techniques for Dealing with Seminar Discussion

First, let us consider a few useful strategies which students with dyslexia said they used to deal with seminar debate (Abbott-Jones, 2022).

10.3.1   Undertaking Preparation

Extensive preparation to compensate for the fear of appearing stupid was a resonant theme in tackling seminar interaction. For example, MA Arts student Debra would ensure that she did her research and had read relevant academic materials likely to be discussed during the seminar. To contribute her own ideas, she would transform notes from her reading into a drawing, so she had visual images to show her peers:

> I'd do a lot of background research before, and if I hadn't done it, I would beat myself up about it. I made sure I read or did all my readings because I don't want to appear stupid. So, I had to really read my reading. If I didn't do my readings, I felt horrible, because I was feeling stupid from that insecurity plus not knowing what everyone was talking about, so I was really, really obsessive. Maybe people did prepare as much as me, but if I want to read a book, I'll kind of draw and stuff, so it's more visual to other people.

349

BA English student Cate would always prepare something to say and would drive herself to speak during the seminar by thoughtfully considering how to express herself:

> So, I tried to always plan to say something in seminars, to push myself, and I did it by putting the right sentence. By preparing a sentence and by really preparing something in my head, so I was not really talking in the blue. Preparation and just, you know, thinking in the seminars, clearly formulating what you want to say, instead of just saying it.

Other students would take notes into the seminar, written in an ordered structure to guide verbalisation of their ideas, like BSc Nursing student Tina:

> I try to have notes to refer back to. I don't have cue cards or anything, but I just like to keep notes. I still have my own kind of structure on the paper and trifle with that.

Below are listed a few ideas you may want to consider to help you with seminar preparation:

- If you have been told by your tutor in advance of the seminar the topic you will be discussing, consider what thoughts, ideas and opinions you have on the topic.
- Using bullet points to make your writing concise, list a few of these ideas. Or use a mind map and express your opinions on the topic using keywords to act as memory joggers for activating what you want to say during the seminar.
- If you are required to read an article for the seminar, do the pre-seminar reading, highlighting any important points.
- Write a summary in your own words of what the article is about and what you think about the article, and list any questions, thoughts or criticisms you have in relation to the article.

- Take these notes along with you to the seminar together with your highlighted article, so you can easily get to the sections of the paper you want to discuss.
- Consider looking at additional sources on your topic so you can bring in other authors' perspectives on the article/subject.
- Get together with some peers from your course, a friend, a parent, your dyslexia tutor, or anybody else willing to help, to hold a pre-discussion of your seminar topic. Their opinions on the subject and the questions that they may ask you should help to clarify your thinking on the topic and will enable you to rehearse the ways in which you verbally express your ideas in connection to the article.

Another effective method for participating in seminar discussion and for demonstrating critical thinking ability in relation to the topic of debate is to use the technique of asking questions.

10.3.2   Method of Asking Questions

Questions asked during seminar discussion can move the talk forwards, can engage the listeners, and can exemplify your analytical skills, particularly if you have a differing perspective on the subject from other members of your group. For example, MSc student Alan, on condition he had prepared for the seminar by researching the topic under discussion, would use a technique involving expressing an opposing opinion from what others in the group had said. This would generate discussion and would make the debate more interesting:

> If it's a topic I know a lot about and they're [the seminar group] saying one thing, I will say, 'Well what about this point of view?' And I will play devil's advocate to someone, as long as I know what I'm talking about in enough detail and I've had enough time to study and look at the information beforehand, I will be fine.

PhD Sciences student Ada would ask a lot of questions during seminar debates. She also asked people to repeat what they had said or asked them to explain themselves more clearly. If one of her peers became angry at her continuous questioning, she would use dyslexia as a defensive strategy and as an explanation of why she needed to query things. Accordingly, her role as cohort questioner evolved into discussion facilitator, as she realised that she was questioning topics that peers in her group were also struggling to understand:

> I found that when I kept asking questions, when I said, 'What does that word mean?', people got really angry with me and then as a defensive strategy, I'd be like, 'Look I'm dyslexic. I don't understand what the words are you're saying. I'm sorry.' Now it's a little bit different. It's evolved a little bit more where I feel like I mediate discussions. I know that I'm not the only one in the room that doesn't understand. There are quite a lot of people who don't always totally understand, it's just they don't want to say, and now it's my excuse. I'm like, 'I'm dyslexic, I don't understand.' I can use it as an excuse to ask really basic questions and I know that it's helped a couple of people that I've been in seminar discussions with.

The moral of the story here from both Ada and Alan is that you should never be afraid to ask questions. There is no such thing as a stupid question, and if you have not understood something clearly, it is highly likely that the speaker needs to clarify their explanation. As such, by being the questioner, you may find that you are looked up to by your peers as being the one to ask when others are also struggling to comprehend, or you may become regarded as the one brave enough to explore an alternative perspective on the subject.

Below are some examples of different type of questions you may consider asking during the seminar.

The Clarification Question

Like Ada's approach during seminars, this type of question is simply asking someone to restate what they said or expand on what they said by providing specific examples for clarification. For instance, this could include:

- I did not quite grasp what you meant in relation to…, could you please go through this again? Ask this when you want the speaker to explain something with added clarity.
- When you said…can you please tell me the specifics? This is effective when you want the speaker to add details of something.
- Can you give me an example of…so I can be sure I understand? This is useful when you want the speaker to provide a practical application of the subject to illustrate the topic further.
- Can you say more about…? Ask this when you want the speaker to elaborate on a particular thing they may have briefly mentioned.

The Alternative Interpretation/Alternative Approach Question

Similar to Alan's method, these types of questions drive discussion forward and quite often take it to a deeper, more analytical level by forcing you and others to think of other perspectives on a topic. Types of questions you could ask include:

- When considering the bigger picture of …, could someone draw a different conclusion from the facts or examples you present? This is a useful question to develop debate as it gets you and others not to take things at face value but to consider alternative viewpoints.
- Some critics argue this view on…. What is your interpretation of their standpoint? This is an effective question if you have prepared before the seminar and have found differing outlooks on the subject, as

this encourages deeper discussion around reasons why others hold different perspectives.

- Is there any evidence out there that could be counter to this author's claims? If you are discussing a set text for the seminar, this is a helpful question to ask as it motivates your peers to exchange views on other sources they may have read, and it also leads to conversations around critiquing evidence.
- What are the weaknesses in the paper/topic/example/evidence? Asking your peers about limitations is a productive way to get yourself and your group to evaluate, identify and address any gaps in the subject, hence developing a higher level of analysis and discussion on the topic.

10.4   Using Multisensory Methods

Seminar discussion, as with all academic tasks so far discussed in this book, also lends itself to being effectively stored in memory through a multisensory approach, particularly at the preparation stage. For example, one productive method is to hear yourself talking through your ideas aloud when you are planning the points you want to discuss. You can capture your articulation on a recording device and play it back so you can hear how you are expressing yourself. You can then rehearse from the recording whilst improvising, amending and improving. Once happy with what you want to say, you can record again, play back the recording, and observe the development in your articulation from the original recording to your later version. You can then repeatedly play your final recording to yourself during moments when you are relaxing, as the brain is more receptive to absorption of auditory information when relaxed. This can be combined with jotting down keywords from the recording to take along to the seminar to act as visual memory joggers. Preparation done in this way should help you to memorise the issues you want to discuss and how you want to convey them to your peers. The time you have invested in rehearsal will also enable you to feel more confident in contributing verbally during the seminar.

One of the advantages with the multisensory approach to preparation is that many students with dyslexia, as in the example of MA Humanities student Charlie from Chapter 1, must hear their ideas expressed aloud, or visually see them in a drawing, for them to make sense, otherwise they remain as abstract and uncoherent concepts. The multisensory method enables you to hear your ideas expressed aloud during an early stage of planning for the seminar. The jotting down of keywords on a mind map or in linear form as drawings, colourful keywords and concept maps put into a structure also enables the necessary visualisation. This helps to transform what was once a complex and confused view of something into a concrete representation of the idea, which leads to enabling a clear and coherent explanation for the seminar. Let us be reminded of how Charlie needed this process:

> If I have an idea, I need to be able to either hear it, or see it, for it to be a complete idea. Otherwise, it's just these images, or concepts, it's nothing coherent. Until it's being spoken, I do have a panicky feeling, because there are ideas buzzing around in my head. Suddenly my head gets quite manic, and the ideas need to come out of my head, so until I can say something, I will be on edge.

As discussed in Chapter 5, because of the memory deficits prevalent for so many students with dyslexia, genius thoughts can randomly flash into the mind, yet can become lost and forgotten and difficult to retrieve in an instant. So, another benefit of carrying around a recording device for capturing ideas to discuss during seminars is that documenting these moments of inspiration removes the frustration caused by having forgotten them.

10.4.1 Drawing Pictures to Explain Points and Showing to Others

Sometimes, rather than just taking along a series of key points jotted down on a notepad to remind you what you want to say, you may find that your peers benefit more if you show them pictures you have drawn to help with expressing your ideas. These can simply be rough sketches in spider diagram/mind map form, or just quick drawings presented in linear format. Not only will these enable you to structure your dialogue more coherently, the presentation of images to your peers will enable them to be more engaged with the points you are delivering.

10.5   Public Speaking

Whilst most universities require students to attend and contribute to seminar discussion and to undertake assessed presentations, public speaking is not usually prioritised and taught at university, even though it is an extremely important skill needed throughout a graduate's future career. The recognition of the lack of development in this area was mentioned by several students with dyslexia when asked what techniques they felt they would like support with. For example, MA Arts student Debra responded with:

> Maybe having techniques of how to speak in public. These kind of very simple group exercises. To give tips and coping mechanisms in these different situations. Mine would be public speaking and exams. Having strategies to help. Working on these insecurities which have been built up because of dyslexia. Maybe supporting the individual insecurities, or fears.

In agreement with Debra, tackling the insecurities derived from thoughts of public speaking is necessary, particularly as presenting is such a common requisite in employment. For instance, Debra recalled her fears of presenting, which led to her belief that she needed strategies to cope, from her employment as museum coordinator:

> I had to present a project that I was coordinating in my last job in a museum, and I had to give a speech in front of everybody. I knew my stuff; I just didn't trust myself to say it clearly and articulate it. When I got up there, I started shaking and I thought, 'Oh my God everyone's listening to me,' and then I started stuttering, so yeah, having strategies to help.

Yet, once given the right methods, people with dyslexia can excel at public speaking, as they have usually developed strong interpersonal skills as a compensation for struggling with written language, as noted by BSc Nursing student Lisa:

> I also think a lot of people with dyslexia are very good communicators verbally because they know they can't do it written. They have a lot more confidence verbally speaking, and from anyone I've met who is dyslexic, normally their vocabulary is quite good.

Whilst strategies were presented above on preparing for seminar discussion and asking questions during seminars, let us now turn to ways of developing confidence in contributing verbally.

10.5.1 Strategies for Contributing Verbally to Seminar Discussion

One of the key techniques used by students with dyslexia to deal with anxiety connected to seminar discussions was being the first to speak.

MA Education student Chloe was so afraid of speaking in seminar discussions, she decided that to overcome the fear, she would force herself to be the first to provide an idea or opinion. This approach worked to her benefit as, given time and experience, she began to find it easier to contribute verbally in her group:

> What I did in all of them (seminars) was I said, 'Okay, the longer you wait the more difficult it will be, make sure you're the first one who says something.' So I was, and as soon as I said something first time it made it easier. I often find that, as soon as first time, the second time will be easier, the third time, and then I was unstoppable. I was always talking.

10.5.2 Strategies for Dealing with Formal Presentations

Although the previous chapter has already provided guidance on techniques for tackling presentations, here, because presentations are a form of public speaking, we note a few additional methods that may help you to feel more comfortable, confident and less anxious when approaching this task.

Timing the Presentation and Practising Speaking It Aloud

When students with dyslexia were asked in Abbott-Jones (2022) about methods they used for addressing presentations, preparation by rehearsing proved to be a consistent theme used for alleviating nervousness and anxiety in connection with the presentation. Twelve out of the 20 students with dyslexia said they would plan and repeatedly perform the presentation. This would be done (as discussed in Chapter 9) whilst timing the presentation to decide whether it needed to be edited down or expanded to meet the allocated time, as explained by MA Humanities student Charlie:

> Usually there is a time limit. I make sure that it is to the time limit, so I will practise it with my mum, and she will time me and then I will cut it if it needs to be shorter.

Testing Out Things to Say and Not to Say

Repeatedly rehearsing also enables you to select the things you want to say and the points you want to leave out, as explained by BSc Medicine student Naomi:

> No, I don't need to say that, or I'll skip that part, maybe I don't need to say it. So, I see what kind of comes out naturally looking at the slides. Obviously, you have to time yourself to make sure you're not taking too much time and cut things out, so I think, yeah, just practising speaking it aloud beforehand helps me.

Join Public Speaking Organisations and Amateur Dramatics Societies

The students with dyslexia in Abbott-Jones (2022) who tended to feel more confident with formal presentations were currently involved in, or had recently been members of, public speaking organisations, such as Toastmasters, a club specifically aiming to develop communication and leadership skills, or they had participated in drama training during their earlier school years, as noted by MSc Humanities student Alison:

> Actually, with presentations I'm relatively good, but I think that's because at school I studied drama, so that really helped my confidence like speaking out loud, so I've never really had an issue with that.

Techniques to Reduce Public Speaking Anxiety

In an article titled 'Anxiety level in students of public speaking: causes and remedies' by Farhan Raja (2017), a list of productive techniques provided for the purpose of supporting higher education tutors in helping their own students to overcome their fears of public speaking is particularly useful in giving pragmatic advice. The list may resonate with you and could also assist in diminishing your own anxieties in relation to public speaking, as Raja has so consciously set out to do:

- The instructor needs to help students realize that being stressful is natural.
- Better preparation and understanding of the topic eliminates the chance of making a mistake or getting off track during a public speaking activity.
- A moment of silence is nothing to be afraid of. If speakers lose track of what they are saying or begin to feel nervous, it is likely that the audience will not mind a pause to consider what the speakers have been saying.
- Practising complete speech several times would certainly give the speakers an edge. They can practise it with a small number of people they are at ease with.
- Speakers should seek feedback from the audience during practice sessions or ask someone to record the talk. Watching it several times for self-criticism also helps facilitate the learning and improvement process.
- Better preparation also helps speakers recover quickly if they go off track or get confused.
- The speakers should anticipate audience responses and queries that may be generated during practice so that they have confident answers.
- It is essential to focus on the material, not on the audience, as people are primarily paying attention to the information being presented.
- The speakers should recognise and acknowledge their success. It may not have been perfect, but chances are that the speakers are far more critical of themselves than the audience is.
- Joining an active public speaking forum would also benefit the students. Once they get into the habit of considering themselves comfortable in an unknown environment while speaking in public, the anxiety would automatically go down and make the speakers feel at ease. (Raja, 2017, pp. 106–107).

360

10.6   Strategies for Dealing with Interaction at Networking Events

Networking involves being invited to a social function where you gather at a set venue, either with a group of professionals from your line of work or with peers from your course. It enables you to establish relationships with other individuals and involves meeting new people both within and outside your industry or course area. Feeling confident in introducing yourself to strangers and having the ability to converse and engage with people at these types of events is important, as networking centres around the exchange of information and ideas with others from your field.

Once over the initial nerves of being out of their comfort zone in having to talk to strangers, people with dyslexia can often excel in these types of situations. That is because, as noted above, communication skills can become highly developed in compensation for deficits with written forms of language (Logan, 2009). Humour for people with dyslexia can also be highly evolved, as it may have been used since childhood as a coping mechanism and a way to distance oneself from stressful and humiliating experiences (Nezlek and Derks, 2021). Consequently, good communication skills and sense of humour were attributes noted by students with dyslexia in Abbott-Jones (2022) when asked what qualities they felt they had developed because of their dyslexia. In fact, 9 out of the 20 students believed that dyslexia had led them to have grown strong verbal communication capability, and BSc Nursing student Lisa felt that people with dyslexia had an ability to laugh at themselves which comes with maturity and acceptance of self:

> A lot of dyslexics have a sense of humour. I love it, because most dyslexics I've met have that slight cynical sense of humour where

it's a bit 'oh God! you know' kind of jokey way about it. Fair enough when you're younger it's the most frustrating thing in the world. You do feel like an idiot, but then when you get my age, or are older, they look back. You can make jokes about when you've written something horrendously rude by accident, or you've written something else which completely changes the meaning of the sentence, and someone read it.

So, in addition to some of the tips below, the advice for dealing with interaction at networking events is to just be yourself and allow your conversation with others to simply be natural and genuine. Other advice is as follows:

10.6.1   Be an Active Listener

When talking to someone, rather than focusing on how you are going to respond to what your speaker is saying, centre your attention completely on listening to the person and trying to understand their point. That way, when you do respond, you will be able to demonstrate your reasoning ability, your sincerity and interest in their viewpoints by replying in a thoughtful manner. By being an active listener rather than a dominant speaker, you are much more likely to engage with your speaker and to leave them with a positive impression of yourself.

10.6.2   Ask People Questions about Themselves

A part of being an active listener is to also show your commitment and attentiveness in getting to know more about a person by asking them questions about themselves. People love talking about themselves and things they are interested in, so by asking questions you are tapping into what motivates and inspires them, which enables them to enjoy their conversation with you. Again, this ensures that they will remember you in a positive light.

10.7   Strategies for Dealing with General Informal Conversation

The more you interact with your peers at your university, the more comfortable you will feel conversing with your tutors, professionals and other experts from within and outside your academic area, at networking events, social functions, or other formal and informal occasions. For example, BSc Medicine student Naomi, who as part of her course had to attend events with qualified medical practitioners, found that owing to regular interaction with peers, these events were not as daunting as she previously expected:

> I guess because I've always been in conversation with peers, if it's just me and a group of experienced clinicians talking about something, I probably wouldn't say much because I don't know a lot, so it's okay. I just, I won't talk unless I have something relevant to say, so I don't think I'd feel too nervous usually.

Consequently, Naomi did not get too anxious at these events, as she was reassured that her conversational ability was strong on account of her interpersonal skills with her peers. Instead, she looked positively at these events, as a way of developing and enriching her knowledge on specific areas from her more experienced colleagues. This leads fundamentally again to the importance of developing the capability of being an active listener, which is just as crucial to use in general informal conversation as it is in all other aspects of social interaction. One technique you could try, to make the person you are talking to more engaged in the conversation and to show them you are interested and care about what they are saying, is to use the strategy of reflective listening.

363

10.7.1   Using Reflective Listening

Reflective listening is simply to paraphrase back to the person speaking a small part of what they have just said. Say for instance, your speaker has just said the following:

> The weather in the UK is getting increasingly hotter every summer.
> This year we saw temperature extremes of up to 40 degrees.

To show the speaker you are paying attention to their dialogue, you could merely respond by saying, 'Yes, temperatures were extremely hot this year.' This helps to develop rapport between yourself and the speaker, as you have established a shared identity on a topic.

Reflective listening is also a useful technique during work situations when your supervisor, boss or employer has given you a set of verbal instructions to act upon. Repeating back to them what they have told you to do allows you to check you have interpreted their direction correctly and prevents any miscommunication between yourself and your supervisor.

Another strategy helpful for initiating conversations and for keeping discussion flowing between yourself and speaker is to ask open-ended questions.

10.7.2   Begin Conversations with Open-Ended Questions

Social anxiety can generally prevent people from initiating conversations with others. One way to attempt to begin discussions with others at social events is to try asking non-personal, open-ended questions, which can help to alleviate the pressure of trying to force a conversation. For example, if you are attending a party, you could try asking another attendee, 'Have you known… (the host) long?' That way, you are not overly personalising the question but are instead getting the person to open up about their acquaintance with the host. This can then become a shared topic, as the likelihood is that they will reciprocate the question by asking you how you also know the host.

10.8   Strategies for Dealing with Specific Forms of Public Speaking

Now let us return to the realm of public speaking in the context of the presentation, the business meeting, the interview, the debate, and the ceremonial occasion where you may be asked to give a speech (at a wedding or a funeral, etc.). These types of situations all place demands upon you by requiring you to speak articulately and coherently to an audience. That audience may be composed of your course peers and tutors, prospective employers, stakeholders whom you are tempting to invest in your business or yourself, or your close family and friends. The four main forms of public speaking include speaking to inform, to persuade, to actuate, and to entertain.

Let us now look a little more closely at each category in terms of reflecting on some strategies that may help to ensure we are delivering the appropriate type of speech for a given situation.

10.9   Strategies for Speaking to Inform

The University of Pittsburgh's Department of Communication have produced a particularly useful guide (www.comm.pitt.edu/informative-speaking) providing advice on techniques to use when speaking to inform an audience, perhaps during a formal presentation.

They state that you should:

10.9.1 Consider the Audience

For example, if you are speaking to peers on your course, they should have the same level of knowledge as you do on a topic, so although you will still need to define terms and concepts in your presentation, you may not need to spend too much time in elaborating exactly what a particular concept is. If, however, you are attending a conference with people outside your topic area, you will need to clarify basic concepts from your topic. You should always speak as you write essays, by never assuming your audience has a thorough background in the subject.

10.9.2 Use Appropriate Language

Only use jargon and specialised language if you know your audience is familiar with those terms. Otherwise, each time you introduce a terminology word in your speech, briefly define what it means.

10.9.3 Explain the Importance of the Topic

In your speech introduction, you can engage your audience's interest by explaining how the information you are delivering will connect with and perhaps benefit them. For example, if you are presenting a topic from your subject area to your peers, you could explain that you are looking at it from the alternative perspective of … author's viewpoint, so your audience know they are gaining a new insight into the area. Or if at a conference of specialists in your field, you could explain, for instance, that your presentation focuses on the topic's practical implementation in the workplace. That way, the audience are aware that the talk can provide them with new knowledge and skills to develop their practice further.

10.9.4   Show, Don't Tell

Most people are more engaged with a speech if they have visual material to see, or if they can use their kinaesthetic strengths by having a go at doing something. If you are talking about processes or procedures, for example, these can be explained more clearly through a series of images. Furthermore, informative speeches, as noted by staff at the University of Pittsburgh, 'often benefit from a demonstration or visual aid'. In other words, if you are explaining about a chemistry experiment and you have the luxury of getting your audience to have a go at the processes involved by holding the talk in a science laboratory, then your audience will benefit more from the talk as they have been actively participating. If, however, this is not feasible, then images and technology will help to bring your talk to life for your audience.

10.9.5   Be Specific

With any concepts, theories, ideas, processes or procedures you are introducing in your talk, you need to provide the detail, so that your audience understands. You could try using the following method of define, describe, demonstrate as a template for helping you to structure your talk for each new concept you present.

Define

Identify and explain what the main characteristics or qualities of the concept are. For example, if the talk was about anxiety, you could say: 'Anxiety is defined as a feeling of worry, nervousness or unease about something with an uncertain outcome.' Immediately, your audience is clear on how you are using the term.

Describe

This is where you will give a more detailed account of the concept, theory or process. Returning to anxiety, for instance, you could elaborate by explaining about different forms of anxiety, such as state and trait anxiety, social anxiety, performance anxiety, and so on.

Demonstrate

To demonstrate, you would provide a practical example or explanation. This helps to transform the theory from an abstract idea to something with real-life meaning. For the concept of anxiety, you could present a case-study of a person diagnosed with anxiety and show a video of that person talking about how anxiety affects them in different situations. If you have introduced a process or procedure, you could demonstrate this practically to your audience. This helps your audience to engage by witnessing an actual example of the concept, which makes the talk more relevant to them.

10.10   Strategies for Speaking to Persuade

Persuasive speaking is used when the speaker/presenter is attempting to persuade and convince the audience to support their view. For example, persuasive speech is often used by politicians and policymakers when lobbying for committees or general audiences to back their ideas. It can also be used in the university environment and in the work setting through presentations when you are wanting to sway your peers to agree with your conclusions or influence your colleagues to support your request to take a specific action. Below are listed a few techniques that you can have a go at implementing if you would like your speech to come across as persuasive.

10.10.1   Establish a Clear Thesis

When you select your topic for a persuasive speech, a few factors should be considered. These include currency, controversy and whether the topic has implications for society. For example, your speech will be more meaningful to your audience if you select from your subject area a topic that is currently being discussed and debated regularly by others in your field. The topic may also be relatively controversial as this will engage your audience's interests and could also be something that has significance for certain groups in society. For example, if you are in the area of medicine, your thesis (which is basically your argument) could be 'It is important for populations to be vaccinated against coronavirus.' If you are studying environmental sciences, your thesis may be 'Global warming is accelerating too rapidly, bringing the world to irreversible change.' Both these statements are current global issues and can be controversial, depending upon different people's opinions.

10.10.2   Answer the Question 'Why?'

After you have introduced your thesis argument to your audience, the next part of your speech should be to provide your listeners with a comprehensive and detailed answer to the question of why. Why should it be important for the population to be vaccinated? Why is global warming accelerating too rapidly? Answering this question supplies the relevant background information for the audience, and it can create a sense of urgency that makes people consider the significance of the topic.

10.10.3   Provide Powerful Evidence to Support Your Point

To connect with your audience's logic and reasoning, you will need to provide strong evidence to support your thesis. This could be in the form of statistics, facts from government and other authoritative organisational reports, quotes from experts on the subject, results from surveys, and information from peer-reviewed research articles. The evidence helps to make the issues real for the audience.

10.10.4   Use Rhetorical Devices

Sometimes the use of rhetorical devices can help to captivate the audience by making the speech more compelling. Some of these are listed below:

Rule of Three

Commonly used by heads of states and politicians, the 'rule of three' is when ideas in speech are presented in threes to make them more memorable for the audience. For example, to support the thesis of why the population should be vaccinated against coronavirus, the rule of three in the speech could be presented as: to protect yourself and loved ones, build immunity, and stop the pandemic. In relation to the issue and effects of global warming, the rule of three could be articulated as: frequent wildfires, droughts, and intense tropical storms. Consequently, the rule of three enables you to get your information across by using a succinct effective method more likely to be digested and remembered by the listener.

Rhetorical Questions

Rhetorical questions in persuasive speech are used to make a point and are asked merely for dramatic effect rather than to get an answer. They can draw emphasis to the issue for the audience. For instance, in relation to the vaccination issue, the speaker could ask the rhetorical question 'How many more people must die before the entire population is vaccinated?' Whilst this is fairly contentious, the speaker has captured the audience's attention and has accentuated the gravity of the topic. In connection to global warming, the rhetorical question could be 'Have we left it too late to stop the destructive effects of global warming?' The question works to absorb the audience as it draws attention by highlighting what could potentially be the catastrophic consequences of the issue if left, whilst engaging the audience as they are keen to know the answer.

10.11 Strategies for Speaking to Actuate

Speaking to actuate, as the name implies, denotes performing a presentation or a speech whereby you motivate the audience to undertake some specific action. Thus, speaking to actuate can vary and can be used in an immense array of differing scenarios: from attempting to influence people to vote for politicians at elections, to speaking to prompt people to donate money to specific charities, to inspiring people to join campaigns for certain causes, to prompting people to part with money for products, and to speaking to convince people to change lifestyle habits. In fact, any form of speech which calls for the listener to either commit to a particular action or undertake an observable changed behaviour is speaking to actuate. Below are a few devices you may want to try using if the aim of your talk is to activate your listener.

10.11.1   Use Ethos

Using ethos in your speech means to demonstrate your credibility, expertise, experience and knowledge of the topic. For example, if you are trying to get someone to change their behaviour and to recycle more, you could explain to the listener that as environmental sciences is the subject you are studying at university (if indeed it is), then you have a deeper understanding of the adverse effects that plastic waste can have on the environment. People tend to be swayed more into action by others if they believe their speaker is qualified to talk about the topic.

10.11.2   Use Pathos

Using pathos in speech to actuate is using language to evoke certain emotions in your listener. If, for instance, you are wanting your audience to subscribe to charity, you could try to elicit sympathy by describing examples of the harsh conditions faced by the people, children or animals that the charity aims to support. Appealing to emotional triggers, both positive and negative, is continuously carried out by television advertising, so if you need to write a speech to actuate, then analysing language used by commercials provides a particularly good starting point.

10.12   Strategies for Speaking to Entertain

Speaking to entertain is usually undertaken on special occasions, such as at weddings, birthdays, award shows, and sometimes at conferences, depending upon the topic and nature of the event. According to the eLearning provider Saylor Academy

(www.saylor.org/), when writing an entertaining speech, four factors need to be considered. These include:

10.12.1   Preparation

Try jotting down some basic notes using bullet points or a mind
map as a plan for what you are going to say. Then rehearse this a
few times, ensuring you are sticking to the allocated time you have
been designated for the speech. The rehearsal of the talk in front of
a few friends and/or family members will help to alleviate nerves and
anxiety when it comes to delivering the speech.

10.12.2   Adapt to the Occasion

Make sure that the content of your speech is appropriate and suitable for the situation. For example, if you are the best man at a wedding and have been asked to deliver a speech at the reception, then
the talk will serve as a lens for the audience to gain a better understanding of the groom and the newlyweds through their significant
position within your life. You could add an element of humour to
various scenarios, such as when you first met the groom, or experiences you have shared, but ultimately the speech should revolve
around sending messages of positivity about the groom and bride to
the wedding guests.

If, in a different scenario, you have been asked to speak after
receiving an award, then your talk will be based on conveying genuine gratitude and will likely focus on thanking all those who supported you in your journey to being granted the commendation. You
are likely to use less humour than in the best man speech and instead
will show more appreciation.

10.12.3   Adapt to the Audience

Do some research on who your audience will be and then you can implement some rapport-building devices into your speech. For instance, if you are receiving an award in front of a group of teachers, you could insert an anecdote in recognition of how hard teachers work and how rewarding the job is, which will enable you to connect in solidarity with your audience.

10.12.4   Be Mindful of the Time

In the preparation stage when practising your speech, make sure that if too long, you have edited it down to the time you have been given for the talk. If too short, then add in more material so the speech is of the appropriate length. If you are unsure about what the expected timeframe for the speech should be, then either ask the person who invited you for advice or do some research to ascertain the usual length for the type of speech you are giving.

Next, we shall move onto looking at strategies for dealing with interviews.

10.13   Strategies for Dealing with Employment Interviews

There are many different types of job interview: the traditional conversational kind where you are being asked direct questions by a panel of one to three interviewers; the competency-based interview requiring you to provide evidence to demonstrate your skills and knowledge meet the specifications of the job role; the behavioural interview centred on asking the candidate to explain how they reacted to certain work situations in the past; the unstructured interview whereby questions are randomly asked based on the participant's previous answer; the stress interview used to assess how the interviewee handles pressure; the practical assessment interview used to see how an applicant performs certain job-specific tasks; or case interviews where the candidate is asked to come up with solutions to a problem. Here we are going to focus on techniques for coping with behavioural interviews, case interviews, unstructured interviews and competency-based interviews.

Many of you will have already gained some initial experience in undertaking interviews, whether for university places, for part-time jobs, or for assessment purposes as a part of your course at university, and you may already have an element of metacognitive awareness of where your strengths and weaknesses lie when it comes to interviews. For example, BSc Veterinary Medicine student Natalie was particularly conscious that at times her character could be domineering, so when it came to group interviews, whereby she was assessed on her ability to work as part of a team, she would make sure she did not take over but instead encouraged other quieter members of the group to have an input.

> The only thing I'm aware of is that I'm not too overbearing, because I know I can be, because I'm quite loud and quite opinionated. I know sometimes, I can be a bit much, like for instance in the Veterinary interviews, one thing that most of them do is they put you in a group and they give you a task to do in the group because they want to see how you do as a group, are you shy? Too quiet? Are you too confident? Are you not listening to others? And in one I was put in a group, and they gave us loads of clinical scenarios and asked us to pick what we felt were the top five. So, being me, I took the lead and said, 'Well why don't we try doing this?' And then I thought, okay, make sure you ask other people their opinion. Then luckily a few other people chipped in, and there's a girl

I noticed was quite quiet, so I said 'Oh, what do you think?' I'm never nervous, I'm just more aware of the fact that you need to let other people speak, and other people have a say. I try to make sure I'm aware that sometimes I do be quiet, or I do bring someone in that's maybe being a bit shy.

This self-awareness exhibited by Natalie enabled her to show that although her natural character was to be assertive in group work scenarios, she also ensured that she motivated others to participate, hence demonstrating her skills as a team-player.

10.14   Disclosing Dyslexia in the Application Process

Another particularly pertinent issue for students with dyslexia when it comes to the job application and interview process is the dilemma of whether to disclose dyslexia. This can be a significant anxiety-provoking quandary for many, because on the one hand, you want your employer to know of your dyslexia so they can manage and support you appropriately in your new role. On the other hand, however, owing to student belief (worryingly often a well-founded belief) that employers' lack of knowledge and under-standing of their learning difference will put them at a disadvan-tage in being considered for the position, they become influenced into non-disclosure. An example of this predicament is described by MA Arts student Cara:

I was hoping to go for a job, which is a temp job. It's basically a tutor-ing job to help other kids with learning difficulties and its autistic children, dyslexic children, and kids with like ADHD, or behavioural problems. But I'm nervous that my dyslexia is going to interfere. My friend is already a teacher there and she said you go for an interview, but you also have to pass a spelling test. So, I don't know whether I should disclose that I am dyslexic, but that it doesn't really affect me that much.

It is this kind of thinking – that employers focus solely on cognitive weaknesses to the detriment of strengths – that prevents so many dyslexic individuals from saying they have dyslexia in the application process. You are under no obligation to disclose your dyslexia. However, considering dyslexia is covered by the Equality Act (2010), and consequently as a dyslexic employee you are protected by law, the advantages of letting your employer know (either through completion of an equal opportunities form, or by raising this as a discussion point during your interview) can outweigh the decision not to disclose. Essentially, this means that because of your disclosure, your employer has a duty to make reasonable adjustments during your interview and in your workplace if selected for the job, so you can carry out your role to the standard expected. For example, reasonable adjustments during interview could include being able to refer to your prepared notes (although this is generally the norm for interviews with non-dyslexic candidates anyway), being allowed extra time to process and respond to questions, and the interviewer being required to ensure that questions are phrased clearly and kept to one question at a time. Reasonable adjustments made once employed could include the provision of assistive technology such as speech-to-text and mind-mapping software, allowing you plenty of time to complete tasks, or reducing distractions by providing a quiet, private workspace. Additionally, if a person with dyslexia feels they have been discriminated against, they have a legal right to take their case to an employment tribunal. So, despite the fears that many people with dyslexia have in relation to disclosure and the assumption that this will go against them in the selection process, because of the level of protection that acknowledging can provide, it is perhaps best to overcome the anxiety and to talk openly and honestly with an employer on how they can effectively support you so you can productively carry out your job.

Now we advance to looking at some key tips for tackling behavioural interviews.

10.15   Strategies for Dealing with Behavioural Interviews

Behavioural interviews are used by an employer as a method to check the consistency of your behavioural reasoning (the way you apply logic, motives, and behaviour) in pressurised, conflicting and stressful situations. You are usually required to demonstrate evidence of high levels of resiliency and perseverance in your character through the types of responses you give to the interviewer. Consequently, types of questions asked in behavioural interviews are generally centred around exploring previous challenges you have encountered and what you did to resolve and deal with those circumstances. This could be based on questions like: 'Tell me about a time you had a conflict with someone within the organisation and what you did to overcome the dispute', 'What was the most challenging team project you have worked on and why?' or 'What is the most difficult problem you have had to solve in a work situation?'

Here are some tips for dealing with these kinds of questions:

10.15.1   Using Challenge/Action/Result as a Method to Structure Your Response

With **challenge** you first describe to the interviewer the specific circumstances of the situation. You secondly explain the **action** you took in handling the situation, and thirdly, you outline the **results** of your action. This enables the interviewer to be given the proof that you can identify challenges, to use resiliency by putting steps in place to reduce the difficulty, and that the measures you put in place based on reasoned logic helped to resolve the situation.

10.15.2   Using Problem-Focused Coping and Emotion-Focused Coping to Structure Your Response

As behavioural interviews are used to assess the consistency of your logic in the actions you have taken to manage specific external demands, yet are also evaluating your levels of durability in dealing with internal demands, you could try structuring your responses by providing an example of problem-focused followed by emotion-focused coping. For instance, for **problem-focused coping**, you first explain to the interviewer how you interpreted the situation and what you did to deal with the problem. For **emotion-focused coping**, you then outline the measures you took to help you reduce your stress, worry, anxiety and so on in relation to the challenges. This could be by providing examples of how you use exercise, walking in nature, cycling, or talking to someone to alleviate your tension. That way, the interviewer is given evidence that you can effectively handle problems and that you also have productive strategies for alleviating work-related pressure.

10.16   Using Strategies for Dealing with Case Interviews

Case interviews are commonly used by management consulting firms when employing new business consultants to assess the candidate's ability to use analytical skills and to produce strategies for solving problems. If you are required to attend this kind of interview, a couple of useful strategies include the following.

10.16.1   Practise Resolving Case Archetypes

According to career platform themuse.com, there are typically a limited number of types of cases that you will be asked to resolve. These comprise: 'entering a new market, developing a new product, growth strategies, pricing strategies, starting a new business, increasing profitability (or increasing sales or reducing costs), acquiring a company, turning around a company, and coming up with a response to a competitor's actions.' (themuse.com). Consequently, with each one of these scenarios, if you practise creating the structure (which in a case interview involves breaking the problem down into its component parts, followed by describing the solution), then you should feel confident that you are prepared to effectively tackle the case delivered to you during the interview. Furthermore, as there are no single correct answers with cases, interviewers are more interested in assessing how you process large amounts of information and how constructively you can apply logical thinking and solutions to a problem. Therefore, practice and preparation should allow you to feel more assured in demonstrating competency and clarity of thinking when it comes to talking through your devised structure and answers to the case with the interviewer.

10.16.2   Develop a Clear Structure in Relation to the Case and Communicate Using Describe, Analyse, Conclude, Recommend/Solve (DACR/S)

Themuse.com argue that a good structure is really the key to doing well with a case as it is your chance to demonstrate to the interviewer 'how you think'. They suggest that an effective structure should break down the problem by identifying the key elements. For instance, if your case is based on how to generate larger profits for a company, you can break this down into evaluation of the factors 'increasing revenue' or 'decreasing costs'. You can then break each of these down further into increasing revenue means 'increasing your price' or 'increasing the number of things you sell', and decreasing costs meaning 'decreasing fixed costs' or 'decreasing variable costs'. These elements can then be coherently explained to the interviewer by DACR/S:

D – Describe the problem, which enables the interviewer to see you have understood and identified the issues.

A – Analyse the information. This is where you explain to the interviewer your interpretation and evaluation of the information and evidence you have been provided in association with the problem.

C – Conclude. You present the interviewer with solutions demonstrating your logical thinking based on the information and evidence. You can also show your critical thinking ability by talking through the strengths and weaknesses of each resolution.

R/S – Recommend/Solve. You outline the other possible solutions displaying your ability to be an astute problem-solver by showing how you recognise that there are always several alternatives to resolving difficulties.

10.17   Strategies for Dealing with Unstructured Interviews

An unstructured interview is spontaneous in nature, and questions are asked based on the candidate's previous responses to earlier questions. Consequently, the unstructured interview feels more like a conversation and is less formal than the behavioural and case interviews discussed above. As such, unstructured interviews are generally used for creative or technical positions, or when assessment of the candidate's personality is a key priority for the employer. Here are a few helpful tips for dealing with unstructured interviews and the types of questions you may be asked.

10.17.1   Do Research and Preparation Beforehand

If you do some research on the company before your interview by finding out as much information as you can around elements like the role you are applying for, the skills and experience that the company values, the latest news and events connected to the employer, the company's culture, mission and values, and the person interviewing you, you will be in a much stronger position to be able to tailor your responses so that they demonstrate how you meet the company's requirements. For example, if the position being advertised states they are looking for someone who is 'customer focused and shows initiative', you can jot down some notes as part of your preparation of the times you exhibited these skills. That way, if you are asked a question such as 'Describe your ideal job', you can interweave in your answer something along the lines of how you enjoy communicating with a variety of people/customers. You can also provide examples of occasions where you have used your initiative when working with people. This allows you to demonstrate through your response evidence of the skills the employer is looking for.

10.17.2   Practise Responses to Questions You May Be Asked, Using the STAR Strategy

The Situation, Task, Action, Results (STAR) method is particularly effective for dealing with certain types of questions asked during unstructured interviews. That is because the approach enables you to provide a well-structured, coherent and logical response and allows you to deliver concrete examples and proof that you possess the capabilities the employer is looking for. For instance, say the interviewer asks, 'What accomplishments are you most proud of and why?', here is an example of how using STAR will ensure that you give a well-thought-out and illustrative answer:

S – Situation. This is where you describe the situation you were in or provide the details of the task you had to accomplish. In relation to the question above, you could respond by giving an example of any number of achievements you feel particularly proud of, from being promoted at work, to gaining a degree, passing an exam, volunteering for a charity, preventing a conflict, or helping a friend.

T – Task. Outline the goal you were working towards. For example, if the accomplishment you are most proud of is completing a project or university degree, then here you can provide the specifics of the project/ degree and examples of the obstacles you overcame to reach your goal.

A – Action. Here you explain the actions you took to succeed. If your example is passing an exam, you can talk about the types of strategies you implemented in your revision and the methods you used to tackle the exam paper which enabled you to achieve. If you are talking about resolving a conflict, you could outline the negotiation methods or the types of communication you used.

R – Result. Here you explain in more detail the outcomes of your action. In the case of the exam or degree award, you could detail the specifics of the grade and any positive feedback you were awarded. In relation to settling the conflict, you could explain the ways in which the parties involved now work or communicate effectively together as a team.

As you can see, the STAR technique used during interviews allows you to supply productive responses illustrated with positive examples of skills you possess to meet the requirements of the post.

10.18   Competency-Based Interviews

Competencies are basically the set of skills, behaviours and knowledge an employer lists in the job description as the abilities the candidate will need to demonstrate as evidence they will be able to do the role successfully and efficiently. The way in which the interviewee shows to the employer they possess these capabilities is through effectively answering the competency-based questions. For example, if the role is looking for someone who can work productively in a team, the interviewer may say, 'Tell me about a time you worked in a team.' This is where you will need to draw upon past experiences that illustrate your success at teamwork to signify to the interviewer your ability to work well as part of a team. Below are a few examples of how you can successfully prepare for and deal with competency-based interviews.

10.18.1   In the Preparation Stage, List the Criteria for the Role

Scrutinise the job description and list the criteria the employer is looking for in a Word document, on a notepad or in mind-map form. You can then reflect on and match examples from your past experience of where you have displayed that ability. The examples you select to match the listed skills do not necessarily have to come from just previous work or university experience but can be more generic and from events in your past life as a whole. For instance, say one of the skills the employer is looking for is leadership, and the question asked is 'Can you describe a situation where you showed leadership?', you could exemplify this by relating it to a time you were on holiday and organised activities and day trips amongst groups of friends, or you could display leadership skills by relating them to your extra-curricular activities or volunteering work.

384

10.18.2   Use STAR Strategy to Structure Responses

The STAR method, as discussed above, is also a particularly effective technique for helping you to prepare answers using specific examples from your experience to match each one of the competencies. STAR provides you with a framework to ensure you have all the essential components in your answer and enables you to deliver a logical response. Furthermore, for some competencies you may want to use STARE, where the E stands for Evaluation. Here you would describe how you would do things differently if you were to do them again. This is a distinctly productive way of exhibiting your reflective and analytical skills.

10.18.3   Ask the Interviewer Questions

A way to exhibit your interest further in the role and in working for the company is to ask the interviewer questions about both the position and the organisation during the interview. This not only displays to the interviewer your keenness in wanting to know more, but if you phrase your questions to integrate information you have read about the organisation's culture, the services offered and the current job opening, you are also demonstrating that you have taken time to do research in preparation for the interview.

10.19   Summary

In summary, this chapter has:

- Specified the types of obstacles students with dyslexia face in relation to seminar discussion and debate.

- Outlined techniques for helping with overcoming barriers to participating in seminar discussion and debate, which included:
  - Undertaking preparation for class discussion by taking brief
  notes into the seminar written in an ordered structure to guide
  verbalisation.
  - Using the method of asking questions to demonstrate critical thinking and to develop debate.
  - Using the multisensory method of hearing ideas spoken aloud
  during preparation stage, capturing these on a recording device,
  playing them back to hear, then jotting down keywords from the
  recording to take along to the seminar to act as visual memory
  joggers.
  - Drawing pictures to explain points and to show to others.
- Delivered a range of strategies to develop confidence when participating in various forms of public speaking.
- Provided advice on preparing for and tackling different types
of job interviews including behavioural, case, unstructured and
competency-based interviews.

11

• • • • •

Emotional Coping Techniques and Looking After Your Wellbeing

11.1   Introduction

Previous chapters have focused on presenting various types of effective cognitive strategies that students with dyslexia say they use to
overcome difficulties with their academic work, in the hope that
this will inspire readers to test out some of these ideas on their own
studies. This chapter, however, centres specifically on types of emotional coping techniques to help students to deal with and attempt
to overcome negative emotion in association with their studies.
The chapter is of fundamental importance, as findings presented
in Abbott-Jones (2022) provided evidence to suggest that students
with dyslexia struggle to find effective strategies for coping emotionally. Although many of the cognitive techniques presented up

to this point in the book do also help to alleviate negative emotion such as anxiety, particularly through organisation, preparation and rehearsal, students with dyslexia need additional methods to supplement these techniques to help them to cope emotionally.

As such, this chapter firstly outlines the types of emotional difficulties experienced by students with dyslexia. This helps us to have a deeper understanding of why these obstacles exist for the dyslexic learner and enables the dyslexic reader to feel less alone as they develop a shared identity with the recognition of these emotional problems. The chapter then moves forward to present a range of valuable emotional coping methods, as specified from the voices of students with dyslexia from the previous book (Abbott-Jones, 2022), that readers may want to consider. These include the types of cognitive techniques that can help to alleviate anxiety and stress in association with your work; learning to identify your anxiety triggers; learning how to apply cognitive restructuring to help to frame situations you fear more positively; talking to someone; planning, identifying and using the right type of learning strategies that match with your learning style and ways in which you process information; implementing breaks; participating in exercise; seeking comfort; and using mental resilience, such as persistence and determination. Specific examples are provided through articulations from dyslexic students, and the dyslexic reader of the book is invited to think about trialling some of these approaches.

11.2   Types of Emotional Difficulties Experienced by Students with Dyslexia

Research work on dyslexia's association with anxiety and on the social/ emotional difficulties for the adult dyslexic student at university has historically been neglected. The focus has been on the cognitive deficits of dyslexia, and the literature has tended to concentrate on implications of disability legislations introduced during the mid-1990s in terms of what this means for higher education institutions and disabled students working within those institutions. Where studies do exist that have looked at the relationship between dyslexia and negative emotional consequences, they have tended to centre on the connection between dyslexia and emotional difficulties in schoolchildren, without looking at how this pans out in adulthood and in the university environment. Very rarely has the association between dyslexia and emotional difficulties from the dyslexic adult student perspective been featured. Yet, we need to develop a deeper understanding of the ways in which the emotional consequences of dyslexia are shaped from childhood into adulthood as an internalised anxiety to fully comprehend the support needs of students with dyslexia in higher education.

Recognition of emotional difficulties in association with dyslexia was further compounded during the research process conducted for *Dyslexia in Higher Education: Anxiety and Coping* (Abbott-Jones, 2022). For instance, during one-to-one interviews with 20 students diagnosed with dyslexia, what was most noticeable, when asking students how dyslexia affected them, was how often they identified an emotional difficulty before any type of cognitive difficulty they had. This reaction suggests that the social/emotional and mental health conditions, and the barriers that these inevitably impose on academic performance, are of major concern for these students.

This was exemplified by MA Arts student Cara, who recognised her difficulty in putting ideas in the right order in her writing, but was more focused on the emotional consequences of her dyslexia, such as the impact on her confidence:

389

> I would say it has quite a significant emotional impact [the dyslexia], mostly in my work. Occasionally, I can get sentences back to front, so I would have all the right words in, which is just something to be aware of if I've got presentations, or I'm trying to learn quotes. I have to make sure that I've got it correct. When I'm writing, I know that it never comes out right the first way. Normally I'm writing all my ideas and they're all in there, but they are in the wrong order, so then I have to rearrange it all. I think it's something that knocks my self-confidence quite a lot. Often, I try and hide it. When you tell people, they don't always understand. Some of my own family don't really understand, so that's quite annoying.

The case of MA Humanities student Debra was similar. Although she specified that she had slow reading and processing speeds, it was self-doubt established by her dyslexia that was affecting her in a more troublesome way than the cognitive deficit:

> I would say, I don't know what the word is, but a lot of self-doubt. I question, I don't really believe that I am able, I question myself academically. I always think others are much more academic than myself and I did consider myself stupid as a child. My sisters were constantly reading books, and I would struggle to finish a book. At school when we had to read out loud, I noticed everyone, I would always compare myself to other people and I noticed that they would be reading out loud fine, or finish. If we had to read together, a chapter, a paragraph, they would read it before me. So, I just noticed that I was slightly behind, and I just thought that was because I was a bit slow.

BSc Nursing student Tina spoke about the emotional stress caused by the prospect of having to read academic work and the difficulties the stress would create for her, over the recognition of her difficulties with reading and writing:

> I think it kind of makes me get stressed out when I have to read. That's how I notice it a lot [the dyslexia], and I don't pick up mistakes in my writing.

What is noticeable about all these statements is that, for adult students with dyslexia, the emotional impact of dyslexia can have a more detrimental effect on learning progression than the cognitive deficits. That is because low self-esteem, self-doubt and stress can interfere with and impede cognitive processes in a more harmful way than learning deficits.

The reason these negative emotions exist for dyslexic leaners is essentially down to life-long difficulties, stemming from early school days, with certain academic tasks. These tasks can vary from spelling, to meeting deadlines, note taking or exams, dependent upon the learner and their dyslexia profile, which manifests frustration, anger, anxiety and stress. This has a causal chain effect leading to low self-confidence, and if not adequately dealt with and addressed can cause mental health problems. The feeling of inadequacy is illustrated here by BA Sciences student Fiona, who spoke about how difficulties with spelling made her feel incompetent:

> I find it frustrating. I'd be frustrated at the task, I'd probably be like, look I'm not good at this. It makes me feel uncomfortable, it makes me feel stupid. But I feel like I'm constantly trying to prove to people that I deserve to be here, so anything that comes under like spelling has an emotional reaction, because I probably get quite defensive. I think sometimes I feel inadequate, I think that's probably...Or, I think I've had a constant kind of thing of do I deserve, should I be here?

Taking the above into consideration, we can be in agreement that in some cases negative emotion, as identified by studies on childhood dyslexia (Dahle, Knivsberg & Andreassen, 2010; Gabrieli, 2009; Habib & Naz, 2015; Humphrey & Mullins, 2002; Knivsberg & Andreassen, 2008; Lima, 2011; Plakopiti and Bellou, 2014; Riddick, 2010), continues into adulthood in the form of internalised anxiety. The anxiety is generally triggered by the activation of damaging emotion stored in memory from adverse earlier childhood educational experiences.

391

Let us now turn to looking at techniques and strategies that can assist with reducing anxiety in relation to your academic work.

11.3   Cognitive Techniques That Help Alleviate Anxiety

11.3.1   Organisation

Cognitive techniques to a great extent have repercussions for alleviating and dealing with the negative emotional consequences of dyslexia. For example, if a student has devised an effective strategy for being able to memorise and retrieve information for an exam, this has a knock-on effect in reducing the anxiety the student has in connection with thoughts of the exam. In fact, eminent coping theorists Folkman and Lazarus (1984) and later Skinner, Edge, Altman, Sherwood, and Cooper (2003) recognised that cognitive coping in the form of problem solving/instrumental coping has a significant role to play in altering negative emotion.

Furthermore, as we have seen in Chapter 2 *Organisation Techniques and Meeting Deadlines*, putting strategies into place to help with planning and keeping organised with your work can have a significant effect on lessening feelings of stress and negativity. This is exemplified in Abbott-Jones (2022) when out of 20 students with dyslexia interviewed on techniques that helped them to remain focused and motivated with their work, 13 students reported that organisation helped to curtail feelings of anxiety, stress and anger. Organisation skills – including using systems to control events, using plans, timetabling, using daily to-do lists, and making timetables into visual posters to display on the wall – were key to students with dyslexia becoming calmer and more engaged with their academic work. This was clearly exemplified in the quote below articulated by Nursing student Lisa:

> When I was younger, I was completely disorganised and angry at everything. I thought I was stupid, and I was a pretty angry child because of everything. Once I started to organise things it calmed down a bit because I was able to focus. My focus was to make sure that everything was organised and then everything did have a place and it was a bit more logical.

11.3.2   Making a Plan of How to Tackle Your Assignment or Revision

As we have seen from Chapter 2 (which also provides further detailed information on how to plan), breaking up larger projects into a series of smaller time-framed steps is key for dissipating anxiety and the feeling of being overwhelmed because of not knowing where to start with your work, or having left several projects accumulating up until the last minute.

Lisa, from the quote above, having learned the benefits of planning for her wellbeing from her younger days, maintained that scheduling her work was the solution for keeping her stimulated and driven in her studies:

> I have a lot of things with schedules and plans, like I have to-do lists for every day, because otherwise I don't focus on anything, or I don't get things done.

As articulated by coping theorists Skinner et al., 'making a plan not only guides problem solving but also calms emotion' (Skinner et al., 2003, p. 227). Hence, problem solving in the form of organisation and planning is a prime example of coping that helps to alleviate cognitive difficulties, yet also helps to reduce negative emotions of anxiety, stress, being disorganised, angry and frustrated.

11.3.3 Making a Timetable and Creating and Sticking to a Routine

Some students with dyslexia, who were able to identify ways they needed to learn to reduce stress and anxiety, pinpointed that the anxiety stemmed from feeling either out of control with their studies or from their lack of organisation. This was recognised by Fiona, a final-year BSc Sciences student, and by Alan, a postgraduate MSc Sciences student:

> I think the disorganisation of myself impacts my anxiety. If I get better at organising, I could limit some of my anxiety or deal with it better. (Alan)

> When I'm not in control it all seems to start to go awry, so I will prepare to organise things. I end up taking control because the anxiety will get too much. (Fiona)

Consequently, for these students, a key to resolving the feeling of uncertainty and being out of control was to timetable their week, which helped them to manage their time in terms of knowing what they would be doing and when. This negated the precariousness and meandering caused by not having a routine. Weekly timetabling helped the students to have more structure in their lives, which created a sense of familiarity and guidance and assisted with reducing stress.

11.4   Productive Emotional Coping

Linking back to the problem of anxiety and its prevalence for students with dyslexia, which was identified through empirical research in Abbott-Jones (2022), negative emotion in dyslexic students is not only concerning because of its ubiquity but also because many of the students interviewed said that they did not know any productive techniques to deal with their anxiety, stress, anger or frustration. In fact, some students stated that they did not know how to cope emotionally, as in the example of BSc Sciences student Helen, who declared:

> I don't cope with it [negative emotion]. I have a breakdown. I don't cope. I try and move on, and I just get stuck. Last Saturday, I wanted to finish this lecture on diabetes. Anyway, there was 75 slides in the whole thing and I'm on slide 36, and I was on slide 36 on Saturday at 9 am, and I was still on slide 36 at 7 pm. I didn't even move on one slide.

Helen's observation here shows that her panic caused by not comprehending her reading, which was forcing her to freeze and, in a cyclical effect, interfering even more with her ability to process the information, was not being dealt with. So, instead of walking away from her work and immersing herself into something to help to calm her mind, instead she was counterproductive and had wasted a day by not attending to her anxiety.

During interviews, students were much less forthcoming on ways they coped emotionally than cognitively. Nevertheless, after much probing and exploration, some students with dyslexia did begin to open up, and a mixture of ways of dealing with destructive emotion began to be identified. Some of these approaches are recorded below.

11.4.1   Learning to Identify Your Anxiety Triggers

MSc Sciences student Alan had, with time and experience, developed an awareness of the types of academic tasks and situations that generated anxiety. Having learned to identify unhelpful techniques which caused stress, he avoided them and instead generated his own alternative methods. For example, it was common for Alan's peers to cram for exams (placing large amounts of information into short-term memory). However, Alan, on recognising that this was not only ineffective for him but also gave rise to unwarranted stress, adopted an alternative revision method that suited how he needed to process and recall information. On cramming, he stated:

> I also can't cram. I've never been able to cram. I never will cram, and I will never put myself in a situation to cram because it doesn't work. It just causes more anxiety and stress and I just need to take my time.

11.4.2   The Anxiety Triggers Questionnaire

An initial method that may help you to begin to identify causes for your stress and anxiety, and to generate a metacognitive awareness of your thoughts, emotions and physical effects during times of distress, is the questionnaire presented below. This is also available on the link to Resources. By undertaking the questionnaire (or any similar online anxiety triggers survey), you will become more informed as to the types of experience that cause distressing emotion. This can then be a useful basis for discussion with your support tutor on situations you are consciously aware of, in relation to triggering the anxiety.

Learning to Recognise Your Anxiety Triggers
What situations trigger stress for you?

- When you have too much work to do?
- When things don't go the way you want?
- When you give yourself unachievable goals?
- Other?

What thoughts do you have in these situations?

- I'm never going to get this done.
- I'm not good enough.
- No one understands what I feel.
- Other?

What emotions do you have?

- Feel anxious.
- Feel depressed.
- Feel irritable, tearful or moody easily.
- Other?

What physical signs do you have?

- Have headaches.
- Feel shaky inside.
- Lie awake at night and worry.
- Other?

11.4.3   Learning How to Apply Cognitive Restructuring

Cognitive restructuring is defined by coping theorists Skinner et al. (2003) as 'active attempts to change one's view of a stressful situation in order to see it in a more positive light'. Cognitive restructuring is used when a stressful situation is impossible to change.

When applied to consider the situation faced by students with dyslexia, whilst it is possible to change approaches to study to find more suitable methods for effectively processing and retaining information, the diagnosis of dyslexia cannot be altered. Whilst more memorable techniques for revision can be adopted, if there are deficits in working memory these will remain. This reality, acknowledged by a few students with dyslexia during interviews for Abbott-Jones (2022), was evidenced by the ways in which problem solving was being used in conjunction with cognitive restructuring in the form of positive thinking to minimise distress This was most notable when students spoke about the advantages of their dyslexia and the qualities they felt it had given them in comparison to their non-dyslexic peers. Examples such as the quote below from BA English student Chloe illuminate the ways in which some students with dyslexia have used cognitive restructuring to embrace their diagnosis:

> The advantage [of dyslexia] is that I have a brilliant imagination and I get lots of ideas. I see things quite differently than maybe a lot of other people. That can be genius at times. I can walk on the street and start laughing because I have so many things bouncing in my head and sometimes, I see things, not because I'm hallucinating, but I just see things and it's quite lively.

11.4.4   Using the Inner Critic Template

The inner critic, our critical inner voice which gives rise to feelings of self-doubt and inadequacy, as experienced above by MA Arts student Debra and BA Sciences student Fiona, can be reformulated through actively applying cognitive restructuring when faced with obstacles. A way of helping to develop the ability for cognitive restructuring could be to use the 'inner critic template' below. You can access the template via the Resources link (www.cambridge.org/abbottjones). That way, when you become familiar with the process, each time you encounter an experience that has left you feeling doubtful or under-confident or has generated other negative emotion, you can use the steps of the exercise to help you with reframing your mindset to feel more positive about the original problem.

Problem situation	
Inner critic says	
Evidence for this	
Evidence against this	
Balanced view	
Future strategy	

First, you think about the problem, challenge or situation that is causing distress. It could be that you have not enough time to complete an assignment, or you got a low grade on an exam paper. It could also be more specifically connected to your emotional state, such as you believe you have not enough confidence to do a presentation, or you have anxiety about reading aloud in class.

In your own words, write about the problem alongside the **Problem situation** box.

The next step is to write what your inner critic says, which could be something along the lines of 'I'm not good enough', or 'I have imposter syndrome'.

You then provide the evidence to support this. This could be reflecting on your previous exam grades or assignment feedback, or it could be your own affirmation that you have not turned up to do a presentation yet, or have not contributed to seminar discussion.

You then make a note of the evidence to support your inner critic in the **Evidence for this** space.

You then begin to flip this thinking around – which is using your cognitive restructuring – by reflecting on the evidence accumulated over your lifetime to suggest the opposite of what you are feeling. In the case of dealing with the low grade for the exam, for example, this could be considering previous exams from your school, or college days, in certain subjects in which you achieved higher grades, which provides the evidence to show you can do them. If your problem situation is related to your fear of reading aloud in front of your peers in class, you may think about times from your past in which you may have read aloud more comfortably in front of your mum, partner or friends, which verifies that doing it in front of your peers could be okay. In the case of avoiding presentations, you may recall the occasions in which you contributed verbally and confidently during class discussions, which confirms that doing a presentation should be possible.

You then note your past achievements and life experiences, showing that you have previously overcome your obstacles, in the **Evidence against this** box.

You next write a balanced view of your situation, such as, 'I may have got a low mark in this exam, but I used the correct type of revision strategies to get higher grades before.'

This effectively leads to the devising of the **Future strategy**, which could be to look at exam techniques used before that worked well; or to continue to practise talking and introducing ideas more regularly in seminar sessions to help with developing confidence in delivering a presentation, and so forth.

Let us now turn to other strategies that students with dyslexia said they were using to alleviate negative emotion.

11.5   Talking to Someone

A consistent theme for coping emotionally, used by 17 out of the 20 students with dyslexia interviewed in Abbott-Jones (2022), was to talk to someone. As MSc Geology student Luke explained, talking to someone for him was an outlet for relieving stress and provided a way to think openly about his concerns:

> I always felt talking with somebody about it always relieved some of the stress because it allowed you to think about the issue.

MSc Humanities student Alison would rely on her mum as the source for relieving pent-up emotion. Her mother not only understood dyslexia, but also motivated Alison by helping to put things into perspective for her, encouraging Alison to regard herself as successful academically:

> I just go to my mum and cry about it, and she'll be like, 'Why are you upset?' When I got diagnosed with dyslexia, she never suspected it. She took it as quite a shock, but because she teaches adults and had to learn a lot about dyslexia herself, she was quite soft about it and was like 'Oh, don't worry, you're doing a master's at Kings, it's okay, you're just over stressing.'

MA Arts student Cara explained how she had previously experienced high levels of anxiety and stress during her undergraduate degree. Yet, after graduating, having children and a supportive partner, followed by returning to postgraduate study some years later as a part-time student, she reflected how her new family had helped to reduce the negative emotions she suffered in her undergraduate studies. Her family support network provided emotional relief and acted to prevent the anxiety she originally encountered during her earlier studies:

> I'm much better now, I'm a part-time student, and I also have a great family to instruct me. That works very well, I can recommend it to everybody.

Charlie, a postgraduate student who also solved her emotional problems through talking to someone, believed there was a barrier to this outlet at her university. She felt that academic staff were not necessarily providing opportunities for talking with regards to emotional difficulties:

> The way that I work out the problems in my mind is to talk about it and that's something that's incredibly limited at University, because it's very rare to find a lecturer who will be willing to give you time to talk about it.

11.5.1 Identifying the Appropriate People to Talk To

In Charlie's case above, university teaching staff should, as part of their role and responsibilities, have a duty of pastoral care to their students. However, because of workload, ethical problems and questions, and some confusion over what exactly university lecturers are qualified to deal with, appropriately and adequately supporting student wellbeing tends to be an area that becomes neglected and overlooked by teaching staff.

Consequently, although initially it may feel daunting to open up to someone about any difficulties you are experiencing, a first step in this is to identify someone you trust and who you would feel safe and supported in talking to. This could, as in Alison's and Cara's examples, be a parent, partner or other family member, or you may feel more secure in talking to a professional, such as a psychologist, or your support tutor.

11.5.2 Sharing Experiences and Anxieties with Dyslexic Peers

Although the Disabled Students' Allowance (DSA) is structured for students with a formal diagnosis of dyslexia to receive one-to-one support with a specialist dyslexia tutor, students with dyslexia have frequently commented on how it would be helpful to have some group meetings with other dyslexic peers from their universities. This would assist in feeling less isolated with any difficulties, and a shared social identity could be established whereby various experiences and anxieties could be talked over with the group. MSc student Alan recognised the benefits of creating this collaborative space.

That possibly would be quite helpful, dyslexics on similar courses meeting and talking about their experiences. Two or three students and somebody who can ask the right questions. That sort of peer sharing could be quite useful in some settings.

This type of support is not provided by the DSA, but any enterprising student could organise and develop their own group. This could be through asking disability centre staff at your university to help you with reaching out to other dyslexic students and with finding a quiet location to hold meetings. Or you could initiate contact with your dyslexic peers via social media, from where you can discuss how to gather somewhere in person to collaborate in talking through various learning experiences.

11.5.3 Helping Others to Develop an Awareness of Difficulties Connected to Dyslexia

Sometimes, helping peers, colleagues and tutors have a greater awareness of the emotional difficulties associated with dyslexia can be achieved by explaining to people the ways in which dyslexia can affect an individual cognitively. For example, MA Education student Chloe had a non-dyslexic friend who thought Chloe was overly anxious about her work and could not understand why she needed to start her dissertation so early in the term. To address this lack of understanding, Chloe confided in her friend by explaining how her dyslexic brain functioned and why she took so long over her work compared with her peers:

> One of my really good friends at Uni was like, 'Well, calm down.' Then one day at lunch, I really explained to her how my brain worked, and she was like, 'Well of course you do this and this.' Then she got it, she understood why I did what I did, and interestingly enough, I started the dissertation long before her and at one point we were at the same stage because she could do things quicker, and I need more time.

So, talking is not only a productive emotional outlet, it also helps to inform your non-dyslexic peers and tutors of the types of difficulties you experience, both emotionally and cognitively. In that sense, the people you encounter daily will appreciate your openness, as they can have a better understanding of how to support you more effectively with your learning and your wellbeing.

11.6   Planning and Using Strategies

As identified in Chapter 2 and in Section 11.3 ('Cognitive Techniques That Help Alleviate Anxiety'), planning and using strategies appropriate for how you think, process information and learn is essential in helping you to deal with stress and alleviate any mental health difficulties, such as unhealthy levels of anxiety. You may ask why we want to revisit the importance of planning as a part of your study life, and why planning is such a productive method for reducing anxiety whilst simultaneously assisting with cognitive difficulties.

The answer to this is, once you have learned to identify your anxiety triggers, by reflecting and using the anxiety triggers questionnaire presented above or a similar measure, you can plan how you are going to tackle your stress in connection to the event that is causing it.

11.6.1   List Your Intentions for How You Will Deal with the Stress

First, consider what you intend to do to address your worries. This ideally should include an amalgamation of actions (behaviours) you will take and strategies (cognitive techniques) you will use to confront the problem. For example, if you are particularly concerned about a forthcoming presentation, exam, deadline, meeting or interview, the actions you may want to take could include talking to your support tutor, finding out more information about the event, or doing some exercise to relieve thoughts of the stressor (the thing that causes the emotional difficulty), which are all behaviours you could pursue. The strategies you can implement in collaboration with your actions might involve rehearsing and timing your presentation, highlighting to break down your exam questions, timetabling to meet your deadline, or making notes for your interview.

When you are stressed and anxious, your ability to think, remember, make decisions, concentrate and focus is highly disrupted, so having a plan listing your intentions for ways of facing the stressor (both actions and learning strategy methods) helps to keep you on track.

11.6.2   Why Problem Solving in the Form of Planning Is Productive

As mentioned above, problem solving (tackling and diminishing the stressor) is what coping theorists, such as Skinner et al. (2003), call a 'higher-order' category of coping (using more sophisticated, productive methods to cope with the stress). Problem solving as a form of coping encompasses what Skinner et al. refer to as 'lower-order' techniques – smaller actions that are taken as part of higher-order problem solving. These include instrumental action (practical steps), strategising, problem solving (rather than the higher-order problem solving of specifically targeting the stressor, this could include smaller actions of investigating the stressor, applying rational thinking, coming up with creative solutions, etc.), planning, logical analysis, effort, persistence, determination. It is clear why problem solving has been conceptualised by

Skinner et al. (2003) in this way, as all of the lower-order strategies specified above are functionally homogeneous: they not only deal with taxing demands in the same way (i.e., through actively approaching the stressor), but also achieve the same coping outcome (i.e., obtaining a desired result). Furthermore, for students with dyslexia, the lower-order technique of planning is particularly productive, and over time, as they learn to recognise causes for anxiety, students often apply it extensively. This is because planning – having a written schedule of how to tackle things in place – cognitively compensates for deficits in working memory and helps to overcome procrastination.

Having to-do lists and calendars with tasks visually and colourfully noted down acts as a tool to keep us focused, outlines the work, makes us feel less overwhelmed because we know the steps and timeframe needed to complete it, and gives us a sense of control, thus reducing and eliminating anxiety, as explained by BSc Sciences student Helen:

> I have a lot of things with schedules and plans, like I have to-do lists for every day, because otherwise I don't focus on anything, or I don't get things done.

Hence, the amount of anxious energy, both draining and exhausting, wasted in worrying that something is going to be lost, due to deficits in memory, become diminished and replaced by a calmness, as illustrated by MA Education student Chloe:

> If I don't have it written down on a to-do list, or a plan, something there I'm scared I'm going to lose it. It's going to disappear. It's one ball is going to be somewhere, and then I spend more energy thinking about if I forget something. Just as soon as I get it down, nicely done. Each week, times daily, and quite often at night before, I will do one for the next day, so I know what's going to happen.

406

11.6.3 Make Your Planning and Use of Strategies for Learning Enjoyable and Creative

As discussed by Helen and Chloe above, and in Chapter 2, having plans and tasks written down in multisensory, colourful and creative ways provides a form of self-help to support our mental health, as was so helpfully described when we revisit the quote provided by BSc Nursing student Lisa:

> When I was younger, I was completely disorganised and angry at everything, I thought I was stupid and I was a pretty angry child because of everything, but once I started to organise things, it calmed down a bit because I was able to focus, and my focus was to make sure that everything was organised and then everything did have a place, and it was a bit more logical.

Accordingly, as planning helps to keep our minds clear of clutter and releases us from internal and external pressure by giving us a clear direction to follow, you will be able to spend more time in being productive, devising fun and engaging strategies for learning. This is because you will procrastinate less, and the reduced anxiety, due to planning and having a logical order for things, will free up space in the mind for creativity and innovation with your learning methods.

Next, we look at the importance of implementing breaks in your work schedule to help with reducing stress and increasing productivity.

11.7 Implementing Breaks

From a practitioner perspective, students with dyslexia who have obtained places at UK universities are generally incredibly hard-working and have high performance expectations. Yet, because of the discrepancy nature of dyslexia (Grant, 2010), whereby levels of intelligence in the average range or higher become undermined by cognitive weaknesses in working memory and information processing ability interfering with academic performance, these students can easily pressurise themselves to overwork as a way of compensating for these difficulties. This is a counterproductive strategy, as it leads to becoming overwhelmed, tired and frustrated. The scenario is usually typical when a dyslexic learner, aware of their intellectual ability, becomes annoyed that they cannot demonstrate this through their academic work, so they assume they must work harder than their non-dyslexic peers to obtain satisfactory grades. This overworking ethos and the way that it can lead to fatigue and burnout was recognised by MA Arts student Cara who declared:

> I know I can do it, but then I tend to burn out a lot and I probably don't have as many rest breaks as I should, but that's because in my mind I know how much I want to do and how much I want to get done.

Over time, as metacognition develops, and knowledge of effective strategies to use for study, teamed with awareness of the mind's receptiveness for absorbing information, becomes evolved, students with dyslexia begin to recognise the complete futility of overworking, as described by MA Arts student Debra:

> I realised breaks were quite important. I think my initial breakdown, my first breakdown, trying to change my bedsheets, was that I had sat in front of the computer for hours. Just trying to do something and it didn't work. Overly tired, just putting too much pressure on myself, far too much pressure and realising that you can only really concentrate for kind of 90 minutes. So, I do a good 90 minutes, this time, I'd go make a cup of tea, or I'd just do something totally different, paint my nails, whatever, then come back, re-read it and do it again.

Whilst Debra here identified that when working on written assignments she could usually concentrate for a period of roughly 90 minutes, every individual is different in relation to concentration span. Concentration span can vary considerably depending on the type of task you are working on, and on how arduous the task is for you to accomplish. Consequently, when scheduling breaks into your daily studies, it is advisable to time yourself initially, so you can get a sense of the rough length of time you can concentrate on something, before you begin to be aware of your thoughts drifting, or you start to feel fatigued. Once you have an idea of your attention span in relation to the task, you can timetable a series of breaks to ensure that your work is broken into bite-size chunks. Also, although Debra found making a cup of tea or painting her nails an effective respite, allowing her to reset her focus on returning to her writing, every person will have their own unique method for resting and regrouping. This may involve changing your scenery by going outside for a quick walk, turning your attention to dipping into an enjoyable novel, TV programme or film for a while, doing a chore such as loading the dishwasher or hoovering, taking some exercise or dancing to re-energise, or playing computer games. Using relaxing activities for the purpose of shifting brain states helps you maintain your mental and physical health. It does not matter what actions you do in your own unique way of enjoying your breaks, as long as you have identified that that particular way of spending your time is effective in enabling you to refocus on work on your return.

11.8   Stepping Back from Pressurised Situations

A variation of the break from work discussed above is the equally important technique of stepping back from highly charged situations. This strategy helps you to stay calm and rational when faced with challenges and is helpful for diminishing negative emotion. For example, some students interviewed in Abbott-Jones (2022), when faced with emotionally demanding or coercive situations, would use the method of stepping away from the scene to regain composure, or to refresh their mind from any unnecessary stress. For example, MA Education student Chloe would take a step back during arguments with friends:

> In fights with friends, I need to step away from the scene. I'm temperamental.

BSc Nursing student Tina, meanwhile, would step away for a few moments to regather herself when in testing situations during hospital placements:

> The only thing is stepping away from it. Sometimes the best thing for me to do is step away from work.

PhD Sciences student Ada's anxiety was so severe during her undergraduate studies that she had undertaken an NHS stress management course. During the course, she had been taught methods for dealing with anxiety. One of the strategies for dealing with arduous situations involved taking deep breaths and extracting herself for a moment from the setting:

> They taught us some really good techniques, you know, just having a deep diaphragm breath, just taking yourself away for a moment. All you have to do is just excuse yourself for a moment. Even, if you need to, you can pretend to take a phone call, just do something like that and also remember something you really enjoy.

The practice of stepping away for a moment or two from circumstances you identify as intense is constructive, as it allows what coping theorists Skinner et al. (2003) refer to as cognitive restructuring. Basically, by stepping back, rather than reacting impulsively, which is the more likely case if you do not step away from the situation, you are able to reflect and ask yourself some simple questions on how you are interpreting the situation. As a result, the time out helps you to view the scenario more positively, enabling you to regain an element of control in terms of how you respond. Accordingly, after careful consideration, you will be able to deal with the testing experience by undertaking calm and thoughtful actions, more so than having not stepped away from the distress.

Stepping back is also productive for emotion regulation (Skinner et al., 2003), as the rethinking involved in briefly withdrawing from a challenging situation provides you with the ability to positively manage and rationally respond to an emotionally taxing experience.

11.9 Participating in Exercise

Exercise is another productive way of relinquishing anxiety, depression, stress and negative emotion, and provides an effective technique for maintaining positive wellbeing. In fact, a recent study (2019), undertaken by researchers Chai, Chen and Stein from Harvard Medical School, found evidence that running for 15 minutes a day, or walking for an hour, reduced the risks of major depression by 26%.

Use of exercise to help to deal with negative emotion and mental health difficulties was also a theme mentioned by 12 out of the 20 dyslexic students interviewed in Abbott-Jones (2022). This varied from going to the gym to going walking, running, using mindfulness (a form of meditation focusing on the present moment rather than the past or future), using meditation and breathing exercises, undertaking yoga, om chanting and listening to Zen music, going cycling, or otherwise spending time outdoors.

However, students who had learned to acknowledge that scheduling time in a typical study day for sports, as this enabled more productivity with work rather than being counterproductive by taking time away from their studies, were generally more experienced students in the final years of their degree courses, or were post-graduates. This is because, as with most techniques provided by this book, it takes time to develop the metacognitive awareness and recognition of strategies that are beneficial for the wellbeing and healthy, effective functioning of our own cognition. This scenario is exemplified by MA Humanities student Charlie when she talked about activities she tried to do to diminish her anxiety:

> Sometimes I went to a psychologist, but that was not very helpful. I also tried to do some sports, it helped, but I was so narrowly minded that I often skipped sport for sitting longer in the library. But it takes a long time to understand that.

11.9.1   Find Out What Activities Are Accessible

Taking out a gym membership at a private club can be expensive. One way to resolve this, if on a budget, is to find out what types of sporting activities you can do for free or cheaply through your university. PhD student Ada discovered a swimming pool on her campus that she could use for free and found that inexpensive yoga classes in the run up to exams helped her to remain calm.

> You know, if you like swimming, go swimming. Because I was at Uni, we could do two quid yoga, so I went and did that a lot and it was really good. And a big part of yoga is breathing, and the moment you can get your breath to just calm down, or just take a nice deep breath, then that was so useful just before exams.

11.9.2 Calming Exercises and Mindfulness

Calming and breathing exercises in the example above can be useful for dealing with anxiety and stress. Other methods that are productive for helping to overcome mental health difficulties include mindfulness. BSc Sciences student Helen would go to the gym and running, to help to relieve stress and frustration; but in addition, during times when she wanted to be less physical, yet was still in need of an outlet to relax and calm her mind, she would participate in mindfulness. Further to buying a book to learn mindfulness techniques, she also participated in mindful colouring, which helped to reduce negative thinking by bringing her awareness and focus to the current moment through a relaxation process:

> Mindfulness is quite good to do. I've got a book on it. I love the colouring-in books.

MSc Humanities student Alison, relatively new to the mindfulness method, explained that if she had known about this approach in her undergraduate years, she would have used mindfulness to help with feeling less anxious before exams. She also suggested that mindfulness and meditation are strategies that universities should provide to help with student wellbeing:

> If I looked at it now, having practised more mindfulness, I would have probably visualised it and got more comfortable during exams. I think mindfulness and meditation are good techniques for students to do. Often when you're doing something, you're so busy thinking 'Oh if I don't get this grade, or I need to pass.' You're not thinking, 'Okay, this is my piece of work, I just have to write this one paragraph first.' If you took it step-by-step, you know it stops the stress. It's something universities should teach.

Whilst some university centres for study skills and wellbeing do provide students with information and guidance on mindfulness techniques, in agreement with Alison above, this really needs to be consistent amongst higher education providers and implemented as a taught component on all university undergraduate and postgraduate degree courses. At present, however, like Helen above, you can still learn about mindfulness methods from books, YouTube videos or extracurricular courses, if you want to discover how this activity can benefit your wellbeing if carried out on a regular basis.

11.9.3   Meditation

MA Arts student Cara had begun practising meditation, building up from 1-minute meditation per day to 20 minutes, which she combined with breathing methods to help to feel more tranquil:

> I discovered a strategy that's 1-minute meditation. You need to breathe out in a prism, calm down. Meditation is like mindfulness. It's where you focus for a minute. I really trained myself. Close the eyes and concentrate on the breathing which goes through the nose and on nothing else. If you force yourself to meditate for 20 minutes, you really relax afterwards. It needs practice.

11.9.4   Combining Different Types of Exercise

Sometimes, depending on your emotion at any point in time, you may want to use a combination of different forms of exercise for different purposes. For example, if you have a lot of nervous energy, or are feeling frustrated, or you want to be re-energised, you could try a more physically demanding sport, such as running, cycling or team sports. If you have anxiety or stress and want to be relaxed and calm, you can try yoga, mindfulness and meditation. Our moods and negative emotions constantly vary and change with the different situations we face daily, so recognising the type of activity that can help to reduce the variation of negativity we are currently experiencing is important for emotional regulation and maintenance of positive wellbeing.

An example of this is provided by PhD Sciences student Ada. Always anxious before exams, she found that cycling to the exam hall helped to transform her apprehension into a comfortable, energised exuberance, and enabled her to focus on the paper more effectively during the exam:

> I cycled there to get rid of the extra adrenaline so that I could focus better when I got there.

11.9.5 Walking to Have a Change of Scene

Being outside and in nature also helps to reduce anxiety and to make the mind more responsive to processing information for studies.

MA Humanities postgraduate Charlie noted that during the writing of her undergraduate thesis, she would take breaks by going walking. The change in environment would help to re-energise her mind and body:

> During my dissertation, I went for quite a lot of walks, and that helped to have a change of scene.

11.10 Seeking Comfort

In addition to exercise, comfort seeking for the purpose of gaining a sense of reassurance and for minimising stress can also be productive. Emotional strategies involving seeking comfort to help with learning, as used by students in Abbott-Jones (2022), varied from being in the right environment, to finding peace and sustenance through drinking coffee and eating chocolate, listening to music as a distraction and a way to block out stressors, using the family pet dog as a comforter and an aid to structuring study sessions, using professional support by talking to a psychologist, and finally to taking calming drops such as rescue remedy to ease nerves and relieve anxiety.

Being in the right environment where you feel healthy, safe and secure is important. This is illuminated by MA Education student Chloe, a secondary school Maths teacher. She reflected that although she was able to present her work confidently in front of a class of school pupils, when it came to performing presentations in front of her university peers, she was unable to do so:

> I've been wondering this for so long, and I still can't come up with a good answer as to why I can do it in one place and not in another.

She finally concluded this was based on situation and atmosphere. For example, she perceived that, unlike with her university peers, she was not being evaluated or judged by her pupils. This is because, over time as a proficient teacher, she had developed a sense of trust, rapport and empathy in her relationship with the pupils. Furthermore, as the students were aware of her dyslexia and how she had developed strategies to overcome this, she was ultimately looked up to as a role model by the schoolchildren.

Admittedly, for Chloe, there is a difference between presenting at university and in front of her pupils with whom she has developed a long-established secure relationship and who, aware of her dyslexia, make her feel comfortable. But the difficulty lies in the fact that her inhibitions about presenting in front of her university peers are based on *perception* only. Chloe's university colleagues are not likely to be assessing her presentation for the purpose of criticising or finding flaws in it, but this is how her negative inner voice has interpreted the situation, so that she becomes highly defensive over her work. Using the inner critic template above to develop more positive cognitive restructuring in these types of circumstances could help to eradicate these harmful thought processes. Additionally, practising mindfulness to focus your complete attention and awareness on the present and only on what you are saying during a presentation, hence eradicating all other interfering thoughts, can also, over time, assist with changing your destructive mindset into one based on positivity.

Continuing with the theme of environment and its importance in feeling comfortable and secure during your studies: the surroundings in which you position yourself to work should be somewhere you feel relaxed enough to process the information you are learning. Many students with dyslexia struggle to absorb new knowledge when they are anxious. This can happen during lectures whilst trying to note take. Consequently, if your university provides a lecture capture service whereby you can replay the recording of the lecture from the comfort of your home, as you are now in this more flexible and cosy space, and as your mind becomes more relaxed, you will find it easier to assimilate information. This can help you to further consolidate the learning you may have been struggling to understand during the live lecture.

On a variation of environment, an appropriate time of day in which to find tranquillity and enjoy nourishment is another key contributor to aid effective learning. MA Arts student Debra discovered that she was able to study productively early in the morning:

> I'm much better in the morning when everyone's asleep and it's peaceful. I make a cup of coffee and I really like that.

BSc Medicine student Naomi would find solace in chocolate:

> I probably just munch on my chocolate pot, like this will do.

417

Although finding comfort in chocolate may not be the healthiest activity, an occasional treat can be effective in lowering levels of stress. Like with everything in life, balance and moderation is important, and giving yourself a gift every now and then – whether that is eating chocolate, going for a meal, having a massage, watching a film or reading an enjoyable novel – should be factored into your working schedule. That way, you are kept motivated with your studies, knowing that at the end of the working week, or whenever you schedule in your treat, you are rewarded with something enjoyable as a thank you to yourself for your productivity.

Other forms of comfort that students with dyslexia spoke about included support from the family dog. MA Humanities student Charlie, whilst studying, would sit with the dog, which provided her with a reassuring companion. When the dog required walking, this signalled to Charlie it was time to break from studies for exercise and fresh air, as she describes:

> Funnily enough, the one thing that used to be the most help was the dog. He was a comfort pet because he would quite happily sit with me. Then I was able to structure my day around him. When he wants a walk, he wouldn't let you stare at a screen for too long. They [dogs] just take stress away. If feeling anxious he would sit on my lap, and I would be reading. That was my main destress thing, but exercise works well as well.

Combining of strategies was used by many students. This indicates that students with dyslexia do not solely rely on one form of emotional coping but amalgamate different types of coping dependent upon the individual's circumstances. Debra, mentioned above, in addition to finding it productive to work in the peace of an early morning whilst drinking coffee, would also combine her knowledge of breathing exercises from yoga with the use of calming drops, such as Rescue Remedy, to help with relieving stress during more anxious moments.

11.11   Developing and Using Mental Resilience

Developing and utilising mental resilience, and having the qualities of persistence and determination, will enable you to be provided with the ability to put skills and strategies into place during times when you face hardship. Also, through cultivating these characteristics, it is more likely that you will be able to stay on track in achieving the goals in life that you set for yourself.

Basically, resilience means having the ability and flexibility to adapt to life's misfortunes and setbacks. For example, the recent coronavirus pandemic brought uncertainty and disruption to everyone's lives. During this time, you may have found that your study plans were affected, and you were no longer able to attend live lectures or to meet and make new friends from your course. The distress induced during this precarious event has been proven (Wathelet et al., 2020; Chirikov et al., 2020) to have had a detrimental effect on the mental health of both undergraduate and postgraduate university students. Whilst the situation caused by the coronavirus was beyond your control, if you were able to maintain a positive mindset by continuing to focus on your study goals through persisting with online learning and reading to develop knowledge on your topic area, you would have been demonstrating resilience during challenging times. Resilient people can also be proactive when it comes to problem-solving, and can make calculated decisions and can put those decisions into action. For example, if you found that during the coronavirus pandemic you were suffering from loneliness and isolation, and this was beginning to affect you mentally, a resilient person would recognise this negative effect and would put processes and techniques into place to help to remedy the situation. For instance, you could arrange a daily FaceTime call with family members or friends to help to feel less isolated, you could think of forming or joining an online community to discuss things you are interested in, you could learn new things to help with keeping you busy and occupied, or you could go for a walk to get fresh air and exercise which can help with loneliness and stress.

No matter what challenges you face or how traumatic, if you can find and devise solutions to problems and can persist in continuing to achieve set goals, even though you may have to be flexible in how you go about achieving them, you are demonstrating resilience. Resilience and mental strength develop over time. If, for example, you have already faced a series of stressors, pressures, challenges or traumatic events in life and still been able to recommence making progress towards your goals, even though these may have changed slightly, you have proven that you will have the capacity to meet any further setbacks during your life by harnessing the inner strength you previously used to bounce back from adversity.

11.12   Resilience in Students with Dyslexia

Having dyslexia makes learning more difficult. As a consequence, students with dyslexia have generally had to work harder than their non-dyslexic peers or have had to develop their own learning strategies to be successful and to make it to university level education. Fortunately, this is already demonstrative of resilience. We have seen throughout the various chapters of this book how students with dyslexia have problem-solved by concocting their own techniques to counterbalance their difficulties in learning something in the traditional way. Accordingly, as a dyslexic learner in higher education, it is likely that an element of resilience is already instilled into you, yet the difficulties you face as an adult will change and may at times become more extreme. For example, you will be exposed to a different set of problems in the workplace than experienced at university, so it is of ultimate importance to maintain and nurture your resilience through different sets of circumstances.

On interviewing students in Abbott-Jones (2022) on the positive effects of dyslexia, it became apparent that the characteristic of resilience is a resource that students with dyslexia have relied upon to achieve. For instance, students described themselves as harder working, more driven, persevering and resilient because of their dyslexia. Thus, it became apparent that mental resilience is used as an emotional coping strategy to overcome barriers to learning. Applying hard work and developing knowledge around mental resilience by reading self-help books to cultivate positive attitudes was a technique employed by MSc Geology student Luke:

> Hard work always solves problems. Mental toughness. I've got a few books on it at home. If you can cultivate the right mental attitude, you can overcome a lot of problems.

The development of mental resilience and persistence enabled students with dyslexia to cope both emotionally and cognitively, again described by Luke:

> The mental resiliency stuff is key because once you get that down everything else kind of shrinks in impact upon your psyche.

Once a level of psychological resilience becomes fostered and instilled, students with dyslexia regard this as a quality enabling them to cope emotionally and cognitively, as observed below by BSc Medicine student Naomi:

> I think the fact that it [dyslexia] makes me work that much harder to find things out is a real bonus. It's made me a really driven and resilient person.

421

Whilst techniques already presented in this chapter will help you to develop resilience, Whitley (2018) suggests three effective resilience-enhancing strategies which may be helpful. These are listed below.

11.12.1   Skill Acquisition

Whitley proposes that 'acquiring new skills can play an important part in building resilience, as it helps to develop a sense of mastery and competency – both of which can be utilised during challenging times, as well as increase one's self-esteem and ability to problem solve' (Whitley, 2018).

He goes on to say that the skills to be learned are dependent upon the individual. Whilst some may benefit from improving cognitive skills, such as working memory or selective attention, others may benefit from learning new hobbies or activities through competency-based learning.

On this note, you could reflect as to what exactly will currently benefit you, either cognitively or emotionally. For example, are there are any elements of your studies where at present you feel under-confident? If so, you may want to dip into any one of the chapters presented in this book to look at ways of developing techniques to support that specific area. Alternatively, you may feel that, at this moment, it is more the emotional difficulties than the cognitive ones interfering with and affecting your self-confidence and esteem. As such, learning something new and enjoyable as a hobby could assist with strengthening your sense of wellbeing and could productively support your mental health.

11.12.2   Goal Setting

Whitley advises: 'the ability to develop goals, actionable steps to achieve those goals, and to execute, all help to develop will-power and mental resilience. Goals can be large or small, related to physical health, emotional wellbeing, career, finance, spirituality, or just about anything. Goals that involve skill-acquisition will have a double benefit. For example, learning to play an instrument or learning a new language' (Whitley, 2018).

We have talked a lot in this book about goals related to studies, and achieving assignments and projects by planning and breaking them down into smaller time-framed goals, yet we have not really discussed other types of goals that will also instil determination and resilience. These extra goals and their implementation in your life are as important as your study goals, and in some cases may help to foster a different type of resilience from persisting with studies. For example, perhaps you want to climb a mountain, run a marathon, volunteer for charities, undertake projects in third-world countries, overcome your fear of heights by trying rock climbing. All these experiences will expose you to testing situations, which, if conquered, will help to strengthen and consolidate your resilience.

11.12.3   Controlled Exposure

Whitley suggests that 'controlled exposure refers to the gradual exposure to anxiety-provoking situations and is used to help individuals overcome their fears. Research indicates that this can foster resilience, and especially so when it involves skill-acquisition and goal setting – a triple benefit' (Whitley, 2018).

Taking controlled exposure into account in relation to how this can benefit the individual by increasing confidence, self-esteem, autonomy and mastery whilst also fortifying resilience, you could perhaps initiate this by thinking of a situation you find anxiety-provoking. For example, if you dread public speaking and presentations, you could practise first in front of a small group of friendly peers. This helps to provide the needed exposure and at the same time gives you the courage to believe you can do it. As such, you have faced your fear in a more comfortable setting, which cultivates the resilience required when you perform the actual presentation.

11.13   Summary

In summary, this chapter has:

- Outlined types of emotional difficulties experienced by students with dyslexia.
- Presented a range of emotional coping methods, which has included:
  - Implementing cognitive techniques that help to alleviate anxiety and stress.
  - Learning to identify your anxiety triggers.
  - Learning how to apply cognitive restructuring.
  - Using the inner critic template.
  - Talking to someone.
  - Planning, identifying and using the right type of learning strategies.
  - Implementing breaks.
  - Participating in exercise.
  - Seeking comfort.
  - Using mental resilience.

Epilogue

One final note. As a brief overview of the contents of this book, let us be reminded of the main ideas presented, together with the original purpose of the work.

The book has *combined* a focus on both cognitive coping strategies and socio-emotional techniques for overcoming negative emotion. As shown in the earlier book *Dyslexia in Higher Education: Anxiety and Coping* (Abbott-Jones, 2022), students with dyslexia have a high prevalence of anxiety, self-doubt and low self-confidence which often interferes with their academic performance and can be more detrimental to student progression than the cognitive deficits associated with dyslexia.

As such, this book has built on the work completed for *Dyslexia in Higher Education: Anxiety and Coping*, but rather than aiming to raise awareness of the prevalence of anxiety and negative emotion, and the effects of dyslexia for the dyslexic learner, it has focused instead on effective cognitive and emotional techniques used by such students. The result is a pragmatic, study skills development book for the purpose of supporting students with dyslexia to deal more effectively with their study tasks and learning experiences whilst at university.

Consequently, the book's main themes have focused on the presentation of strategies for overcoming the cognitive and emotional barriers prevalent for the dyslexic learner. These have included:

- Ways in which technology can be utilised.
- Making learning multisensory.
- Applying practicality to study tasks.
- Examples of favourite ways of studying to make learning enjoyable, as described by students with dyslexia.
- Improving metacognition and metacognitive awareness.
- Helping to reduce scotopic sensitivity.

Ultimately, all these strategies have been intended to help the reader to cope with academic life both cognitively and emotionally.

Importantly, the main motivation for the book was to provide a shared platform for students with dyslexia to have something to identify with, which has previously been lacking.

This collective space is offered throughout the book. This is because both emotional and cognitive difficulties have been featured, together with productive strategies to deal with the range of study tasks demanded from students during their time in higher education. The strategies are tried and tested by students with dyslexia, and delivered from the perspectives of people who have learned to successfully cope with dyslexia in the academic world. I hope that, together, the dyslexic student voice and the dyslexic author have given a layer of distinctiveness to the work.

References

Abbott-Jones, A. (2022). *Dyslexia in Higher Education: Anxiety and Coping Skills*. Cambridge University Press.

Ahmad, S. Z., Ludin, N. N. A. A. N., Ekhsan, H. M., Rosmani, A. F. & Ismail, M. H. (2012). Bijak Membaca – applying phonic reading technique and multisensory approach with interactive multimedia for dyslexia children. In *CHUSER 2012 – 2012 IEEE Colloquium on Humanities, Science and Engineering Research*. IEEE.

Akhavan Tafti, M., Hameedy, M. A. & Mohammadi Baghal, N. (2009). Dyslexia, a deficit or a difference: comparing the creativity and memory skills of dyslexic and nondyslexic students in Iran. *Social Behavior and Personality: An International Journal*, 37, 1009–1016.

Alexander-Passe, N. (2010). *Dyslexia and Depression: The Hidden Sorrow*. Nova Science Publishers.

Alexander-Passe, N. (2012). *Dyslexia: Dating, Marriage and Parenthood*. Nova Science Publishers.

Alexander-Passe, N. (2015a). *Dyslexia and Mental Health: Helping People to Overcome Depressive, Self-Harming and Other Adverse Emotional Coping Strategies*. Jessica Kingsley Publishers

Alexander-Passe, N. (2015b). Investigating post-traumatic stress disorder (PTSD) triggered by the experience of dyslexia in mainstream school education? *Journal of Psychology & Psychotherapy*, 5, 215.

Alexander-Passe, N. (2016). Dyslexia, success and post-traumatic growth. *Asia Pacific Journal of Developmental Differences*, 3, 87–130.

Ali, S. (2012). Teaching reading and spelling to adult learners: the multisensory approach. *English Language Teaching*, 5, 40–45.

Alley, M. & Neeley, K. A. (2005). Rethinking the design of presentation slides: a case for sentence headlines and visual evidence. *Technical Communication*, 52, 417–426.

References

Baddeley, A. D. (1999). *Essentials of Human Memory*. Psychology Press.

Bonwell, C. & Eison, J. (1991). *Active Learning: Creating Excitement in the Classroom*. ASHE-ERIC Higher Education Report. School of Education and Human Development, George Washington University.

Boyle, R., Rosen, S. & Forchelli, G. (2016). Exploring metacognitive strategy use during note-takin for students with learning disabilities, *Education 3–13*, 44, 161–180.

British Dyslexia Association (2007) (www.bdadyslexia.org.uk).

British Psychological Society (1999) (www.bps.org.uk/).

Brosnan, M., Demetre, J., Hamill, S., et al. (2002). Executive functioning in adults and children with developmental dyslexia. *Neuropsychologia*, 40, 2144–2155.

Brown, I. W. (1991). To learn is to teach is to create the final exam. *College Teaching*, 39, 150–153.

Bruck, M. & Parke, R. D. (1992). Persistence of dyslexics' phonological awareness deficits. *Developmental Psychology*, 28, 874–886.

Burke, J. (1999). *The English Teacher's Companion: A Complete Guide to Classroom, Curriculum, and the Profession*. Heinemann Educational Books.

Burke, J. (2000) (www.englishcompanion.com).

Businessballs. www.businessballs.com/self-awareness/vak-learning-styles/

Buzan, T., & Buzan, B. (1993). *The Mind Mapping Book; Radiant Thinking – The Major Evolution in Human Thought*. BBC Books.

Camilleri, S., Chetcuti, D. & Falzon, R. (2019). 'They Labeled Me Ignorant': narratives of Maltese youth with dyslexia on national examinations. *SAGE Open*.

Carney, R. N. & Levin, J. R. (2003). Promoting higher-order learning benefits by building lowerorder mnemonic connections. *Applied Cognitive Psychology*, 17, 563–575.

Carroll, J. & Iles, J. (2006). An assessment of anxiety levels in dyslexic students in higher education. *British Journal of Educational Psychology*, 76, 651–662.

Chai, K. W., Chen, C-Y. & Stein, M. (2019). Assessment of bidirectional relationships between physical activity and depression among adults. *JAMA Psychiatry*, 76, 399–408.

Chirikov, I., Soria, K. M., Horgos, B. & Jones-White, D. (2020). *Undergraduate and Graduate Students' Mental Health during the COVID-19 Pandemic. SERU Consortium Report.* University of California – Berkeley and University of Minnesota.

Cottrell, S. (2008). *The Study Skills Handbook* (3rd ed.). Palgrave Macmillan.

Cronnell, B. & Humes, A. (1980). Elementary spelling: what's really taught. *The Elementary School Journal*, 81, 59–64.

Culler, R. E. & Holahan, C. J. (1980). Test anxiety and academic performance: The effects of study-related behaviors. *Journal of Educational Psychology*, 72, 16–20.

Dahle, A., Knivsberg, A. & Andreassen, A. (2010). Coexisting problem behaviour in severe dyslexia. *Journal of Research in Special Educational Needs*, 11, 162–170.

Darke, S. (1988b). Effects of anxiety on inferential reasoning task performance. *Journal of Personality and Social Psychology*, 55, 499–505.

Dash, J. (1991). *Daughters of the Dust.* Kino International.

Dent, H. C. (1961). *Teaching as a Career.* Batsford.

Divine, M. (2015). *Unbeatable Mind: Forge Resiliency and Mental Toughness to Succeed at an Elite Level* (3rd ed.). Mark Divine.

Donovan, J. L. & Marshall, C. R. (2016). Comparing the verbal self-reports of spelling strategies used by children with and without dyslexia. *International Journal of Disability, Development and Education*, 63, 27–44.

Dweck, C. S. (1975). The role of expectations and attributions in the alleviation of learned helplessness. *Journal of Personality and Social Psychology*, 31, 674–685.

Dweck, C. S. & Licht, B. G. (1980). Learned helplessness and intellectual achievement. In J. Garber & M. E. P. Seligman (Eds.), *Human Helplessness.* Academic.

Dyslexia Action (2009) (www.dyslexiaaction.org.uk/).

Edutopia (2022) (www.edutopia.org).

Edwards, J. (1994). *The Scars of Dyslexia: Eight Case Studies in Emotional Reactions.* Cassell.

Eysenck, M. W. (1984). Anxiety and the worry process. *Bulletin of the Psychonomic Society*, 22, 545–548.

429

Equality Act. (2010). (www.legislation.gov.uk/).

Farmer, M., Riddick, B. & Sterling, C. (2002). *Dyslexia and Inclusion: Assessment and Support for Subject Teachers*. Whurr.

Flavell, J., Miller, P. & Miller, S. (2002). *Cognitive Development*. Prentice Hall.

Folkman, S. & Lazarus, R. S. (1984). If it changes it must be a process: study of emotion and coping during three stages of a college examination. *Journal of Personality and Social Psychology*, 48, 150–170.

Frase, L. T. & Schwartz, B. J. (1975). Effect of question production and answering on prose recall. *Journal of Educational Psychology*, 67, 628–635.

Fuller, M., Healey, M., Bradley, A. & Hall, T. (2004). Barriers to learning: a systematic study of the experience of disabled students in one university, *Studies in Higher Education*, 29, 303–318.

Ganz, B. & Ganz, M. N. (1988). Overcoming the problem of learned helpless. *College Teaching*, 36, 14–15.

Gabrieli, J. (2009). Dyslexia: a new synergy between education and cognitive neuroscience. *Science*, 325, 280–283.

Ghisi, M., Bottesi, G., Re, A. M., Cerea, S. & Mammarella, I. C. (2016). Socioemotional features and resilience in Italian university students with and without dyslexia. *Frontiers in Psychology*, 7, 478.

Golub, E. (2005). On audience activities during presentations. *Journal of Computing Sciences in Colleges*, 20, 38–46.

Grant, D. (2010). *That's the Way I Think: Dyslexia, Dyspraxia and ADHD Explained* (2nd ed.). Routledge.

Grskovic, J. A. & Belfiore, P. J. (1996). Improving the spelling performance of students with disabilities. *Journal of Behavioral Education*, 6, 343–354.

Habib, A. & Naz, F. (2015). Cognitive failure, teacher's rejection and interpersonal relationship anxiety in children with dyslexia. *Pakistan Journal of Medical Sciences*, 31, 662–666.

Hargreaves, S. (2012). *Study Skill for Students with Dyslexia* (2nd ed.). SAGE.

Hodapp, V. & Henneberger, A. (1983). Test anxiety, study habits and academic performance. In H. M. Vander Ploeg, R. Schwarzer & C. D. Spiel (Eds.), *Advances in Test Anxiety Research Vol. 2*. Erlbaum.

Hulme, C. & Snowling, M. J. (2009). *Developmental Disorders of Language, Learning and Cognition*. Wiley-Blackwell.

Hume, M. (1997). *Feminism and Film*. Edinburgh University Press.

Humphrey, N. & Mullins, P. (2002). Personal constructs and attribution for academic success and failure in dyslexics, *British Journal of Special Education*, 29, 196–203.

Indeed (2022) (https://indeed.com/).

Ingesson, S. G. (2007). Growing up with dyslexia. *School Psychology International*, 574–539.

International Dyslexia Association (2000) (https://dyslexiaida.org).

Ismail, S. S., Ismail, R., Mohd Mahidin, E. M., et al. (2010). E-Z disleksia for dyslexic children. In *Proceedings of Regional Conference on Knowledge Integration in ICT*. Kolej Universiti Islam Antarabangsa Selangor (KUIS).

Jobs, A., Twesten, C., Göbel, A., et al. (2013). Question-writing as a learning tool for students – outcomes from curricular exams. *BMC Medical Education*, 13, 89.

Jordan, J.A., McGladdery, G. & Dyer, K. (2014). Dyslexia in higher education: implications for maths anxiety, statistics anxiety and psychological well-being. *Dyslexia*, 20, 225–240.

Jones, A. C., Wardlow, L., Pan, S. C., et al. (2015). Beyond the rainbow: retrieval practice leads to better learning than does rainbow writing. *Educational Psychology Review*, 28, 385–400.

Jones, M. W., Obregon, M., Kelly, M. L. & Branigan, H. P. (2008). Elucidating the component processes involved in dyslexic and non-dyslexic reading fluency: an eye tracking study. *Cognition*, 109, 389–407.

Kernaghan, K. & Woloshyn, V. E. (1995). Providing grade one students with multiple spelling strategies: comparisons between strategy instruction with metacognitive information, and traditional language arts. *Applied Cognitive Psychology*, 9, 157–166.

Klein, C. (1993). *Diagnosing Dyslexia*. Avanti.

Knivsberg, A. & Andreassen, A. B. (2008). Behaviour, attention and cognition in severe dyslexia. *Nordic Journal of Psychiatry*, 62, 59–65.

Latham, G.P. & Seijts, G.H. (2016). Distinguished scholar invited essay. *Journal of Leadership and Organizational Studies*, 23, 225–233.

Lefly, D. & Pennington, B. (1991). Spelling errors and reading fluency in compensated adult dyslexics. *Annals of Dyslexia*, 41, 143–162.

Lima, R. (2011). Depressive symptoms and cognitive functions in children with developmental dyslexia. *Arquivos de Neuro-Psiquiatria*, 69, 854–854.

Locke, R., Alexander, G., Mann, R., Kibble, S. and Scallan, S. (2015). Doctors with dyslexia: strategies and support. *The Clinical Teacher*, 14: 355–359.

Logan, J. (2009). Dyslexic entrepreneurs: the incidence; their coping strategies and their business skills. *Dyslexia*, 15, 328–346.

MacLeod, W., Butler, D. & Syer, K. (1996). Beyond achievement data: assessing changes in metacognition and strategic learning. Presented as part of a coordinated symposium at the annual meeting of the American Educational Research Association, New York City.

Mandler, G. (1984). *Mind and Body: Psychology of Emotion and Stress*. Norton.

Mann, T. B., Bushell, D. Jr. & Morris, E. K. (2010). Use of sounding out to improve spelling in young children. *Journal of Applied Behavioural Analysis*, 43, 89–93.

McDougall, S., Hulme, C., Ellis, A. W. & Monk, A. (1994). Learning to read: the role of short-term memory and phonological skills. *Journal of Experimental Child Psychology*, 58, 112–123.

McGuffin, M. E., Martz, S. A. & Heron, T. E. (1997). The effects of self-correction versus traditional spelling on the spelling performance and maintenance of third grade students. *Journal of Behavioral Education*, 7, 463–476.

McKeachie, W. J., Pollie, D. & Spiesman, J. (1986). Relieving anxiety in classroom examinations. *Journal of Abnormal and Social Psychology*, 50, 93–98.

Mealey, D. L. & Host, T. R. (1992). Coping with test anxiety. *College Teaching*, 40, 147–150.

Mehta, R. & Zhu, R. (2009). Blue or red? exploring the effect of color on cognitive task performances. *Science*, 323, 1226–1229.

Mortimore, T. (2008). *Dyslexia and Learning Style: A Practitioner's Handbook* (2nd ed.). Wiley.

Mortimore, T. & Crozier, W. R. (2006). Dyslexia and difficulties with study skills in higher education, *Studies in Higher Education*, 13, 235–251.

Nalavany, B., Carawan, L. & Rennick, R. (2011). Psychosocial experiences associated with confirmed and self-identified dyslexia: a participant-driven concept map of adult perspectives. *Journal of Learning Disabilities*, 44, 63–79.

National Council for Osteopathic Research (2022) (https://ncor.org.uk/).

Nelson, J., Lindstrom, W. & Foels, P. (2015). Test anxiety among college students with specific reading disability (dyslexia): nonverbal ability and working memory as predictors. *Journal of Learning Disabilities*, 48, 422–432.

Neumann, F., Oberhauser, V. & Kornmeier, J. (2020). How odor cues help to optimize learning during sleep in real life-setting. *Scientific Reports*, 10, 1227.

Newman, I. (2019). When saying 'go read it again' won't work: multisensory ideas for more inclusive teaching & learning. *Nurse Education in Practice*, 34, 12–16.

Nezlek, J. B. & Derks, P. (2001). Use of humor as a coping mechanism, psychological adjustment, and social interaction. *Humor: Internation Journal of Humor Research*, 14, 395–413.

Orton, S. T. & Gillingham, A. Orton–Gillingham (www.orton.gillingham .com/).

Oxford University Press. (n.d.). Wellbeing. *Oxford English Dictionary* (www .oed.com/).

Ormrod, J. E. & Jenkins, L. (1989). Study strategies for learning spelling: correlations with achievement and developmental changes. *Perceptual and Motor Skills*, 68, 643–650.

Pan, S. C., Rubin, B. R. & Rickard, T. C. (2015). Does testing with feedback improve adult spelling skills relative to copying and reading? *Journal of Experimental Psychology: Applied*, 21, 356–369.

Parker, L. E. & Lepper, M. R. (1992). Effects of fantasy contexts on children's learning and motivation: making learning more fun. *Journal of Personality and Social Psychology*, 62, 625–633.

Pearson, N. A., Rashotte, C., Torgsen, J. & Wagner, R. (2013). *Comprehensive Test of Phonological Processing* (2nd ed.). (www.pearsonassements .com/).

Plakopiti, A. & Bellou, I. (2014). Text configuration and the impact of anxiety on pupils with dyslexia. *Procedia Computer Science*, 27, 130–137.

Putnam, A. L. (2015). Mnemonics in education: current research and applications. *Translational Issues in Psychological Science*, 1, 130.

Raja, F. (2017). Anxiety level in students of public speaking. *Journal of Education and Educational Development*, 4, 94–110.

References

Ramus, F. & Szenkovits, G. (2008). What phonological deficit? *Quarterly Journal of Experimental Psychology*, 61, 129–141.

Rash, A. M. (1997). An alternative method of assessment: using student-created problems. *Primus*, 7, 89–95.

Rea, D. W. (2000). Optimal motivation for talent development. *Journal for the Education of the Gifted*, 23, 187–216.

Reason, R., Woods, K., Frederickson, N., Heffernan, M. & Martin, C. (1999). *Dyslexia, Literacy and Psychological Assessment*. A report of a working party of the British Psychological Society Division of Educational and Child Psychology. British Psychological Society.

Reynolds, C. R., Richmond, B. O. & Lowe, P. A. (2003). *Adult Manifest Anxiety Scale –College Version*. Western Psychological Services.

Riddick, B., Farmer, M. & Sterling, C. (1997). *Students and Dyslexia, Growing Up with a Specific Learning Difficulty*. Whurr.

Riddick, B., Sterling, C., Farmer, M. & Morgan, S. (1999). Self-esteem and anxiety in the educational histories of adult dyslexic students. *Dyslexia*, 5, 227–248.

Riddick, B. (2010). An examination of the relationship between labelling and stigmatisation with special reference to dyslexia. *Disability & Society*, 15, 653–667.

Rome, H. (1971). The psychiatric aspects of dyslexia. *Bulletin of the Orton Society*, 21, 64–70.

Rose, J. (2009). *Identifying and Teaching Children and Young People with Dyslexia and Literacy Difficulties*. An independent report from Sir Jim Rose to the Secretary of State for Children, Schools and Families.

Ruberto, N., Daigle, D. & Ammar, A. (2016). The spelling strategies of francophone dyslexic students. *Reading and Writing*, 29, 659–681.

Sako, E. (2016). The emotional and social effects of dyslexia. *European Journal of Interdisciplinary Studies*, 2, 231–239.

Sarason, I. G. (1984). Stress, anxiety, and cognitive interference: reactions to tests. *Journal of Personality and Social Psychology*, 46, 929–938.

Saylor Academy (2022) (www.saylor.org/).

Schwarzer, R., Jerusalem, M. & Schwarzer, C. (1983). Self-related and situation related cognitions in test anxiety and helplessness: a longitudinal analysis with structural equations. In H. M. Vander Ploeg,

R. Schwarzer & C. D. Spielberger (Eds.), *Advances in Test Anxiety Research* Vol. 2. Erlbaum.

Schwarzer, R., Jerusalem, M. & Striksrud, A. (1984). The developmental relationship between test anxiety and helplessness. In H. M. Vander Ploeg, R. Schwarzer & C. D. Spielberger (Eds.), *Advances in Test Anxiety Research* Vol. 2. Erlbaum.

Scott, R. (2004). *Dyslexia and Counselling*. Whurr.

Seligman, M. E. P. (1975). *Helplessness*. W. H. Freeman.

Shaywitz, S. E. (1996). Dyslexia. *Scientific American*, 275, 98–104.

Singleton, C. (2003). *Understanding Dyslexia*. Lucid Research.

Skinner, E., Edge, K., Altman, J., Sherwood, H. & Cooper, H. (2003). Searching for the structure of coping: a review and critique of category systems for classifying ways of coping. *Psychological Bulletin*, 129, 216–269.

Smith-Spark, J. H. & Fisk, J. (2007). Working memory functioning in developmental dyslexia. *Memory*, 15, 34–56.

Spencer, K. (2000). Is English a dyslexic language? *Dyslexia*, 6, 152–162.

Spielberger, C. D. (1980). *Test Anxiety Inventory*. Consulting Psychologists Press.

Stipek, D. J. (1988). *Motivation to Learn: From Theory to Practice*. Prentice Hall.

The Muse (www.themuse.com/).

The Dyslexia Shop (2022) (www.thedyslexiashop.co.uk/).

University of Reading LibGuide (2022) (www.libguides.reading.ac.uk/).

University of Pittsburgh Department of Communication (2022) (www.comm.pitt.edu/informative-speaking).

Vanderswalmen, R., Vrijders, J. & Desoete, A. (2010). Metacognition and spelling performance in college students. In A. Efklides & P. Misailidi (Eds.), *Trends and Prospects in Metacognition Research*, 367–394. Springer.

Warnick, K. & Caldarella, P. (2016). Using multisensory phonics to foster reading skills of adolescent delinquents. *Reading & Writing Quarterly: Overcoming Learning Difficulties*, 32, 317–335.

Wathelet, M., Duhem, S., Vaiva, G., et al. (2020). Factors associated with mental health disorders among university students in France confirmed during the COVID-19 pandemic. *JAMA Network Open*, 3, 1–13.

References

Wechsler, D. (2008). *Wechsler Adult Intelligence Scale* (4th ed.). Pearson.

Whitley R. (2018). Men's mental health: beyond victim blaming. *The Canadian Journal of Psychiatry*, 63, 577–580.

WikiHow (www.wikihow.com/).

Wine, J. (1971). Test anxiety and direction of attention. *Psychological Bulletin*, 76, 92–104.

Wirtz, C. L., Gardner, R., Weber, K. & Bullara, D. (1996). Using self-correction to improve the spelling performance of low-achieving third graders. *Remedial and Special Education*, 17, 48–58.

Wiseheart, R., Altmann, L. J. P., Park, H. & Lombardino, L. J. (2009). Sentence comprehension in young adults with developmental dyslexia. *Annals of Dyslexia*, 59, 151–167.

Wittmaier, B. (1972). Test anxiety and study habits. *Journal of Educational Research*, 46, 929–38.

Xing, M., Wang, J. & Spencer, K. (2008). Metacognitive beliefs and strategies in learning Chinese. *System*, 37, 46–56.

Zago, S., Poletti, B., Corbo, M., Adobbati, L. & Silani, S. (2008). Dysgraphia in patients with primary lateral sclerosis: a speech-based rehearsal deficit? *Behavioural Neurology*, 19, 169–175.

Index

439

Index

443

444

445

Index

447

For EU product safety concerns, contact us at Calle de José Abascal, 56–1°, 28003 Madrid, Spain or eugpsr@cambridge.org.

www.ingramcontent.com/pod-product-compliance
Ingram Content Group UK Ltd.
Pitfield, Milton Keynes, MK11 3LW, UK
UKHW020404140625
459647UK00020B/2633